DESIGN THINKING

FOR
STUDENT PROJECTS

Sara Miller McCune founded SAGE Publishing in 1965 to support the dissemination of usable knowledge and educate a global community. SAGE publishes more than 1000 journals and over 800 new books each year, spanning a wide range of subject areas. Our growing selection of library products includes archives, data, case studies and video. SAGE remains majority owned by our founder and after her lifetime will become owned by a charitable trust that secures the company's continued independence.

Los Angeles | London | New Delhi | Singapore | Washington DC | Melbourne

TONY MORGAN · LENA J. JASPERSEN

DESIGN THINKING
FOR
STUDENT PROJECTS

⑤SAGE

Los Angeles | London | New Delhi
Singapore | Washington DC | Melbourne

Los Angeles | London | New Delhi
Singapore | Washington DC | Melbourne

SAGE Publications Ltd
1 Oliver's Yard
55 City Road
London EC1Y 1SP

SAGE Publications Inc.
2455 Teller Road
Thousand Oaks, California 91020

SAGE Publications India Pvt Ltd
B 1/I 1 Mohan Cooperative Industrial Area
Mathura Road
New Delhi 110 044

SAGE Publications Asia-Pacific Pte Ltd
3 Church Street
#10-04 Samsung Hub
Singapore 049483

Editor: Ruth Stitt
Assistant editor: Jessica Moran
Assistant editor, digital: Mandy Gao
Production editor: Sarah Cooke
Copyeditor: Tom Bedford
Proofreader: Katie Forsythe
Indexer: Silvia Benvenuto
Marketing manager: Kimberley Simpson
Cover design: Naomi Robinson
Typeset by: C&M Digitals (P) Ltd, Chennai, India
Printed in the UK

Library of Congress Control Number: 2021946817

British Library Cataloguing in Publication data

A catalogue record for this book is available from the British Library

ISBN 978-1-5297-6170-2
ISBN 978-1-5297-6169-6 (pbk)

At SAGE we take sustainability seriously. Most of our products are printed in the UK using responsibly sourced papers and boards. When we print overseas we ensure sustainable papers are used as measured by the PREPS grading system. We undertake an annual audit to monitor our sustainability.

CONTENTS

EXTENDED CONTENTS

ABOUT
THE AUTHORS

TONY MORGAN is an Associate Professor in Innovation Management Practice at the University of Leeds, where he co-developed and teaches the flagship interdisciplinary Innovation Thinking and Practice module with Lena Jaspersen. He also leads the Masters' level Innovation Management in Practice module and works with external organisations on the application of innovation and Design Thinking techniques. His interests include innovation, Design Thinking, the practical application of emerging technologies and employability skills.

Prior to joining the University of Leeds, Tony held a three-year Visiting Professor role at the university, as part of the Royal Academy of Engineering's scheme to infuse practical industry experience into academia. His thirty-year career in the IT industry included twenty years at IBM. His roles included IBM Innovation Centre Leader for a global banking client and Chief Innovation Officer for IBM's Global Technology Services business unit in the UK and Ireland, where he led a successful programme to instil innovation into IBM's relationships across a large portfolio of clients.

At IBM, Tony trained experienced leaders and early career professionals in applying innovation-related approaches and techniques to address client needs, increase client satisfaction and generate additional revenue. He's the author of *Collaborative Innovation: How Clients and Service Providers Can Work by Design to Achieve It* (Business Expert Publishing, 2017). He is currently part of a team at the Leeds Institute of Teaching Excellence carrying out pedagogical research into interdisciplinary team-based teaching and learning with a focus on digital and employability skills.

LENA J. JASPERSEN is a University Academic
Fellow in Innovation Management at the University of
Leeds, where she co-developed and teaches the flagship
interdisciplinary Innovation Thinking and Practice module
with Tony Morgan and teaches qualitative research methods at
the PhD level. Her main research interests include collaborative research and innovation,
and the role of partnerships in addressing global development challenges.

Lena's background brings an international and interdisciplinary dimension to her
writing, teaching and research. She holds Masters' degrees in Sociology and International
Relations and was awarded a PhD with Recommendation of Research Excellence from the
University of Leeds. Lena is also currently part of the team at the Leeds Institute of Teaching
Excellence carrying out pedagogical research into interdisciplinary team-based teaching
and learning with a focus on digital and employability skills.

Lena has a strong interest in innovation and research methods. She's a co-author of the
seventh edition of the bestselling *Management and Business Research* (Sage, 2021), which
provides readers with a clear and comprehensive overview of methods for conducting
management and business research. Lena's other publications include a recent article in the
British Journal of Management, containing a systematic overview of methods for qualitative
network research, *Understanding Global Development Research* (Sage, 2017) and the *UNreal
World of Human Rights* (Nomos, 2012).

ABOUT THE ILLUSTRATORS

SHRIYA PANKHANIA graduated from the University of Leeds in 2021. Her degree in Art and Design includes a focus on illustration and UI/UX design. Shriya has a passion for building solutions and visual designs that create better experiences for all users.

MADELEINE (MADDIE) KNIGHT is a Design student at the University of Leeds, specialising in digital design and installation art. Her interests include using design to benefit individuals and wider society. Maddie's other passion is sustainability. She's undertaking a graphic design placement with a sustainable design house and development consultancy in London.

ACKNOWLEDGEMENTS

We've learned so much and been inspired by our past and present students. When you tell us how much you've taken from our modules and how you've used the contents in your applications and careers, it means so much to us. Thank you. Much of your feedback has gone into the book.

Before we began writing the words, we ran some Design Thinking workshops with students to find out what they'd like to see (and not see) in a book. Although we haven't been able to action everything, we've consistently used your input to guide us – from scan reading to space for reflections. Thanks too to the five great former students – Dilan Uludag, Poonam Parmar, Taras Lanchev, Lorennzo Zanutto and Charlotte Gray – who we interviewed for the final chapter. Your inputs are inspired and inspiring.

A special word for our two great illustrators, Shriya Pankhania and Madeleine Knight. Your drawings and designs have often brought our words to life. Thank you! We wish you every success in your future careers.

The impact of both the module and the book would be much diminished without the input and passion of the leading industry experts who've supported us and our students. For space, we need to limit the named acknowledgements to the experts we've interviewed in the book, but we thank you all. Thanks especially then to:

Helen Sherwood	Michael Lewrick	John James
Stephen Isherwood	Ian Smith	Carly Gilbert-Patrick
Gisela Abbam	Kat Owens	Paul Hallett
Tim Kastelle	Jeanne Liedtka	Eva-Marie Muller-Stuler
Doug Dietz	Gary Wilson	
Ulrich Weinberg	Mark Fearn	

Many academic colleagues have also provided input and/or peer reviewed the contents of the book. We thank you, and trust you'll find the published content useful for your students. Thanks too to Ruth Stitt, Jessica Moran and Sarah Cooke at SAGE Publishing for all your support and, at times, let's be honest, your patience.

This book was inspired by the authors' experience of developing and delivering the Innovation Thinking and Practice module at the University of Leeds. This interdisciplinary team-based module is one of the key highlights of our careers. We'd like to thank the following for their support in establishing the module: The Royal Academy of Engineering Visiting Professorship Scheme, Prof Peter Jimack, Prof Krsto Pandza, Prof Andy Bulpitt and Prof Kerrie Unsworth.

Lastly, we'd like to thank our friends and families for all their patience and support when we've been writing this book. We hope what we've created will make it worthwhile.

ONLINE RESOURCES

Design Thinking for Student Projects is accompanied by a wealth of online resources that have been carefully developed to aid teaching and support learning. Visit **study.sagepub.com/designthinking** to access:

FOR INSTRUCTORS

A **Teaching Guide** providing practical guidance and additional materials for those using the book in their teaching.

Facilitation Guides for In-person and Online Workshops containing advice on how to plan and run workshops, as well as useful tips for both facilitators and attendees.

An **Assignment Paper Example** and a **Marking Guidelines Example** that can be used when setting and assessing coursework.

A **Student Reflection Template** providing instructions and a framework for completing weekly reflective reviews.

Digital Collaboration Tool Practice Instructions that can be adapted and shared among attendees in preparation for workshops.

FOR STUDENTS

A Personal Learning Journal that can be used to document key takeaways from each chapter.

Answers to Exercises in the book.

Facilitation Guides for In-person and Online Workshops containing advice on how to plan and run workshops, as well as useful tips for both facilitators and attendees.

MURAL Practice Instructions providing information on how to use the digital collaboration tool MURAL, as well as a **Sample Project on MURAL** showing how a populated MURAL wall looks.

Questions for Developing Commercial Awareness, as well as a **Template for Developing a Business Case**, providing readers with practical skills and understanding.

A **List of Employability Skills** necessary for the world of work, including a description and examples of each one.

A **Personal Learning Review and Skills Profile** encouraging readers to reflect on what they have learnt and identify skills gaps.

LIST OF ICONS

 KEY LEARNING POINT

 REFLECTION POINT

 EXPERT LEARNING

 EXERCISE

 TEAM ACTIVITY

 SAMPLE PROJECT

 MORE IN-DEPTH

PREFACE

First, welcome to the first edition of *Design Thinking for Student Projects*. This book is about how to:

- run team-based student projects successfully
- develop innovative solutions to address real-world challenges
- use Design Thinking and associated innovation and project management techniques
- develop key employability skills.

Using practical Design Thinking and other techniques, this book will walk you through all the steps necessary to deliver an innovation project and gain vital employability skills at the same time. It's suitable for undergraduates and postgraduates across all disciplines, especially those undertaking team-based modules and courses. The content can also be used independently by students and others seeking to gain and improve their skills. Using the book's LinkedIn group, readers can even reach out and connect with each other to create their own projects and teams.

There's a good reason we've written this book. Employers are looking for graduates who can creatively solve problems, manage change, demonstrate commercial awareness and collaborate and communicate at different levels, but often it's not quite so easy to gain these skills. Universities are increasingly helping their students do so by using team-based projects, utilising innovation to solve real-world problems with or without external partners.

As academics and students are seeking new ways to teach and learn in the classroom and online, they need textbooks that support them in this effort. This book does exactly that. Before we began writing, we ran a number of Design Thinking workshops, with students as our end users. Our goal was to generate empathy and understand what they (and hopefully you) would really like to see (and not see) in a new textbook. We've consistently used their input to guide us – from making the book easy to scan read to including space for making notes and reflections.

We've generated empathy for the teachers and academics who may be supervising you. The online resources accompanying this book have been designed to make it easy for them to use the content to help and to improve their existing courses and modules and, where applicable, create new ones. Course leaders may ask you to make good use of specific chapters or sections of the book or read and follow through the whole thing.

Lastly, our student users told us they wanted to hear not just from us as authors but from many others with real-world experience, so you'll find the book's packed full of advice and guidance from a range of leading industry leaders, experts and academics.

Welcome to the new essential guide for learning the practical employability and Design Thinking skills demanded by today's and tomorrow's graduate recruiters. We wish you well in your studies and future careers.

CHAPTER

1

INTRODUCTION

Chapter contents

Goals

- To introduce the book and its authors.

- To highlight how you may benefit from this book.

- To introduce you to reflective learning.

- To consider the seven skill gaps addressed in this book.

- To provide an overview of the content of this book.

WELCOME

Welcome to ***Design Thinking for Student Projects***. We hope you will enjoy reading this book, and that this book will inspire you to develop new skills. You will soon note that this may not be the kind of textbook you are used to. Our book is different, because we believe that everyone who studies these days would benefit from learning more about innovation, Design Thinking and employability skills, and that the best way to achieve this is not by reading about it – but by *doing* it.

Who are we to say that? 'We' are Tony Morgan and Dr Lena Jaspersen. Tony is an experienced Innovation Leader who worked at IBM for over 20 years in senior client-facing roles including business unit Chief Innovation Officer and Innovation Centre Leader for a global banking client. Tony used his experiences to create new innovation training courses in IBM and write a book focused on collaborative innovation aimed at employees and future leaders. Now he is an Associate Professor in Innovation Management Practice at Leeds University Business School working with students and companies to help them harness the power of innovation and Design Thinking approaches.

Lena is an academic researcher who studies collaborative research and innovation at the same department. Lena has co-authored several books on research methods and has published in leading academic journals. Together we teach students from across our university to develop their own innovation projects by engaging with industry leaders and policy makers. Many of our students have told us how much they have enjoyed taking part in our programme, how it has inspired them and how it has helped them develop key skills needed for their professional careers. You'll hear from some of these students later on.

It was their encouragement and that of some of our colleagues which made us decide to write this book, which is based upon our experience of learning with and from our students.

Before creating the book, we ran Design Thinking workshops with students from different universities to find out what they like and don't like about textbooks. Our conclusions included a better understanding of why many students don't wish to engage with lengthy and dense academic texts. Instead, they told us that they prefer something which is easy to read, offers practical recommendations and is visually appealing. If this approach works for you, please read on. We appreciate that some of our colleagues will find this approach somewhat surprising. We are often so used to textbooks heavy on theory and academic discourse. We hope they will give this a chance. We are not out to replace such valuable resources but to complement them. We believe it is important to attend to both theory and practice and that there is a beauty in keeping things simple and accessible where possible. Sometimes, we need a dialogue instead of a lecture, or an activity rather than a case study.

One student advised us to 'use humour to turn this book into a cult classic'. However, we feel the world might not quite be ready for this. Let us know what you think! Perhaps through the medium of interpretive dance or a short video on TikTok? Or, failing that, how about sending us a message on our LinkedIn group? We would love to hear from you.

WHAT THIS BOOK IS ABOUT

This book is intended to be a **practical learning aid for students seeking to develop Design Thinking, innovation and employability skills by working on a team-based project**. So, working with this book means you will engage in an actual team-based project tackling a real-world innovation challenge!

For those of you relatively new to Design Thinking, we'll look at this more in detail in Chapter 3. For now, think of it as an incredibly versatile methodology used by companies like Google, IBM and many others for defining and tackling problems following a user-centric and iterative approach.

This is not a book targeted purely at students studying for a specific Engineering, Business or IT related degree. It is a book for *everyone* who wishes to strengthen their career prospects by improving their employability skills. So, there's a good chance this book is for you!

Today's graduate employers want more from new hires than purely an in-depth knowledge of their core degree discipline. As we'll see, they want people who can be creative, manage innovation and change, solve problems, understand commercial implications, and effectively communicate and collaborate with diverse teams and individuals in rapidly changing and uncertain times (WEF, 2020).

Each of the subsequent chapters of this book covers one or more of the skills listed above, which we have translated into the **seven skill areas** we describe below. The primary aim of this book for readers is to guide your development of these skills to help you prepare to get the job you want – and to help you succeed in it.

The second aim of this book is to enable readers to take part in an **exciting innovation project** that addresses one or more of the problems of our time. Working on this project will be an engaging experience and – judging from the experience shared by our students – it may provide you with a new perspective on what you want to do professionally. This can be really helpful, particularly if you find the prospect of deciding on your future career a little bit daunting and scary!

HOW TO WORK WITH THIS BOOK

The book can be used in conjunction with university and professional development modules, courses and programmes, including those involving Design Thinking, and project-based or team-based learning. The book can also be used by self-learners with an interest in increasing their knowledge of innovation projects, Design Thinking and attractiveness to employers. This is one of the reasons why this book has its own **community on LinkedIn**. We encourage you to engage with this community and to connect with other learners all over the world as you embark on your first (and subsequent) team-based

innovation challenges. Self-learners can also use the community to look for team members. Research shows that diverse teams tend to be more creative and testifies to the power of open and collaborative approaches to innovation (something we will have a closer look at in Chapter 2). What better way to learn from such insights than by putting them into practice!

On our LinkedIn group you may also come across our Design Thinking competition, something we hope to do upon publication of this book. It will offer a great opportunity to showcase your work to others and perhaps even win an award.

HOW WILL I LEARN?

The book will aid your learning by using a **combination of experiential and reflective approaches**. The book takes you through the early stages of an actual innovation project and follows a simple but effective innovation management process. We invite you to work in a team with other students to tackle an innovation challenge, typically as part of a course or module, or even if using the book independently. Such project-based learning has been shown to be highly effective in higher education (Guo et al., 2020).

While a lot of the project activities in this book are team-based, the way we encourage you to learn has a much more personal dimension. We show to you how to use a four-step approach to reflective learning.

Learning is facilitated by using a four-step approach – see Figure 1.1.

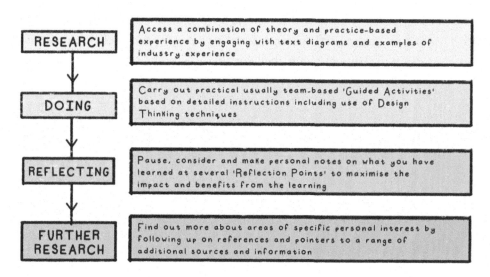

RESEARCH → Access a combination of theory and practice-based experience by engaging with text diagrams and examples of industry experience

DOING → Carry out practical usually team-based 'Guided Activities' based on detailed instructions including use of Design Thinking techniques

REFLECTING → Pause, consider and make personal notes on what you have learned at several 'Reflection Points' to maximise the impact and benefits from the learning

FURTHER RESEARCH → Find out more about areas of specific personal interest by following up on references and pointers to a range of additional sources and information

FIGURE 1.1: Four-step approach to learning

We are often asked about why the reflection part is so important. Our answer is simple – how can you learn from successes and mistakes if you do not understand why they happened? When you engage in a project, you and your teammates will inevitably make mistakes. That's part and parcel of learning by doing. Many of the experts from industry we work with tell us the successes they have achieved in their careers have been directly linked to reflecting on and learning from the mistakes they've inevitably made along the way. They tell us that to learn from our mistakes (and to deal with them), we must sit back and decide what we will do differently next time. Often our first hunch as to why something has gone wrong is not a good guide to further action. We actually need to think about and analyse where we went wrong – and that is where reflection comes in. Learning, like innovation and Design Thinking, is an iterative process.

Many people find that they learn best from experience. Reflective writing is a very effective method for making sense of this. It allows you to stop and organise your thoughts, evaluate what you do and learn from this experience. Contrary to what many of our students think when they start working with us, reflective writing does not take much time. It is not like academic writing – yet it can still make you a better writer. So, it is a win–win exercise!

As part of the learning experience facilitated by this book, we encourage you to reflect on what you have learned by maintaining a **personal reflective journal**. You can do this digitally (we provide a starter template in our online resources for students) and/or by writing in the spaces provided in the **reflection points** included in each chapter of the book. You'll find the first reflection point at the end of this chapter.

We encourage you to work with us through the text, activities, reflection points, further reading and resources as this will enable you to benefit more fully from the book. If you really want to skip something, then our advice is to skip some of the reading but not the reflection.

MORE IN-DEPTH: GIBBS' REFLECTIVE CYCLE

One of the most prominent models of reflective learning is Gibbs' Reflective Cycle. In his book *Learning by Doing*, Gibbs (1988) presented learning as a cyclic process involving six steps, as illustrated in Figure 1.2.

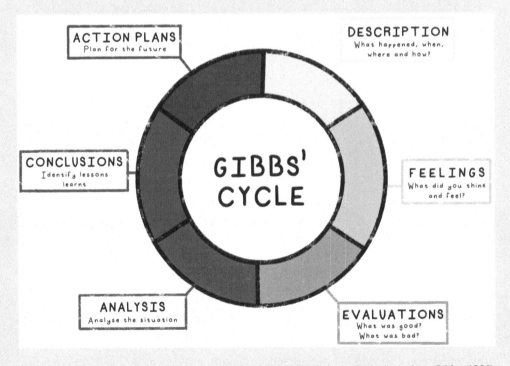

FIGURE 1.2: Gibbs' Reflective Cycle (based on Gibbs, 1988)

Some of our readers may feel that six steps is a lot and we appreciate that many will choose to collapse some of the points. In our experience that is not a problem, as long as there is a descriptive element, an evaluative/analytic element and some 'lessons learnt'. This is why we have adopted a somewhat simplified four-step approach to learning in this book.

THE SEVEN SKILL AREAS

Professional bodies and industry leaders often suggest that there is a mismatch between the more theoretical knowledge students acquire at university and the skills they need to succeed in a graduate job (Jackson, 2010; Suleman, 2018). The resulting skill gaps have something to do with how we teach, study and assess. While in-depth knowledge of a core degree discipline is important, sometimes the more foundational and 'soft' skills are key for

FIGURE 1.3: The seven skill areas

graduates to succeed when they (re)enter the labour market. In many degree programmes, these skills are not taught as such.

This book addresses this gap in graduate learning. It focuses on seven key skill areas that have been identified as of particular importance, which we introduce below.

1. **Innovation and Design Thinking**: This is a skill area that relates more broadly to the ability to identify problems and opportunities, and to develop and implement new solutions in a strategic way (WEF, 2020). Innovation management and Design Thinking skills can be applied in a range of different contexts. As we'll see, innovation is not just about developing new technologies and products. We also need innovation in services, operations and business models, amongst many other things! Design Thinking is a methodology for innovation that starts by generating empathy for people, particularly the people who will be using the solutions we're looking to create. It focuses on really understanding a problem before jumping into ideas and solutions. Design Thinking includes techniques for generating and prioritising diverse ideas, some of which will be developed further, prototyped, and tested using an iterative approach. Throughout the process, we need to be able to communicate in a clear and engaging way to convince others to invest in and implement our chosen idea(s). After all, if the idea remains just an idea, it's not innovation! It will not come as a surprise that such a multi-stage innovation process needs to be managed. Therefore, innovation and Design Thinking draw upon (and lead to the development of) key organisational skills.

2. **Collaboration and teaming**: This about working 'constructively with others on a task' (Knight & Yorke, 2004, p. 8), very often working in diverse teams. It is one of the most synergistic of graduate skill areas. While it is often linked to leadership, we see it more closely aligned with emotional intelligence and being understanding and helpful on the job (aka soft skills!). 'Teaming is a verb. It is a dynamic activity, not a bounded, static entity' writes Professor Amy Edmondson in a blog post (2012; see further resources section at the end of the chapter). Teaming requires good organisational skills, for example relating to coordination and time management, as well as communication skills. It also requires a degree of reflexivity. While talking about collaboration is a nice thing to do – putting it into practice can be harder! Sometimes we need to take a step back and ask ourselves who we are in a given team; sometimes we find it difficult to relate to others in a positive way. Many of our students report that they have had little and/or negative previous experiences with teamwork, and they try to avoid it. In our view this is not a helpful strategy. Most graduate jobs involve a great deal of teamwork,

so improving your skills in this area before entering the job market can make a huge difference to your career and your life more generally.

3. **Critical thinking and problem solving**: This refers to the ability to use available information as a basis to develop, evaluate and implement solutions (Hambur et al., 2002; WEF, 2020). Although this may well sound quite abstract, it involves tackling very practical problems! Complexity in the workplace and the wider world continues to increase, which is why we face increasingly 'wicked' problems. Often, we do not even know where to start, as the way we define a problem depends on our strategy for solving it. We need to hone our analytical thinking skills and be prepared to evaluate and question 'given facts', as well as being open and creative when addressing problems. Often, there is not just one optimal solution – this is why firms tell us they hire graduates – because they look at problems with fresh eyes, think critically and suggest new ideas. What is deemed best will depend on the perspective you adopt. So, while the application of a certain rationale and logic is important in analytic thinking, this skill area is equally about lateral thinking, creativity and, linking back to Design Thinking, empathy too.

4. **Commercial awareness**: This relates to having a more fundamental understanding of priorities and practical implications. Commercial awareness (or business acumen) is one of the key skill gaps most frequently cited by employers in industry, who expect graduates to understand the need to balance costs with income and the importance of satisfying customers (Archer & Davison, 2008). Commercial awareness also relates to numerical skills but ultimately it is more about having a practical sense for what is possible whilst maintaining an entrepreneurial spirit. This is not something one has or has not got – it is something we can all learn! Commercial awareness is often seen as relating to 'business issues' but of course it is also important for those who wish to work in government, public healthcare organisations, NGOs and the so-called third or 'voluntary' sector. You may feel if you haven't got any work experience, then you haven't had chance to develop this – we disagree! Whilst reading this book and completing the thinking exercises, you will recognise and build these skills.

5. **Empathy and communication**: The ability to communicate effectively in different situations and with different audiences is key for virtually all jobs. This is another synergistic skill area where multiple studies have identified large satisfaction gaps between what employers expect and what graduates can provide (Jackson, 2010). In the literature, there is often an emphasis on the communication of outcomes in the form of presentations and reports. While we have included content on presentation skills in this book, in our experience wider communication skills, such as stakeholder engagement, team communication or meeting skills, are just as

important. Graduates are also expected to know how to engage and manage themselves in a professional way with diverse internal and external organisations. There are also many practical challenges associated with interviews. So, we have included additional content that examines communication skills from a broader perspective.

6. **Resilience and managing change**: Coping with challenges, changes or setbacks can be difficult (Griggs et al., 2018). While many degree programmes may be seen as an exercise in resilience in their own right, they also tend to be quite predictable. There are clear criteria and deadlines to be met. Most graduate jobs involve working in much more dynamic environments. Uncertainty, misunderstandings, rejections and setbacks can hit hard! Therefore, it is important to have developed the resilience and skills needed to address them with adaptability, foresight and professionalism. This links to our evidence that we can learn a lot from failure. While setbacks are always frustrating, we can all learn how to deal with them better and turn them into opportunities (well, perhaps not always but much more often than one might think).

7. **Initiative and active learning**: Given the fast pace at which economies are changing, we need to understand the implications for 'both current and future problem-solving and decision-making' (WEF, 2020, p. 153). Lifelong learning is a fundamental requirement to succeed in this environment. By the time we are in higher education, we often assume that we know how to learn. Yet, when we look at pedagogical research this is far from always the case. As automation and artificial intelligence are changing the very jobs we wish to succeed in, we do not just need to ensure digital fluency but also to develop new ways of learning. Such learning is not just about absorbing knowledge and passing exams but also about engaging with others and learning from experience. We need skills that enable us to engage, to analyse what we have done to succeed or fail, and to adapt so that we know how to do better. These skills won't develop when we wait to be taught. They require us to take initiative and to reflect on who we are and what we want to do.

Each chapter will include additional material about the seven skill areas. We've also included interviews with leading industry and academic experts to provide their practical insights in these skill areas. The experts will discuss why these skills are important, how they have used and developed such skills themselves, and even what they look out for when they recruit. You will find at least one of these interviews in each chapter of the book. Just look out for our 'Expert Input' icon! And why not start right now? Let's meet Helen Sherwood and find out what she has to say about the role of employability skills when recruiting graduates.

EXPERT

RECRUITING GRADUATES

Helen Sherwood worked for IBM, a major graduate recruiter, for 25 years. She spent six years recruiting and placing early career professionals. After interviewing nearly 3,000 university students and reviewing many more application forms, Helen can tell us a great deal about the importance of 'employability' skills.

1. WHAT GENERAL ADVICE WOULD YOU GIVE STUDENTS ABOUT EMPLOYABILITY?

A student might think a job advert looks great, the role looks good and they like the company, but there might be hundreds, perhaps even thousands, of other applicants. They really need to focus on what will set them apart. In my experience, graduate recruiters are seeking a good degree, but they are also on the look-out for a combination of attitude and aptitude. The old-fashioned phrase 'common sense' comes to mind.

A student's ability to show they've developed certain skills beyond their core degree discipline – such as commercial awareness, communication skills and confronting change – are key differentiators. If they can demonstrate to a recruiter that they've got some of these wider skills, it can really set them apart from many of the other applicants.

2. SO, IT'S NOT ALL ABOUT THE DEGREE?

Absolutely not! Contrary to what some people think, most recruiters don't focus purely on results. A great degree can demonstrate an ability to learn and think at a certain level, but it's even more important for students to show they can apply their knowledge in a meaningful way.

(Continued)

3. HOW CAN STUDENTS AND NEW GRADUATE HIRES DO THIS?

An applicant who clearly demonstrates they've had a range of experiences, and very importantly learned from them, makes a very compelling candidate. These experiences can vary widely – roles in university societies, volunteering, travelling, placements and so on. Most employers will want to verify their new hires are going to be able to work well and collaborate with a variety of people.

Many employers use assessment centres with scenarios to simulate their working environments. Of course, the employers will be assessing how tasks are approached and addressed, but they'll also be looking for other things, such as the candidate's ability to interact with others and their verbal and non-verbal communication skills. They're looking for well-rounded people, who listen and encourage the less vocal team members, not just those who come up with a perfect solution. The way you get these skills is generally through experience and reflection.

When working with early career professionals, employers hope to see a proactive and honest attitude. They like new employees who, when faced with a challenge, say, 'I don't know how to do this, but I will do my research, find a way and get back to you' – and then actually follow-up on their promises. These people will be more successful in their careers than those who pretend they know everything, over-commit and under-deliver.

4. WHY IS COMMERCIAL AWARENESS IMPORTANT?

When faced with two otherwise identical candidates the most compelling is always the one who understands the company, the competition, the history and the vision. Sometimes, it's all very well knowing how something works, let's say quantum computing, but unless you're tasked with developing it, what the employer really wants to know is 'How can it be used in my business?'. If you're able to spend time understanding the organisation's objectives and work out how the tech can be applied to them, you're onto a winner.

TOP TIP

When thinking about why an employer should choose you, remember your grades definitely matter, but it's your employability skills which will really count. Before you submit your application always read it one more time, taking the view of the organisation you are applying to. Ask yourself, 'Why should they hire me? Does the application highlight my employability skills?' Good luck!

We don't usually place two of these interviews together, but we've done so here, simply because we believe the area of employability skills is so important. So, in addition to Helen, we've asked Stephen Isherwood of the Institute of Student Employers to share his view on why you really should care about these skills and how to acquire them.

EXPERT

EMPLOYABILITY SKILLS

Stephen Isherwood is the Chief Executive at the Institute of Student Employers (ISE), having previously been the Head of Graduate Recruitment at Ernst & Young, one of the largest graduate recruiters in the UK. The ISE promotes excellence and innovation in the resourcing, assessment and development of emerging talent and undertakes research into the education sector and student employment.

1. WHICH SKILLS, BEYOND A CORE DEGREE DISCIPLINE, DO YOU BELIEVE ARE MOST IMPORTANT FOR EMPLOYERS SEEKING TO RECRUIT NEW GRADUATE HIRES?

Our research shows over 80% of graduate employers don't recruit by subject discipline. Of course, there are specialist roles and exceptions to this, but for many employers a degree subject is less important than a number of other factors. Employers tell us they're looking to recruit graduates because of their intellectual ability but, over and above that, they're

(Continued)

also looking for people who can work effectively with others, get things done and solve real-world problems.

Employers want graduates who are on an upward trajectory, people who demonstrate the potential to learn, grow and develop over time. This makes self-awareness even more important. The ability to self-analyse, reflect and learn from one's experience is crucial. Graduate recruiters want to hire people who can show they're self-motivated and have the ability to be resilient when things go wrong.

2. HOW CAN STUDENTS GAIN THESE SKILLS DURING THEIR TIME AT UNIVERSITY?

Students can do this in a number of ways, for example by getting involved in inter-disciplinary activities and projects, such as those highlighted in this book.

At other times, students may gain these skills without even realising they've done so, hence the importance of reflection. Do things which have you working with other people and solving problems which you can use to demonstrate your initiative and motivation. Employers want people who are self-starters.

Within a university context, there's a wide range of extra-curricular activities available. For example, you could get involved in a club or society, or work on a supermarket checkout or in a bar or restaurant. Effectively you're in a business, you've been given responsibility and you're working with people. How you tackled the role and overcame problems can be a goldmine for evidence to share with prospective employers. Sometimes students may think employers don't value this type of thing, but they really do.

3. HOW DO EMPLOYERS VERIFY THEIR APPLICANTS HAVE GOT THESE SKILLS DURING THE RECRUITMENT PROCESS?

Employers who run graduate recruitment programmes normally design and build their recruitment processes around the skills they're looking for. If you unpick an employer's selection process, the application form, online tests, interviews and assessment centre activities are usually focused on a core set of competencies. The good news is most employers are open about what they're looking for, so as an applicant you can find this out.

Of course, employers may use a variety of ways to find what they seek. They may ask, for example, in an interview for you to talk about a situation where you were part of a team and had to address a problem, or about what you did when something went wrong. Students sometimes shy away from talking about things going wrong, but this is often where great learning happens, so talking about what you learned from the experience can be very good.

Alternatively, in an assessment centre, employers are looking to test some of this in practice. In a group exercise, it's not about being able to talk about how you might work with other people to get stuff done but actually showing you can do it.

4. GIVEN THIS, HOW CAN APPLICANTS BEST CONVINCE PROSPECTIVE EMPLOYERS THEY POSSESS SOME OR ALL OF THESE SKILLS THEY'RE LOOKING FOR?

Do your preparation. Have your evidence ready for what the employer is looking for.

Employers, in general, aren't looking to trip you up. Read or listen to the question and answer it directly. Don't do the politician's approach of, 'You've asked me this, but I'm going to talk about that'. This doesn't work.

For a written application form or an interview, it's about having good examples. Talk about your real-life past experiences to provide great evidence. Don't say you're great at problem solving. Talk about a problem you've solved and what you learned from doing this.

Remember, employers would much rather recruit you than reject you. The easier you can make it for an employer, by giving them all the evidence they need, the more likely it is you'll succeed and get the job offer.

5. CAN YOU THINK OF A STORY OR AN EXAMPLE TO BRING THE TOPIC TO LIFE?

I'll start with a not so good example. A recruiter met with a student, who was interested in a role in their company. The student was off the scale in terms of intelligence, but one of the things they said was, 'I want to solve problems, but I don't want to talk to clients. If the company brings me problems, I'm sure I can address them'. Obviously, this didn't go down too well. To solve a client's problems, you need to speak to them to understand their issues and communicate what you believe needs to be done. The student demonstrated they didn't really understand the real world.

(Continued)

Here's a more positive example. One applicant went to university, having previously set up their own business running a market stall. The applicant described how and why the business failed, and how he'd stepped back, analysed the situation and re-evaluated what to do. It was a fascinating insight into the applicant's commercial awareness and the wider skills he'd gained from experiencing failure. He got the job.

TOP TIP

Do stuff! There's not one specific thing which will make you more employable. The candidates who get through in a competitive jobs market are those who show they've done things, that they've developed and pushed themselves and they've been motivated to do this through their own volition, rather than being told what to do.

And when you do stuff, reflect on and learn from it. Use the experience to create examples and stories as evidence in the recruitment process.

Some very clear and consistent messages there from both Helen and Stephen. We trust you found their insights useful, and we hope they've already got you thinking. There are more interviews like these in every chapter. Every interview also ends with a simple 'Top tip', so if you're a scan reader, please do remember to pick these out!

LEARNING FEATURES

By now, you have already come across some of the key learning features of this book. We have created these as our students have shown to us that there are many **different types of learners**. Perhaps you are one of those who are keen on reading and seek guidance to engage with more theoretical content to support your learning. Or perhaps you just want to do your project and read as little as possible. Either way, you will be well catered for!

In order to support you in the way you want to learn, we use different icons to flag different types of content. We include an overview of these icons below and in the opening pages of the book. We hope that this will make it easier for you to have the learning experience *you* want.

FIGURE 1.4: Learning icons

- **Key learning points** flag content that is particularly relevant. They make it easy to revise and catch up.
- In all chapters, we have also incorporated interviews with industry experts that will provide you with additional insights and guidance. Look out for the **expert learning** icon!
- **Team activities** are all about your innovation project. They form the core of this book and your project. According to our students, most of them are fun, too!
- **More in-depth sections** provide additional and deeper insights in relation to the topic of the chapter. In this chapter, we introduced you to Gibb's Cycle (even though our four-step learning model will do for now).
- **Reflection points** invite you to stop and reflect on your activities and learning. Usually, we provide a few questions that will help you to come to a deeper understanding of what you have learnt, and how this may help you in future.
- There are also additional **exercises** – both individual and team-based – which aid your learning.

- We have created a **sample project** for this book with all the team activity outputs. We hope that this will help you to understand how to approach certain activities and use different templates.

ONLINE RESOURCES FOR STUDENTS

This takes us to the next point – the **online resources for students**! The QR codes flag content that you can access online. Some of these resources were created specially for this book and are available via our companion website (see **https://study.sagepub.com/ designthinking**). These include:

- **facilitation guides** for **in-person and online delivery** of team activities
- some **useful templates** for a **personal learning journal** and some of the activities
- **Design Thinking templates and sample outputs**
- **sample solutions** for some of the exercises included in the book.
- templates for a **personal learning review** and **skills profile**, an **employability skills list** and **questions for developing commercial awareness**

ONLINE RESOURCES FOR INSTRUCTORS

Note to instructors: We haven't forgotten you! Our accompanying companion website for instructors (see **https://study.sagepub.com/designthinking**) provides a practical set of resources to enable you to use this book to support your own courses and modules. Resources include:

- a **teaching guide** with practical guidance, materials and options for developing and updating existing modules, courses or training programmes and creating new ones in areas related to the content
- **facilitation guide** for running and supporting Design Thinking and related workshops in a **classroom environment**
- **facilitation guide** for running Design Thinking activities **online**, including **templates and instructions** for using the MURAL tool for online collaboration
- templates for creating a **reflective journal**, an example **assignment paper** and corresponding **marking guidelines**.

We hope you find them useful.

STRUCTURE OF THE BOOK

This book is structured in a way that takes you step-by-step through an **innovation project** all the way up to a pitch to investors, internal project sponsors or other decision makers. We will take you through this process in eleven short chapters. Each chapter takes you to the next level of your project whilst at the same time supporting you in the development of key employability skills.

Following this introductory chapter, we continue with two foundational chapters that may involve a bit more reading than the others.

- **Chapter 2** introduces **innovation and innovation management**. We discuss definitions of innovation and highlight why innovation is important to organisations. We examine different types of innovations and key enablers. We explain how innovation can be managed and have a closer look at approaches to open and collaborative innovation.
- **Chapter 3** then introduces **Design Thinking** for innovation and creative problem solving. We introduce you to key Design Thinking concepts, discuss the importance of teamwork and invite you to take part in an exercise that gives you a first impression of the magic of Design Thinking.

Having established the foundations, we then invite you and your teams to embark on your projects. The next two chapters take you to the first steps of the innovation management lifecycle.

- **Chapter 4** focuses on team building and the concept of an **innovation challenge**, problem or opportunity. We introduce some sample innovation challenges and provide some instructions as to how you may define your own. We have a look at stakeholder mapping and discuss how to research innovation challenges. We invite you and your team to run the prominent Design Thinking activities entitled 'End-user Persona' and 'Empathy Map'.
- **Chapter 5** is then all about **idea generation and idea prioritisation** which are key stages in the Design Thinking process. Activities include the prominent Design Thinking methods 'As Is Scenario', 'Big Ideas' and 'Prioritisation Grid'.

The next four chapters are all about developing, validating and refining your ideas.

- **Chapter 6** is about **communication skills**. After all, we can have the best idea in the world but if we can't communicate the idea and its value, it will go nowhere. Good communication skills are also key for teamwork and user engagement.
- In **Chapter 7** we examine the **capability aspects** of the development stage of the innovation management lifecycle. We introduce techniques used for idea validation and development. Guided learning activities include de Bono's 'Six Thinking Hats' technique, Design Thinking 'Hills' and rapid prototyping.

- **Chapter 8** is about **commercial development** and commercial awareness. Guided learning activities include business case development (sponsor focus) and value proposition development (end user focus).
- In **Chapter 9** we have a closer look at **managing change** and the power of Design Thinking as an iterative process.

The final project stage involves communicating your idea and evaluating your project. We cover this in two short chapters:

- **Chapter 10** is all about how to communicate your idea in a **compelling pitch** to secure funding or further development of your project.
- **Chapter 11** is about **applying the learning**, including activities to assist personal and team reflection on what you have learned, and the skills developed. A number of former students will share how they've applied these skills in the early stages of their own careers, and we close with wider thoughts about future use of Design Thinking and lifelong learning.

RESOURCES NEEDED

If you're using this book linked to a course or module, your instructor(s) will usually summarise the resources you need. Whether you're undertaking every activity or selecting a subset as directed by your instructor, you'll find detailed instructions in every chapter of the book.

Ideally, when you're working your way through the book you will be collaborating with others in a diverse team. Usually, we suggest a team size of between four and eight team members. In our experience, five to seven team members works best. Typically, you'll also be assigned to your team as part of your course or module. If you're working independently, and perhaps have no idea where to find such a team, you might wish to join our LinkedIn group community and reach out to others who have also done so.

This brings us to the next question – where and how will you meet your team? Again, your course or module leaders will usually define this. Ideally, we'd suggest teams be physically co-located from time to time in a room, so they can work together on Design Thinking and other activities. Being in the same space will make many of the tasks easier – and also help you to develop a great team spirit!

This said, we are aware **face-to-face interaction** is not always an option. Global communications can also increase the diversity of our teams, which is almost always a good thing. This is why we have written this book in a way which explains how to run the activities in a classroom setting and also in a way which supports **remote working and online collaboration**.

How do we do that? We propose a combination of video conferencing using tools (examples include Zoom, Microsoft Teams and so on) and an online collaboration platform for Design Thinking and other workshop-based activities (leading examples used in industry include MURAL, Miro and other tools). We have created **facilitation guides** for running workshops both face-to-face and online, which you can access on our companion website (see QR code). The facilitation guides include lists of resources for running the activities in both face-to-face and online settings.

CONCLUSION

This book is a practical learning aid for students working on team-based projects and/or seeking to develop innovation, Design Thinking and employability skills. In this chapter, we have provided a brief introduction to the book. We identified seven key graduate skill areas which we invite you to strengthen by working with us through the book and on own your course or module, or even by (co)creating your own independent innovation project. One of the key skill gaps we specifically addressed was initiative and active learning, where we've highlighted the importance of combining experimental and reflective approaches to learning, through the use of reflective writing and a personal learning journal.

KEY LEARNING POINTS

- Many graduates lack key employability skills in the seven skill areas covered by this book: innovation and Design Thinking; critical thinking and problem solving; empathy and communication; collaboration and teaming; commercial awareness; resilience and managing change; initiative and active learning.

- The best way to improve these skills is not by reading about them but to engage in learning by doing.

- Learning, like innovation and Design Thinking, is an iterative process.

- In this book, learning is facilitated by a four-step approach centred on reading, doing, reflecting and further research.

- It involves teamwork that may be conducted face to face or online.

ACTION POINTS

☐ Join our LinkedIn group to connect with the authors and other students.

☐ Familiarise yourself with the online resources for students which accompany this book.

☐ Set up your own personal reflective journal. Use the template available from our online resources or use the blank space provided in the reflection points in the book to make a note of your reflections. You'll find the first reflection point immediately below.

REFLECTION POINT: REFLECTIVE LEARNING

Reflect on the questions below. Make a note of your answers in the space provided and/or in your personal reflective journal.

REFLECTING ON THE SEVEN SKILL AREAS DESCRIBED EARLIER IN THIS CHAPTER, WHICH SKILL AREAS DO YOU THINK WILL BE MOST IMPORTANT FOR YOUR DREAM JOB AND FUTURE CAREER?

WHICH SKILL AREAS DO YOU THINK YOU NEED TO IMPROVE THE MOST?

FURTHER RESOURCES

The following report explores the jobs and skills of the future, shedding light on the pandemic-related disruptions in 2020 in a much wider socio-technical, economic and political context. It includes an interesting appendix where you can look up more particular considerations and skill gaps for different countries and industries.

WEF. 2020. *The Future of Jobs Report*. World Economic Forum.

The following website by the British Office for Students provides some really useful resources on graduate employment and skills:

OfS. 2021. *Graduate Employment and Skills Guide*. Office for Students.

In this short blog post Amy Edmondson discusses the importance of teaming in the knowledge economy:

Edmondson, A. 2012. *The Importance of Teaming*. Harvard Business School: Working Knowledge.

This is a brief introduction to the notion of 'wicked problems' and how they inspire a different approach to research and innovation:

de Almeida Kumlien, A.C., & Coughlan, P. 2018. Wicked problems and how to solve them. *The Conversation*, 18 October.

A short and useful guide to reflective writing with some useful tips and references:

University of Birmingham. n.d. *A Short Guide to Reflective Writing*.

A recent report about skill gaps in the UK that brings together the perspectives of employers, educators and the working-age population:

Griggs, J., Scandone, B., & Battherham, J. 2018. *How Employable is the UK? Meeting the Future Skills Challenge*.

CHAPTER

2

INNOVATION

Chapter contents

Goals

- To introduce you to what you need to know about innovation to embark on your own project.
- To examine definitions, motivations, types and levels of innovation.
- To explain how innovation can be managed.
- To explore approaches for collaborative and open innovation.
- To identify the main enablers of innovation.

INTRODUCTION

This chapter tells you about key things you need to know about innovation to embark on your first innovation project. As we cannot know how much you *already* know about innovation, we assume one of the reasons you have picked up this book is because your knowledge is limited. This makes this chapter a bit longer and heavier than the others. After we promised you a different kind of textbook, we now start with a lot of reading – but the knowledge gained from this will provide you with a very good grounding in innovation and useful reference points when progressing through the subsequent chapters, where you'll follow the lifecycle of a typical innovation project.

We have structured this chapter like a section of 'Frequently Asked Questions' (FAQ). We seek to answer the questions our students usually ask – many of whom have no prior training in management. This approach will make it easy for you to skim read the chapter if you think you already know quite a lot about the material covered. This was one of the things students told us they wanted to see more of in textbooks. We have included reflection points and exercises throughout, and for students particularly interested in this area we have included a list of further resources at the end.

INNOVATION

WHAT IS INNOVATION?

If you ask ten different people in ten different organisations or industries to define what innovation means to them or their organisation, you might get ten different answers. Despite standard dictionary definitions of the word, views on what innovation means vary. For example, the use of a new digital scanning tool to automate the transcription of hand-written names and addresses from pieces of paper into a database may be considered an important 'innovation' by one individual, team or organisation. In contrast, another organisation may well view it as a 'service improvement' and definitely not 'innovation'.

When working collaboratively with others, it is beneficial to collectively agree a working definition of innovation which the whole team can understand and abide by. In this way, when the team delivers 'innovation', everyone will concur that it has. This approach is particularly useful when working to deliver innovation with other organisations. When Tony worked as an Innovation Leader at IBM, his mantra was 'my favourite definition of innovation is whatever the client says it is'. This might sound a little bit like cheating, but there can be benefits to such an approach as both parties (in this example IBM and the client) need to have a shared understanding of what innovation constitutes in order to work together and make it happen! This said, it is of course also useful to have a good working definition to begin the conversation with. So let us now consider the meaning of innovation.

According to our colleague Tim Kastelle, innovation expert from the University of Queensland Business School, there are three areas of study that look at how ideas create change in a business environment: creativity, entrepreneurship and innovation. He argues that creativity is about the development of new and useful *ideas*. Entrepreneurship is about the creation of tangible *value* (and any entrepreneur will tell you that this involves a lot more than just having ideas!). Innovation in turn is about *'making new ideas real, so that they can create value'* (Kastelle, 2014).

We like this definition because it highlights that the idea is just the start! Ideas need to be developed (so that they become *'real'*) and they need to deliver *value*. This value is not necessarily monetary. It can consist of many things – increased sales, reduced costs, less pollution, improved customer service, better policy, regulatory compliance, enhanced patient outcomes and so on.

The next step in understanding the concept of innovation relates to the qualifier 'new'. Sometimes innovation involves invention; that is the creation of *entirely new* ideas, capabilities or technologies. This can sometimes be what stops us from putting forward new ideas, because we fear that we have not thought of anything really 'new'. Often though, innovation entails the application of *existing ideas* in a *new context*. Let us give you an example. A laser (or 'light amplification by stimulated emission of radiation') is a device which stimulates atoms or molecules to emit amplified light at particular wavelengths to produce a narrow beam of radiation.

When the laser was first invented in the early 1960s, it was acknowledged as a breakthrough *invention*. However, shining an amplified beam of light at something doesn't really add any value. The value was generated later, as people began to apply the new laser technology to address challenges and opportunities in different industries. Since its invention, many innovations have made using laser technology. The barcode scanner is a great example. Light from a laser is scanned across a barcode. The data received from the scanner is then decoded and transmitted to a computer system.

In the retail industry, the data can be used to price individual products at a checkout, update stock levels and track items through supply chains and so on. In healthcare, the same technology is used to confirm patient identities, track and match medication and do other things.

Application of the barcode scanner, using laser technology, has driven change and added value in multiple industries. Each use of the laser-based barcode has been an innovation in its own right. What this example illustrates is that innovation is as much about novel ideas as it is about *understanding the contexts* in which these ideas can be deployed to create value. Therefore, our definition of innovation is:

'**Innovation is the application of new ideas,**
or existing ideas in a new context,
which results in change
that delivers value'.

If you want to learn more about how other innovation experts define innovation, have a look at the further resources section at the end of the chapter where we have included some very useful resources and references.

REFLECTION POINT: DEFINING INNOVATION

Now that you've reviewed what innovation is in an industry context and seen how it is different to invention, reflect for a few minutes and consider the following questions.

Make a note of your answers in the space provided and/or in your journal.

1. HOW WOULD YOU PERSONALLY DEFINE INNOVATION IN AN INDUSTRY CONTEXT? FOR EXAMPLE, IN TECHNOLOGY, BANKING, GOVERNMENT, HEALTH OR MUSIC? OR SOME OTHER INDUSTRY OR SECTOR YOU ARE INTERESTED IN?

2. WHAT DO YOU CONSIDER ARE TWO OR THREE GOOD EXAMPLES OF INNOVATION?

3. WHY DO YOU THINK THEY ARE GOOD EXAMPLES?

WHY IS INNOVATION IMPORTANT?

When we define innovation as we do above, we assume that the value created is of benefit to someone or something. Over the years, many of us have become more critical in our assessment of what can be considered as a benefit. We all know about innovations that have had a questionable impact on our world (take social media – is it good or bad?). You may find some extreme examples, such as innovation in the arms trades or insecticides, but also others such as unsustainable plastic packaging or social media tools facilitating the spread of fake news. These innovations were realised because *someone* expected to derive value from them, and often did. The fact that there have been innovations that we see as of questionable value is not a reason to give up innovating. Quite the opposite!

We need to innovate to address many of the grand challenges of our time. But we should always try to be clear about how we define value, and for whom. For organisations such as government agencies, charities and indeed businesses, innovation is very important not just to address the challenges of our time but also for the organisation to achieve its purpose of flourishing in a given environment when tangible resources might be tight. For businesses, innovation is a strategic resource and a survival imperative. In order to illustrate this point, we would like to highlight these words which **Bernie Meyerson** in his role as global **Chief Innovation Officer of IBM** shared with us:

- 'Innovation is required to stay alive. You need to eat, live and breathe in the present. But you should never ever close your eyes against what's coming, because when you stand there in the tunnel, it's of vital importance to know if that light is the end of a tunnel or an oncoming train'.

- 'Embracing innovation is vital because your competitors are doing it. The world is competitive. If you don't keep reinventing yourself as the world changes, you're simply left behind. Innovation has become more vital as the rate and pace of change has accelerated'.
- 'Those who stand still actually fall behind more quickly, so you either innovate or die'.

Bernie's message is clear. In today's fast-paced world, where things keep changing, virtually all organisations need to continually innovate if they are to compete, prosper and survive – they need to 'innovate or die', a phrase that was introduced by Peter Drucker and others (Ignatius, 2014).

Innovation helps organisations respond to changes in the environment. It is important in all industries and for all organisations – from small start-ups to large enterprises, from charities to governmental agencies and even universities!

REFLECTION POINT: SUCCESSFUL INNOVATORS

Reflecting on Bernie's 'Innovate or die!' message, think about the implications for different organisations and industries. Ask yourself the following questions. Make a note of your answers in the space provided and/or in your journal for future reference.

1. WHICH ORGANISATIONS DO YOU THINK MOST SUCCESSFULLY DEVELOP AND DELIVER INNOVATION ON AN ONGOING BASIS?

2. WHAT DO YOU CONSIDER SETS THEM APART?

WHICH ORGANISATIONS ARE THE MOST INNOVATIVE?

The answer to this question is a little subjective. After all, it depends on how we measure innovation! However, there are a number of studies created on an annual basis that rank how innovative businesses are. Some studies focus on larger enterprises, whilst others place their emphasis on start-ups and/or small and medium-sized enterprises. We think innovation is something much more universal.

The Boston Consulting Group (BCG, 2021) has been running a global survey each year since 2005 to understand which organisations key executives most admire in terms of their innovation capabilities. The results are combined with a series of additional factors and published in the Boston Consulting Group's annual 'Most Innovative Companies' index report, with the results tending to focus on larger companies.

In 2021, the top 10 organisations were as follows:

1. Apple
2. Alphabet/Google
3. Amazon
4. Microsoft
5. Tesla
6. Samsung
7. IBM
8. Huawei
9. Sony
10. Pfizer

You can look up the full list of the top 50 organisations online, as well as details of the selection criteria used to create the list. Perhaps you highlighted some of the top 10 in your answers to the questions in the previous reflection point? If so, you were probably targeting technology companies in your thinking, right?

Although the top 10 is admittedly dominated by larger well-known technology companies, if we look at the top 50 as a whole, we can see there are organisations from many other industries. To those interested in industry trends, the Boston Consulting Group annual innovation index is interesting for a number of reasons. As we can track the results back until its inception in 2005, we can see how the top 10 and top 50 have changed over time. It's interesting to note that between the years 2005 and 2020, 162 different organisations were listed in the annual charts. Of these, only eight (Alphabet/Google, Amazon, Apple, HP, IBM, Microsoft, Samsung and Toyota) appeared in the top 50 every year. Approximately 30% of the organisations appeared only once, and nearly 60% appeared three times or less. These figures demonstrate how challenging it is for organisations to successfully innovate on an ongoing basis.

There are of course other ways to measure how innovative an organisation is. For example, there is the number of patents an organisation files or owns. The Organisation for Economic Co-operation and Development (OECD) collects and analyses examples of public sector innovation and advises governments on how to make innovations work. The Massachusetts Institute of Technology (MIT) in the USA and the KU Leuven in Europe tend to do well in rankings of the 'most innovative university' as compiled by Reuters (Ewalt, 2019). The World Intellectual Property Organization runs a 'Global Innovation Index' for entire countries, which makes for an interesting read (see further resources section at the end of the chapter). If you spend a little bit of time online, you will also find rankings and awards for start-ups and social enterprises, and all sorts of organisations. There are also competitions and challenges for students to demonstrate their innovativeness such as Enactus, UN SDG Awards and many more. Take a look for inspiration!

ARE THERE DIFFERENT TYPES AND LEVELS OF INNOVATION?

Yes. In the past, many people thought innovation was mostly about developing new products and services. In more recent times, it has been recognised that, in fact, there are multiple types of innovation.

Types of innovation include:

- **Product and service innovation** – A great example here is Apple. The organisation has been responsible for a series of groundbreaking product innovations, from the iPod to the iPad and the iPhone and so on. Apple has designed its organisation to focus on driving innovation on an ongoing basis (Podolny & Hansen, 2020): the company is led by experts rather than by general managers. These leaders understand and focus on the use of technology and new products and immerse themselves in the details involved. There's also a more general willingness to collaborate and focus on product or service innovation for Apple's customers.

- **Operational or process innovation** – Toyota, for example, is famed for the systematic and ongoing operational improvements it makes in its manufacturing processes. The 'Toyota Production System' was created with the objective of making vehicles ordered by customers in the quickest and most efficient way. The system is based upon a number of key concepts, including 'kaizen', which is about proactively identifying and making continuous improvements to continually improve and simplify operations. You can read more about Toyota's production system following the QR code provided.

- **Business model innovation** – Companies like IBM constantly change their organisation and what they make and sell. They evolve their business model in line with changing markets and customers. For example, when the company identified that selling personal computers and printers was becoming a commodity low-margin business, it sold these business units off and focused on selling and delivering higher value business and technology services to its clients. In the early 2020s, it has made the decision to spin off its technology services division and to focus on areas such as integrating cloud computing services and artificial intelligence. Another example in this area has been the movement many companies are making from selling products to providing subscription-based services. Whereas consumers used to buy CDs and DVDs, companies like Spotify and Netflix now provide paid subscription services for music and video content.

Some argue we should distinguish between innovations that relate to the market or market segments ('position innovation' – for example, Ryanair targeting a less affluent segment of the market) and innovations that are about how firms frame what they do ('paradigm innovation' – for instance, IBM shifted from a company selling hardware to more of a software and then services model) (Bessant & Tidd, 2015). In our view, these **types of innovations are often related, and can hence be collapsed into business (model) innovation**.

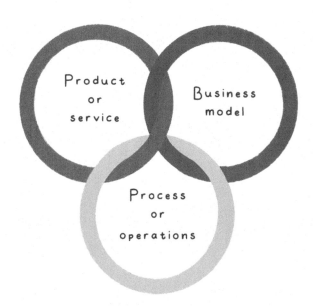

FIGURE 2.1: Types of innovation

When we look at innovation in the governmental or voluntary sector, the terminology can be a little different. Often, we read about 'social innovation' or 'innovation in policy'. However, when we look at innovations at the organisational level, there is a lot of overlap. Many innovations in public administration could be classified as process innovations, for example innovations aiming at the simplification and digitalisation of administrative procedures. Charities may innovate in the services they provide, the business model they use to balance income and expenses, as well as in their operational processes.

Innovation can also occur at different levels. In their much-cited *Harvard Business Review* article 'Managing your innovation portfolio', Tuff and Nagji (2012) described an **Innovation Ambition Matrix**. This categorised an organisation's innovation activities into three levels, as shown below.

- **Core innovation** – here the organisation optimises and improves its existing products, services and processes for its existing customers and markets.
- **Adjacent innovation** – where the organisation builds out from existing activities to create 'new to the company' business, such as new products and services linked to the existing portfolio for existing customers and/or existing products and services for new customers and markets.
- **Transformational innovation** – developing new breakthroughs and inventions, and potentially taking them to totally new markets.

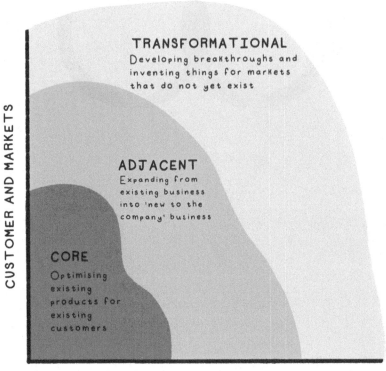

FIGURE 2.2: Levels of innovation (based on Tuff & Nagji, 2012)

Which level(s) of innovation organisations focus on can vary depending on the specific organisation, their strategic aims and the wider context they are operating within. Sometimes, however, innovation occurs when they were working on something unrelated, and it is 'serendipitous' (accidental).

Some organisations systematically try to innovate at the core level across one or more of the types of innovation, with the objective of improving their existing products, services, operations and/or business models step by step. Such *incremental* changes can make a big difference, particularly when they're added together. This is known as the 'aggregation of marginal gains', a term coined by Sir David Brailsford, a British cycling coach whose teams achieved astonishing success by combining many small improvements – saving half a second here, a tenth of a second there and so on – to make team members faster than the competition. Toyota also pioneered such an approach in the motor industry, and there are examples in other areas including surgery (Fleming et al., 2020).

Many organisations drive adjacent innovation to expand the size and scope of their business over time. For example, they may expand their product and service range by creating new offerings, linked to what they already do. An example of this occurred in the financial services industry when traditional banks expanded their customer offerings to provide insurance and other financial products to existing customers, in addition to providing savings and loan accounts.

A smaller subset of organisations places a special emphasis on transformational innovation. Some may argue that the first iPhone transformed the way we communicate. Netflix is another example, as it transformed its business model from one that was about subscribing to a DVD rental service to a subscription-based streaming solution and now even the creation of content. Sometimes, transformational innovation is also described as *radical* and/or *disruptive* innovation, meaning that such innovation doesn't just transform an organisation's business model but an entire field or industry, as in the example of Netflix. For a more detailed introduction to different types of innovation, such as incremental and radical innovation, have a look at the further resources section where we have included a video of our colleague Professor Krsto Pandza explaining these and related concepts.

Many organisations innovate at different levels. Google's parent company Alphabet has introduced a 70:20:10 rule. The company seeks to spend 70% of its innovation effort on core innovation, 20% on adjacent and 10% on transformational innovation. The rationale for this is that most of today's business and revenue is driven in the core level, so it needs to be the major area of focus, but tomorrow's opportunities are likely to be at the adjacent and transformational levels, so this is critically important too. Large companies that make a large share of their revenue in shrinking markets – such as perhaps Konica Minolta (who started out in the photography world), now in the field of photocopiers – are well advised to innovate at higher levels than those who have a strong foothold in growing markets.

This leads us nicely on to our final point, which is important to consider. If successful, something which is transformational level innovation today will move to the core in the future. For example, IBM created artificial intelligence capabilities when it developed 'Watson', a computer system capable of answering questions posed in natural language. At the time, the company was developing breakthrough transformational level innovation, yet ten years later, the technology underpinning Watson was a central part of IBM's business. At this stage, any further innovation on Watson would be considered innovation at the core level.

We hope that this section helps you to recognise the importance of *understanding context* and the *strategic dimension* of innovation. We innovate because we want to deliver value in the future. Our ability to anticipate the future and to know what will be of value depends on our understanding of our environment today, and our values, strategies and objectives, as much as it depends on our ability to develop and apply new ideas. The United Nations Sustainable Development Goals remind us all to think of planet and people before profit, however.

REFLECTION POINT: TYPES AND LEVELS OF INNOVATION

Reflecting on the information above, think about the types and levels of innovation. Ask yourself the following questions. Make a note of your answers in the space provided and/or in your journal for future reference.

CONSIDER THE ORGANISATIONS THAT YOU HIGHLIGHTED IN THE PREVIOUS REFLECTION POINT AS SUCCESSFUL INNOVATORS. WHAT TYPES AND/OR LEVELS OF INNOVATION DO YOU THINK THEY EXCEL AT MOST? WHY DO YOU THINK THAT?

INNOVATION MANAGEMENT

WHAT IS INNOVATION MANAGEMENT?

No matter what type or level of innovation an organisation focuses on, innovation needs to be managed. There are a lot of planning and other activities behind the development and evaluation of ideas, which then need to be translated into plans for action. Usually, there is research to be done and a business case to be made. Although innovation can and sometimes has occurred almost 'by accident', increasingly organisations are looking to manage, develop and deliver their innovation activities 'by design'.

'Innovation management is the process of generating, developing, and applying new ideas and capabilities, with the objective of delivering specific value.'

Organisations sometimes employ specialist innovation managers and specialist innovation teams to systematically manage their innovation-related activities. Such teams use an innovation management process to review, prioritise and track which ideas should or shouldn't be progressed beyond various check points, sometimes called 'stage gates'. This means project development is organised around distinct stages or phases, and at the end of each phase there is a review and a decision point (or 'gate') that a project needs to pass through. Often, business unit leaders and other sponsors will be involved in these reviews, particularly when major investment decisions are to be made.

The objectives of innovation management vary between and within organisations. In general, though, the objective is to accelerate and support the development of new capabilities. In this context, a capability is about the actual ability to deliver something. When we have an innovative idea, we may not immediately know how to develop it, let alone implement it. We first need to work on the idea, understand what is involved and 'develop the capability'. Innovation management is about capability development – we need it so that the best ideas can be developed and delivered as soon as possible, and the value and benefits can be realised by the organisation. By focusing on innovation management, organisations look to do this systematically and consistently, 'by design' rather than haphazardly or by accident.

EXPERT

MANAGING INNOVATION

Tim Kastelle is Director of Entrepreneurship & Innovation at the Business School of The University of Queensland (UQ). Tim's research, teaching and engagement work are all based on his study of innovation management. Tim has worked extensively with a wide range of organisations. He is currently the Director of MBA & Executive Education for the UQ Business School.

1. IN YOUR VIEW, WHAT IS INNOVATION MANAGEMENT ABOUT?

People often get a funny look on their face when I tell them I study and teach innovation management – they'll ask 'How can you manage innovation?' And if you think that innovation is only about having great ideas, then this is a very reasonable question. But, of course, innovation is more than that. I talk about it as executing new ideas to create value – you need all three of those things (ideas, execution and value creation) to genuinely innovate.

This definition implies a process, and this process can, and I'd argue should, be managed. We usually begin with a problem or an opportunity. Once we understand the focus area, we generate ideas. From there, we select the best ideas and begin to develop them. As we move forward, it becomes clearer which ideas are most likely to generate value, and focus on these. Others we set aside but take away the learning from working on them. At the end of the process, we deliver a range of new or updated products, services or processes and so on and use these to derive value. The ultimate objectives of the innovation management process are twofold. Firstly, to create value in as quick and cost-effective a manner as possible, and secondly to do this using a systematic and repeatable approach. A really good innovation management process will support this for products, for services, for ways of doing things and for business models.

2. IN YOUR EXPERIENCE, WHAT DO MOST PEOPLE GET WRONG ABOUT INNOVATION MANAGEMENT?

The most common mistake is one I already mentioned – to believe that innovation is only about having ideas. It's not just that. Humans are idea-generating machines, and so are our organisations. We rarely have a shortage of ideas. But to innovate, we need to be able to choose the ideas worth pursuing, to execute these ideas and to do this in a way that creates value for people we care about. In many ways, ideas are the easy part.

The second big mistake is to think that we can make our organisations more innovative without actually changing the way that we act. You can't treat innovation management as a box-ticking exercise, or buy some magic software that will make the whole thing work. You need to genuinely change the way you think and act on a day-to-day basis if you want to be more creative and more innovative.

3. HOW CAN WE BEST LEARN ABOUT INNOVATION MANAGEMENT?

Innovation is definitely a learning-by-doing activity. In fact, the most dangerous thing you can do is to just learn some of the concepts without engaging in the practice. You need to engage with stakeholders directly, to learn what value means for them, and then work on building out ideas that address this. As you do this more, your creativity and skill in innovation will grow – it takes practice, just like playing an instrument or a sport.

TOP TIP

One of the most important innovation skills is learning how to discover what people need. Most of the time, you can't ask them this directly. Instead, you have to talk about their experiences or observe them, and learn from that. You can't act empathetically without first building empathy – and you do this through conversation and engagement.

WHAT DOES INNOVATION MANAGEMENT INVOLVE?

A simple example of an innovation management process is shown in Figure 2.3 below.

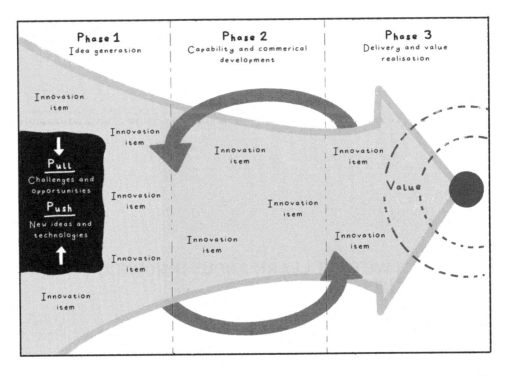

FIGURE 2.3: Simple innovation management process model

 The model above is a simple version of a three-phase 'stage gate' innovation management process that is used by organisations all over the world. You'll soon become very familiar with this, as we use it throughout the book! But let's first have a look at each of the three phases in turn.

PHASE 1 – IDEA GENERATION AND IDENTIFICATION OF OPPORTUNITY

The first phase is all about the initial research, scoping and idea generation. It aims at identifying meaningful innovation opportunities in the form of 'innovation items'. In the beginning, we usually have quite a few of such innovation items in the pipeline. Innovation items are created in response to an innovation pull or an innovation push.

An **innovation pull** happens when new ideas and solutions are needed to address certain challenges or opportunities. You may think of this like a demand *pulling* in new ideas, so to speak. In contrast, an **innovation push** describes a situation where there are new ideas and/or technologies and an organisation is seeking to identify the best challenges and opportunities to apply them to. You can visualise this as someone trying to push an idea or technology onto a consumer. We have a closer look at innovation pull and push in Chapter 5. For now, the main point is that in the first phase ideas ('innovation items') are generated and that they are then reviewed. At the end of the first phase, we reach the first transition point or 'stage gate' where innovation items are prioritised. The most promising ones are selected for the second phase.

PHASE 2 – CAPABILITY AND COMMERCIAL DEVELOPMENT

A smaller number of innovation items are then developed further. This includes two parallel streams of activity. First, we have **capability development**. This means that enough research and development take place for the ideas to be developed in a way that they can be proven up to an agreed point. This may take the form of a prototype, proof of concept, pilot, minimum viable product solution, etc., depending on the specific innovation. Some students find the term 'capability development' confusing. However, we need both knowledge and capabilities to evaluate whether an idea would really work, and we need to develop such understanding in order to decide which idea is the best one to progress further.

The second and related activity at this stage is **commercial development**. Here, we try to demonstrate how the innovation item (such as a product, service or policy) will deliver value to an end user as well as to the business sponsor and wider organisation. Typically, we do this in the form of a business case. Only when the capability and commercial value is proven will the sponsor and organisation be likely to invest in further development and delivery of the innovation. And this takes us to the next transition point or 'stage gate'. Only one or a small number of innovation items will pass through this gate and will be developed so that they deliver value.

PHASE 3 – DELIVERY AND VALUE REALISATION

Innovations with proven capability and commercial value – and that have sufficiently wowed the innovation sponsors – are progressed to the final stage of the process.

Delivery activities are all about the realisation and implementation of the idea. Let's take the example of an app. A prototype is usually created at the second stage to demonstrate the potential value. At the third stage this is developed into the full-blown app with full functionality At the same time, activities are underway that ensure that this app can be distributed, installed and used. Maintenance and support are put in place. Marketing gets involved. All of these activities are often summarised as being part of the delivery and (if the innovation is to be sold externally) commercialisation process.

Typically only when the innovation has been delivered and realised will **value** be derived. For innovations requiring a significant investment for development and delivery, it may be some time before a break-even point is reached, and a positive return is made on the investment. These things need to be considered in the first and second stages, when the more promising innovation items are identified.

Please note that more often than not, innovation projects go through iterations or development 'loops'. In Figure 2.3 this is illustrated in the shape of two orange arrows. For example, capability development (Phase 2) may reveal flaws in the initial idea so that everyone has to go back to the drawing board and come up with new ideas (Phase 1). Or in the context of preparing for the actual delivery (Phase 3), new opportunities to capitalise on certain benefits may be identified, requiring more commercial development (Phase 2). So, anyone who works in innovation will tell you that there are usually many of such loops and obstacles to overcome before a great idea or invention has been transformed into an innovation.

In a number of industries, much more detailed models are used. For example, NASA has developed the 'Technology Readiness Level' model to ensure new technologies are suitably robust prior to deployment. Only once a new technology has been 'flight proven' during a successful mission can it be judged to have reached the highest level, TRL 9. Similarly, a number of regulated industries, such as pharmaceuticals and healthcare, have rigorous and detailed processes, with many stage gates for assessments and decisions of whether to continue or abandon the innovation.

MORE IN-DEPTH: INNOVATION AND CHANGE MANAGEMENT

If you've been studying management (and maybe even if not!), you may be wondering what the difference is between 'change management' and 'innovation management'. There is obviously a close link between the two and potentially a long discussion to be had, which we appreciate you probably don't want to read, so we'll give you a summary instead. 'Change management' typically refers to a set of planned activities to move something (an organisation, a business model, a technology, etc.) from a current to a planned future state. In many ways, 'innovation management' is about doing the same thing. The main difference is that with innovation management we often face more uncertainty. We're focusing on new ideas and capabilities, and throughout the process we are less clear about what the future state will be.

A simple stage gate process can help us to establish where we are in the process. However, we have to be careful that we do not become focused only on the stage or step we're in. For example, as our next industry expert emphasises, we do need to consider issues around delivery and adoption already in the first and second phase and not develop an innovation item with the expectation that it will then be implemented by magic somehow.

EXPERT

UNDERSTANDING CONTEXT

Gisela Abbam is Senior Director for Government Affairs at PerkinElmer, a multinational company serving customers in 190 countries. A global advocate for the prioritisation of health, Gisela worked in several roles which involved close collaboration with governments and international organisations such as the World Health Organization and the World Bank.

1. IN YOUR EXPERIENCE, WHAT ARE COMMON BARRIERS TO AN INNOVATION SUCCEEDING?

In my experience, we need to have a closer look at adoption to better understand some of the most common (and most overlooked!) barriers to adoption.

(Continued)

First of all, users can be reluctant to change the status quo even when there is evidence to show the innovation will improve outcomes. Therefore, we really need to understand adoption from the perspective of those who adopt the product. Do they want to use the product? Will they want to use the product as intended? If not, what additional information about the ease of use can be provided to enable them to adopt the new innovation?

We also need to consider market barriers and regulatory barriers. These should be considered during the product development and actions should be taken to reduce these barriers.

2. CAN YOU PLEASE EXPLAIN THIS A LITTLE MORE?

Yes of course. For example, not every company can just sell a new medical device in any market. First, regulatory approval must be sought and there are different rules and procedures for different products and markets.

Then, achieving accreditation as a supplier to a healthcare service can be difficult. Some countries have a highly centralised service, and one may face a lot of red tape before one is added to the list of official suppliers. Other healthcare services are more fragmented and then one might need to approach individual hospitals, practices and doctors, which again is a different game altogether.

We also need to know about healthcare policy and clinical priorities. For example, if there is funding for prevention as well as diagnosis and treatment.

So, we need to understand how our innovation will be adopted in a given context – a medical context, an administrative context, and a political context! And we need to consider how we can work with relevant stakeholders in these contexts.

3. WOW, THIS SOUNDS LIKE A LOT OF WORK!

Yes, and we need to remember that any additional stage in the adoption process takes time and can hence cost a lot of money! Many adoption processes incur additional costs which we need to be aware of early on – and not just the costs of research and development. This is why it is important to pay attention to the adoption process and the context of adoption when working on an innovation project.

TOP TIP

Focus on identifying and addressing a gap in the market. If you can clearly articulate why and how the innovation should be adopted, then you are on the right track.

OPEN INNOVATION

WHAT IS OPEN INNOVATION?

Open innovation focuses on how organisations can, and should, collaborate with other organisations and external stakeholders to develop new ideas and technologies. At this point, many of our students ask us why organisations choose to innovate together when they seek to derive competitive advantage from their innovations? Bill Joy, co-founder of Sun Microsystems and one of the early pioneers of Linux, answered this question in the following way: 'No matter who you are, most of the smartest people work for someone else' (Lakhani & Panetta, 2007), a principle which is now known as 'Joy's Law'.

The best innovators – you may of think Apple, Google or others – work with other organisations to develop new products and services and to improve existing operations, business models and so on. This gives these companies access to the capabilities and 'smart people' they don't have themselves, but other organisations do. However, as you can imagine, the decision to engage in open innovation has important implications for the way organisations capture value – and for how the innovation process is organised. Have a look for Gartner Group content in your university's online library databases for some examples of how such alliances have brought benefits.

We will discuss some of the benefits of two types of open innovation in the next sub-section. If you are not into management, we appreciate that this is a lot to take in. However, we believe that this understanding of open innovation and innovation management will be very beneficial to you. Learning how to draw on or bring in ideas and capabilities from outside your organisation is a key employability skill. Consider the following: wherever you will work, most of the most talented and interesting people in the world won't be there. So, it really pays off (sometimes even literally) to know how to engage with others when you want to make new ideas real, so that they can create value – whatever this value will be!

HOW DOES OPEN INNOVATION WORK?

Some of the leading academic theory in this area was initially led by Professor Henry Chesbrough from Berkeley University in the US, who defined open innovation in two ways:

- 'Firms can and should use external ideas as well as internal ideas, and internal and external paths to market, as they look to advance their technology' (Chesbrough et al., 2006, p. 1).
- 'Purposive inflows and outflows of knowledge to accelerate internal innovation and expand the markets for external use of innovation' (Chesbrough et al., 2006, p. vii).

What does he mean by this? It is not as complex as it may sound. Professor Chesbrough basically argued that **there are two types of open innovation: outside-in and inside-out.**

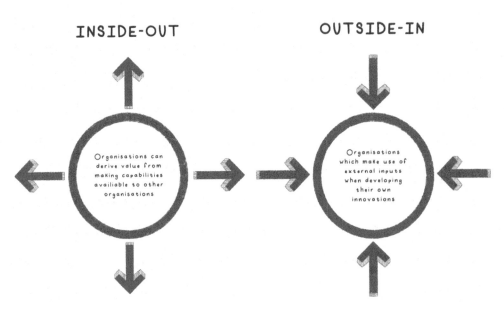

INSIDE-OUT

OUTSIDE-IN

Organisations can derive value from making capabilities available to other organisations

Organisations which make use of external inputs when developing their own innovations

FIGURE 2.4: Open innovation

Let us have a closer look at these two types and see how they work.

In **outside-in open innovation**, external ideas and technologies are brought into the organisation's own innovation process. Mechanisms for this include approaches which some of you may be familiar with, or may have even been involved in. Others may be new to you. As you'll see, there's often a level of overlap between the various mechanisms.

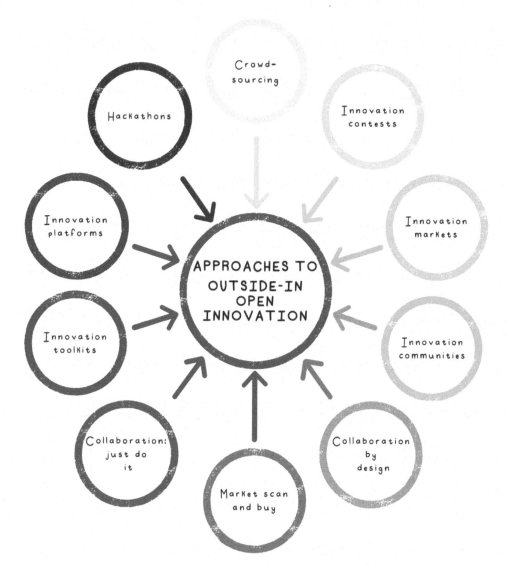

FIGURE 2.5: Examples of approaches to outside-in open innovation

- **Crowdsourcing** is about obtaining something (in this context ideas) from a large group of individuals. A good example of this is 'LEGO Ideas' where anyone can submit an idea for a new Lego product – and those whose proposals are implemented receive 1% of the royalties.
- **Innovation contests** usually highlight a specific challenge and create a competition to address it. For example, the Longitude Prize has a £10 million prize

fund for the development of point-of-care diagnostic tests to conserve antibiotics for future generations. You might find competitions online on all sorts of challenges as innovation contests have become quite a prominent approach to outside-in innovations.

- **Innovation markets** connect organisations that have challenges for inventors and others who have ideas and solve problems. One example is InnoCentive, which provides an online platform for connecting organisations with challenges and problem solvers.
- **Innovation communities** are groups of people, often with similar interests, who develop new ideas usually in a particular field. Some may argue 'LEGO Ideas' has created an innovation community of Lego enthusiasts. In the world of software development, there are many examples of 'open source' communities, who create and maintain source code for computer programs, languages and operating systems, such as Linux, making them free of charge for others to use, distribute and change.
- **Innovation toolkits and platforms** open up spaces where ideas can be shared and developed. Today, many organisations use online platforms and tools where users can submit projects or ideas. Another example here could be the tools provided by companies like Apple and Google to allow developers to create new apps for their platforms. Apple are considered pioneering by the operating system market because new updates to their systems are tested by real users before being launched to the public. (But we are not getting into the Mac vs Windows debate here...)
- **Hackathons** are individual events where multiple teams try to develop a new solution to a problem in a collaborative effort. Hackathons are similar to innovation contests in that they often involve some element of competition, but they usually run over a shorter period of time, from a few hours up to a few days.

Finally, we need to consider the practical aspect of how people and businesses outside the organisation can engage and submit ideas and proposals. In the context of a student project, this perspective may appear less relevant. However, as you develop your career, you will find it is really useful to know about the most common ways in which organisations source innovative ideas in their environment. You may be able to draw on this knowledge much sooner than you think – in your next job interview for example!

- **Collaboration: just do it** is when organisations work with suppliers, partners and/or other organisations to find and develop new ideas and capabilities as part of normal business operations, without any conscious planning. An example of this might be when a retailer works with many suppliers and delivery companies to find new ways to optimise stock levels, so the shelves are never empty.

- **Collaboration by design** involves organisations planning collaborative innovation activities very carefully, including targeting which specific suppliers, partners and/or other organisations to work with, and which areas to focus on when finding and developing new ideas and capabilities. For example, a retailer may select only its most innovative suppliers to work with in this way.

- **Market scan and buy** is about organisations identifying priority areas for innovation and acquiring capability and/or organisations (rather than collaborating with them). For example, when IBM wanted to move more quickly into the cloud computing market, it acquired Red Hat, an American multinational software company that provides storage, open source software products and related services to enterprises. The intention was to help IBM to develop new capabilities and market share in cloud computing more quickly than it otherwise might have.

The second type is called **inside-out open innovation**. This is where ideas and technologies created within the organisation are allowed to go outside to be used by other organisations, on the basis the organisation can derive some value by allowing this. This often occurs when an organisation doesn't plan to make direct use of a new idea or technology it has created but believes that it can benefit financially or in other ways by making it available for other organisations to use and take to market. Approaches that enable this are shown in Figure 2.6. If you wonder why you need to know this, our main answer is that this really helps you to develop your commercial awareness. It can be really useful to understand why an organisation may wish to allow others to use its innovation, and what the common approaches are for doing so.

- **Intellectual property (IP) licensing** involves allowing other organisations to make use of an organisation's protected intellectual property, usually for a fee, to develop, use and/or sell in their own offerings.

- **Joint ventures** are where two or more organisations make a commercial arrangement to undertake a task such as a specific innovation project or large change programme.

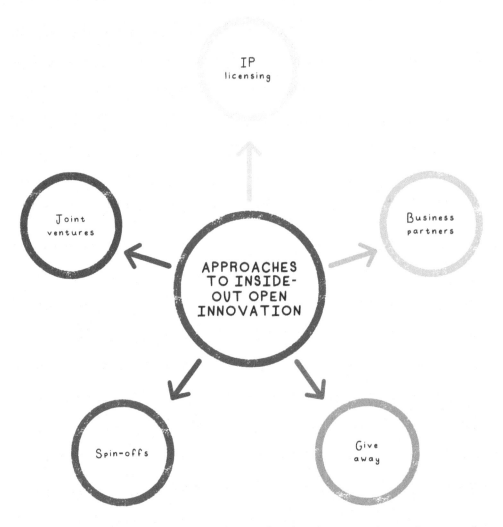

FIGURE 2.6: Examples of inside-out open innovation approaches

- **Business partners** – sometimes organisations develop a commercial agreement where one takes another's innovations to market. For example, sometimes software vendors sell their software products via the consultancy firms which install them.
- **Spin-off companies** involve the creation of a new firm, which will take new innovations or product and service offerings to market, independently of the organisation which created them.

You may wonder why there's also an item called **'Give away'** in Figure 2.6. Sometimes, organisations may make their ideas, intellectual property or technology available to other organisations to use without charge. This could be for purely altruistic reasons, or because the organisation determines they can derive a wider benefit from others using their technology. Industry examples include Volvo opening access to the patent for the three-point seatbelt due to its life-saving value and Tesla making many of its patents for electrical vehicles available to other companies. Arguably, in the case of Tesla such a move may be designed not just to encourage a more sustainable vehicle industry, but to accelerate the development of the wider innovation ecosystem for electric cars and vehicles, which will be good for the company too.

HOW DOES OPEN INNOVATION IMPACT THE INNOVATION MANAGEMENT PROCESS?

When you think of it, outside-in innovation and inside-out innovation make more sense at *different stages of the innovation process*. Outside-in usually starts in the earlier stages – for example, LEGO asks for ideas and not fully developed kits ready to be shipped! Inside-out innovation usually makes more sense when the idea and related capabilities are more developed or even at the commercialisation stage (for example, when one seeks to license or sell the capability). The following diagram illustrates how outside-in and inside-out open innovation activities can be integrated into an organisation's innovation management process.

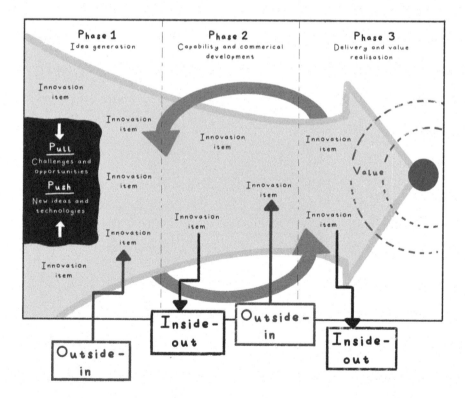

FIGURE 2.7: Simple innovation management process model incorporating open innovation

This figure may look a little complex but don't worry. If you follow the 'outside-in' arrow on the left, this is happening during the idea generation phase. This may represent a new idea which has come from outside the organisation via a hackathon or an innovation context. Alternatively, the 'inside-out' arrow on the right might be a decision not to directly deliver an innovation to market, but instead to license the intellectual property created to another organisation. The original organisation will still realise some value, probably through receiving a payment from the other organisation.

REFLECTION POINT: OPEN INNOVATION

Reflecting on the information above, think about open innovation. Ask yourself the following questions. Note down your answers in the space provided and/or in your journal for future reference.

OTHER THAN THE EXAMPLES PROVIDED, CAN YOU THINK OF SOME POSITIVE EXAMPLES OF OPEN INNOVATION?

WHAT DO YOU THINK SOME OF THE CHALLENGES OF OPEN INNOVATION MAY BE FOR ORGANISATIONS?

Note: If you have problems with one of the questions you can look up some sample solutions on our companion website.

INNOVATION ENABLERS

You may wonder now, what can organisations do to more successfully enable innovation. Many reports and studies have been developed which include recommendations on improving innovation capability. In this section we present a framework of six key innovation enablers, which are based on some of the key learning points identified above, industry reports and the authors' experience.

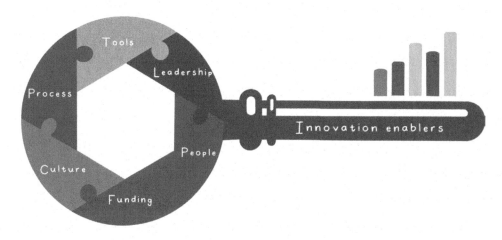

FIGURE 2.8: Innovation enablers

Let us have a closer look at each of the enablers in turn:

1. **Leadership**: The first key enabler is leadership. In order to innovate systematically an organisation needs leaders with an appetite for change. Innovation can be challenging; it often involves changes in outlook or practices that are difficult to implement. Innovation asks people to contemplate the future and leads to decisions fraught with uncertainty. Innovation can go wrong, which is why so many people perceive it as risky. Leaders need to make and communicate innovation as a strategic priority. After all, the organisation needs to 'innovate or die'. But as well as communicating innovation as a priority (and not just marketing bullsh*t), the leaders must take proactive steps to put all of the other five enablers into place, as without them, there will be no, or at best very little, innovation. It will be the organisation's people, not the leaders, who will make innovation happen. They need to be supported by processes, funding, platforms and tools to ensure innovation really is driven as a priority. And the leaders need to nurture an organisational culture conducive to innovation. Leadership is hence a catalyst for all the other five enablers: people, process, culture, funding and platforms and tools. And don't forget, today's leaders also started out in junior roles and progressed over time...

2. **People**: Organisations need people to generate new ideas, develop and deliver on them. Due to the importance of open innovation, they will also need to develop relationships with people and organisations beyond organisational boundaries. Many organisations create specialist innovation units or teams, with responsibility for making innovation happen. Larger firms such as SAP, Ericsson or PayPal have dedicated creative labs or 'play' spaces for employees to just try out new tech and think of ways it could bring benefit to their role, firm or customers. In general, the function of an innovation team is not to 'do' all the innovation themselves (imagine the pressure!), but to accelerate the generation, selection, development and delivery of new ideas and technologies. Innovation managers may be given this or other job titles, but it's what they do which is important, not what their job is called. Often, innovation teams and managers are embedded within a business unit, particularly when working on core and adjacent innovation. The role here may be to act as a catalyst and an enabler for all the other people in the organisation – to ensure that the best ideas, wherever they come from, are identified, developed and delivered. Sometimes innovation teams are established within specialist units. This is often the case when the role is focused on transformational innovation. This separates the team from current daily operations and performance targets, to enable them to focus on developing the new business of tomorrow. Whichever way you look at it, people are at the heart of any innovation project – they make 'new ideas real, so that they can create value'. The remaining enablers are all about supporting the organisation's people to do this.

3. **Process**: 'What, more process?' we hear you cry! To innovate, people need to have the ability to ideate and develop, and to test and learn. As described earlier in this chapter, organisations use innovation management processes to deliver new ideas and capabilities. These processes may sit at the overall organisation level, business unit and/or local team level. One of the simplest (yet most widely used) models for innovation processes is the stage gate process we introduced in the previous section. With the rise of open innovation, we see more innovation management processes making use of external ideas and technologies.

4. **Culture**: Although perhaps less tangible than the other enablers, the development of an innovation culture within an organisation is very important. Sometimes organisations include 'innovation' in their organisational vision, mission or value statement. IBM, for example, has three corporate values, one of which is 'Innovation that matters – for our company and for the world'; Philips' mission statement is 'We strive to make the world healthier and more sustainable through innovation'; whilst Nike's mission statement is 'To bring inspiration and innovation to every athlete in

the world (If you have a body, you are an athlete)'. A positive innovation culture instils belief that the organisation considers innovation to be a priority. It is reflected in the way certain tasks and projects are organised as well as in the physical environment. An innovation culture will be even more effective if it spans beyond the organisation's direct workforce to include a wider ecosystem, including customers, suppliers and business partners. Positive communications and rewards for successful innovations are key elements of an innovation culture, as is a wider organisational culture that cherishes diversity, creativity and engagement. Some organisations achieve this by NOT putting the word 'innovation' into people's role titles, thereby indicating that everyone is an innovator.

5. **Funding**: Innovation needs funding, i.e., money! If everyone is too busy with day-to-day operations, there will be no time for innovative ideas to be developed and explored. This is why some organisations have introduced initiatives where staff can dedicate a set percentage of their time to work on new ideas. Time is important but is not enough by itself, as other resources may also be needed to engage users, develop capabilities, build prototypes, conduct market research and so on. All these things usually cost money – that's why funding is important. Funding for the early stages of the development of new innovations is an issue for many organisations, as the potential benefits and business case aren't yet fully clear. But if there isn't a way for teams to get money to fund such experimentation, how will the organisation find and develop anything new? That's why some companies provide special innovation funds or budgets targeted at supporting early-stage innovation. Once the capability and business case for an emerging technology, or other innovation, is proven, sponsors may decide to put their hands in their pockets and find the money to fund further development and delivery, on the basis that they have clear sight of the likely value and benefits.

6. **Innovation platforms and tools**: To support people, process, funding and culture, organisations need innovation 'platforms' and 'tools'. What do we mean by this? With increased focus on digital innovation and transformation, organisations need agile platforms and mechanisms to identify ideas, create prototypes and experiment with new and emerging technologies. The focus of innovation platforms can be wide ranging. They can include online systems to capture ideas, research labs, 'sandpit' events (discussion forums where free thinking is encouraged), cloud computing based platforms to enable fast development of prototypes and apps and other mechanisms for developing new ideas and technologies, such as those focused on driving open innovation. There are also many tools and techniques which can be used to manage,

develop and deliver innovation. For example, Design Thinking provides a wide range of techniques for developing and enabling innovation. Design Thinking will be explored in more detail in the next chapter.

CONCLUSION

Despite it being one of the longer chapters of the book, we have only scratched the surface of innovation as we have focused on the main principles and the most important things you need to know. After all, this is a book that focuses mainly on a combination of experiential and reflective learning rather than reading! However, we do feel that this chapter gives you the beginning of a solid foundation in innovation theory on which to build in the following chapters.

Perhaps without even noticing it, you have also started to address some of the seven skill areas and gaps. The first gap was of course about *innovation*. Throughout the chapter we have also introduced and discussed key concepts associated with *commercial awareness* – for example, when we reflected on the different levels of innovation and their implications for business development. We also looked at innovation management and discussed the importance of developing capabilities. In the section on open innovation, we explained how organisations may benefit from different forms of open innovation. In the final section describing enablers, we had a closer look at how innovation requires resources such as funding, time and platforms, and how it can be a challenge to obtain these for the early stages of the innovation process.

The reflection points have hopefully helped you to develop your journal and to notice a bit more what you will actually take away from reading a text such as this with (or without) reflective thinking and writing. They will also help you to revisit key learning points as you develop your own project.

KEY LEARNING POINTS

- Innovation is the application of new ideas, or existing ideas in a new context, which results in change that delivers value.

- For all organisations, including businesses and non-profit generating organisations, innovation is very important, not just to address the challenges of our time but also for the organisation to achieve its purpose of flourishing in its given environment.

- There are different types of innovation including product and service innovation, operational and process innovation, and business (model) innovation.

- Organisations may innovate in their core activity or business (core innovation); they may innovate to develop related products/enter neighbouring markets (adjacent innovation); and/or they develop new breakthroughs and inventions (transformative innovation).

- Innovation management is the process of generating, developing and applying new ideas and capabilities, with the objective of delivering specific value.

- A simple stage gate innovation process may involve three stages: a) idea generation/identification of opportunity; b) capability and commercial development; and c) delivery and value realisation.

- Open innovation focuses on how organisations can, and should, innovate with other organisations and external stakeholders to develop new ideas and technologies. There are two types of open innovation: outside-in and inside-out.

- Six key innovation enablers are: leadership, people, process, culture, funding and platforms, and tools.

ACTION POINTS

☐ In order to get the most out of the effort you've spent reading this far, please make notes in your personal reflective journal and/or the space provided in the learning points.

☐ Complete the exercises below to verify your learning.

EXERCISES

1. Proctor & Gamble is an example of a leading organisation which has embraced open innovation. P&G's Connect + Develop website provides a platform for the company to share its challenges and get ideas and inputs

from external inventors and organisations. At the time of going to press, the website address is: www.pgconnectdevelop.com.

A quick internet search will also uncover studies, articles and YouTube videos, etc. describing P&G's approach, including many successes. Select one example of open innovation at P&G from these sources and make a note of why you believe it is a good demonstration of open innovation.

2. Have a look at the table below and indicate whether each activity is more about inside-out or outside-in open innovation. It may also be helpful to identify some examples for each.

	Inside-out open innovation	*Outside-in* open innovation
Market scan and buy		
Hackathon		
Collaboration by design		
Spin-off		
Innovation market		
Innovation platform		
IP licensing		
Joint venture		
Crowdsourcing		

Note: Sample answers for this exercise are available online.

FURTHER RESOURCES

If you want to see some more definitions of innovation visit the following website, where you can look up the definitions of another 15 leading innovation experts:

www.ideatovalue.com/inno/nickskillicorn/2016/03/innovation-15-experts-share-innovation-definition/

Our colleague at Leeds, Professor Krsto Pandza, has put together this video with a quick introduction to different types of innovation:

www.youtube.com/watch?v=h5Zapw9DhmM&t=7s

You can look up the most innovative firms as ranked by Boston Consultant Group here:

www.bcg.com/publications/2021/most-innovative-companies-overview

A short article about Apple's functional organisation and how it is geared towards innovation:

Podolny, J.M., & Hansen, M.T. 2020. How Apple is organized for innovation. *Harvard Business Review*, 98(6), 86–95.

The World Intellectual Property Organization runs a 'Global Innovation Index' for entire countries, which makes for a really interesting read:

Dutta, S., Lanvion, B., & Wunsch-Vincent, S. 2020. *Global Innovation Index 2020. Who Will Finance Innovation?* World Intellectual Property Organization.

Here's a nice blog post on different types of innovation:

Zapfl, D. 2018. What types of innovation are there? *LEAD Innovation blog.*

It could be useful to have a closer look at Tuff and Nagji's original article on levels of innovation:

Tuff, G., & Nagji, G. 2012. Managing your innovation portfolio. *Harvard Business Review.*

To find out more about key enablers for innovation and what makes some organisations more successful at delivering innovation than others, you can read and review this IBM report:

Ikeda, K., Majumdar, A., & Marshall, A. 2013. *More Than Magic. How the Most Successful Organizations Innovate.* IBM Institute for Business Value.

Tim Kastelle who we interviewed above has a great innovation blog:

https://timkastelle.org/theblog/

To find out more about how organisations can 'collaborate by design' to deliver innovation together, you can read this publication. It was written by Tony, based upon his practical experience from working on joint innovation activities with clients at IBM:

Morgan, T. 2017. *Collaborative Innovation: How Clients and Service Providers Can Work by Design to Achieve It*. New York: Business Expert Press.

We are often asked about the difference between open innovation and open source – and that is an important point! Have a look how Chesbrough himself explains it:

Chesbrough, H. 2016. *Open Innovation vs. Open Source*. UC Berkeley Executive Education.

And for those who want to know more, this blog explains it in a bit more detail:

Grams, C., & Lindegaard, S. 2010. *Open Innovation and Open Source Innovation: What Do They Share and Where Do They Differ?*

If you are interested in a solid textbook on innovation management because you want to develop a deeper understanding of what it involves, we recommend the following:

Tidd, J., & Bessant, J. 2018. *Managing Innovation: Integrating Technological, Market and Organizational Change*. 6th edn. Hoboken, NJ: Wiley.

CHAPTER

3

DESIGN
THINKING

Chapter contents

Goals

- To introduce you to Design Thinking and illustrate what it involves.

- To explain the process and key principles of Design Thinking.

- To present a useful example of Design Thinking and indicate where you can find more.

- To get you set to start learning about Design Thinking by doing it (a little)!

- To explore the important role of teamwork in Design Thinking.

INTRODUCTION

Now that we have established what innovation and innovation management are and what they entail, we'd like to introduce you to *Design Thinking*.

Depending on who you ask, Design Thinking is a prominent approach, a process or a broad set of techniques – some may even say an ideology – for solving complex problems. By itself, that does not say much – after all there are many ways to approach problem solving! So, what makes Design Thinking so special, or at least different? Why has it been adopted by innovation leaders all over the world, including Google, IBM and Apple? In the first section of this chapter, we'll take a closer look at these questions to examine the origin, process and principal concepts of Design Thinking. In the second section, we will begin to explore how Design Thinking *is carried out* and explore why teamwork is such an important element – so that by reading this, you can see how it can be relevant to you for now and your future employability journey. At the end of the chapter, we will discuss some of the practicalities to consider when using Design Thinking techniques as part of a project, so that in the next chapter you can finally start working on your challenge! From then on, you'll be learning about Design Thinking activities by doing them!

Before we take a closer look at the meaning of Design Thinking, we would like you to carry out a short exercise, or call it an experiment if you like. It may appear to be a bit strange at first – but don't worry! You'll soon see why we've asked you to do it!

EXERCISE: DESIGN A VASE

First, we would like you to design a vase with flowers in it. This will be for a 75-year-old person with limited mobility who lives in their own house and wants to enjoy fresh flowers.

Take a few minutes out and develop some ideas for different designs. Select one of your ideas, and then use a pen or pencil to draw your vase of flowers in the space on the following page. It doesn't need to be detailed or elaborate – this is not a drawing test! Just sketch something you think the person would enjoy. Once you've done that, move on, and we'll return to this later.

UNDERSTANDING DESIGN THINKING

WHAT IS DESIGN THINKING?

As with innovation, there is no single definition of Design Thinking, so let us have a look at two which we believe when considered together succinctly describe what Design Thinking is all about:

- '**Design Thinking is a human-centred approach to innovation.** It draws from the designer's toolkit to integrate the needs of people, the possibilities of technology, and the requirements for business success' (Brown, 2021).
- 'Designers resist the temptation to jump immediately to a solution to the stated problem. Instead, they first spend time determining what the basic, fundamental (root) issue is that needs to be addressed. They don't try to search for a solution **until they have determined the real problem**, and even then, instead of solving that problem, they stop to consider a wide range of potential solutions. Only then will they finally converge upon their proposal. This process is called "Design Thinking"' (Norman, 2018).

Don't be put off by the word 'designer'. Although Design Thinking originated in the design world, it can, and is, applied in many different contexts by many people in different roles. In this book, you will develop innovation and Design Thinking related techniques to address challenges and opportunities across a wide range of industries – so you are the the innovator or 'designer'!

MORE IN-DEPTH: THE ORIGINS OF DESIGN THINKING

In its origins, Design Thinking was about how designers thought when they addressed a problem, and how thinking relates to doing. This was a topic of much academic debate in design disciplines. In the past decade or so, Design Thinking has really taken off in business and related disciplines, where some of the methods developed by designers were found to be really useful for addressing a much wider range of problems, including those related to innovation and strategy (Johansson-Sköldberg et al., 2013).

Design Thinking was adopted and promoted by the large innovation and consulting company IDEO, with the IDEO CEO even writing a book about it (Brown, 2009), which has become one of the go-to sources ever since. Other large technology companies such as IBM and Google followed suit, and some of the more prominent business schools also discovered the 'magic' of Design Thinking. In 2009, Roger Martin, from the Rotman School of Management, published another prominent book that examined Design Thinking as a source of competitive advantage. A flurry of publications followed that described how Design Thinking could be used to create and grow a start-up business – or even develop one's career! If you want to find out more have a look at the further resources at the end of the chapter.

THE DESIGN THINKING PROCESS

The different methods and techniques associated with Design Thinking can be used in isolation or in combination. When they are used in combination, they form the Design Thinking *process*, as shown in Figure 3.1.

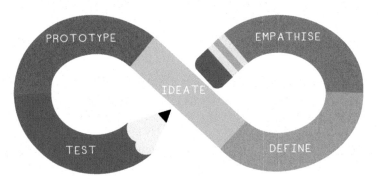

FIGURE 3.1: The Design Thinking process

As you can see, **the Design Thinking process consists of five stages:**

1. **Empathise** – Have empathy for and understand the needs of the end users who will use our solutions and the sponsor(s) and other stakeholders who will fund and derive benefit from them.

2. **Define** – Define and understand the problems, challenges and/or opportunities we will be developing solutions to address. This will be difficult if insufficient time has been spent on the empathy stage.

3. **Ideate** – Generate diverse ideas to address the problem in ways which will meet the needs of the end user and create value for the sponsor(s), analyse and prioritise the ideas and select specific ideas to develop solutions for. Having some 'outside the box' ideas at this stage is really useful!

4. **Prototype** – Quickly create, demonstrate and communicate the value of prototype solutions for selected ideas. There is a parallel activity also needed here to develop the value and commercial viability of the solution.

5. **Test** – Test, prove and enhance the solution, gather feedback from the end users and sponsor(s), improve iteratively as required.

In the previous chapter, we highlighted the importance of the innovation management process. The Design Thinking process is different, but in many ways the two are complementary. This will become much more apparent as you work through the following chapters.

In Design Thinking we start with the actual users, the people who have got a need or a problem that needs to be addressed, rather than the technology or solution. As a 'designer', we ask you not just to *analyse* the users but to have *empathy* with them, to really put yourself into their shoes as much as you can. In order to do so, it is usually helpful to listen and observe and find out more about the lives of those you want to innovate for and with!

You will also note that the process does not start with an elaborate design brief with a long and detailed list of requirements. Although we are provided with a problem area, issue or challenge to address, we only develop our detailed 'requirements' *after* we have developed a better understanding of the needs of the user. This is important, as otherwise we run the risk that we assume requirements that are not accurate or miss others that are important.

The problem definition happens at the second stage and is often framed around a particular challenge or opportunity. Why? All too often, when faced with a challenge or opportunity, people and organisations focus on the first solution that comes to mind or the one they're most familiar with or favour. They do this without really understanding the problem, and before determining if the solution will really address the problem and meet the needs of the people (the end users) who will use it. Design Thinking is a great way of avoiding this pitfall. Design Thinking can also be applied where there is no known 'problem', just an aim to review how things are done in case the process uncovers some hidden gem ideas or opportunities for improvement. Design Thinking therefore equips us with some great methods for researching challenges and defining them in collaboration with users and other stakeholders. This is a great skill to have and, of course, it helps you to hone employability skills in many of the skill areas highlighted in Chapter 1, including empathy and communication, collaboration and teaming, and critical thinking and problem solving!

The third stage is where creativity really kicks in. We use diverse teams of people ideally from different roles and levels of experience with the 'problem', and we ask them to come up with a wide range of creative ideas, the more and wilder the better! Then we confront these ideas with reality to assess how valuable they are in terms of really addressing the challenge and how feasible they are to deliver. This is a very exciting stage and one that requires skills not just in creativity and ideation, but also skills in other areas, such as collaboration and teaming. It is really important not to stem the flow of ideas by being overly critical at this stage. However, the aim or output of this stage is to agree one or more selected ideas to progress to the next stage.

In the fourth stage, we challenge and develop the ideas to transform them into real capabilities. We create prototypes (often mockups) which can be demonstrated and tested. This stage provides a great opportunity to strengthen communication skills and commercial awareness. You might think prototyping sounds like a lot of hard work but there are some great techniques to simplify it, and it's also a lot of fun. As you will see, it's about understanding 'how much is enough?' After all, you are not being asked to fully implement the idea at this stage – rather you are just developing it to a certain level. Remember the vase we asked you to draw? Making prototypes of physical or tangible ideas can be really exciting; however, it can be harder to do for vague concepts or intangible service ideas.

The fifth and final stage involves further testing as we move towards implementation. Hardly any projects get to this stage without having gone through some level of iteration. In many projects, we seek to gain constant feedback from end users and other stakeholders, so we continue to improve our ideas and prototypes. In one project Tony (one of the authors) worked on there was constant interaction with users in a UK retail supply chain business for several weeks until the prototype functioned, looked and felt exactly the way the users wanted, as this made their jobs much easier and so drove efficiency savings across the supply chain.

As you may have noticed by now, this process can also be used to develop a start-up, and indeed, Design Thinking has become a key approach for start-up programmes. Just look up 'lean start-up'! One key reason why Design Thinking works so well at all stages of start-up development is that it is so adaptable and iterative. What do we mean by this? Design Thinking is a very iterative process in that we do not work from start to finish in a linear way. Often, we need to go back and forth between the stages. Sometimes we need to repeat a certain activity. Often, we need to do more research or verify our key assumptions at a later stage.

Innovation projects in general, including the ones which make use of Design Thinking techniques, rarely proceed in a straight line. We may encounter many problems along the way, and we can use Design Thinking and other techniques to fix them. This gives us great practical experience in developing critical employability skills in the areas of resilience and managing change. It can even help us to fall in to love with problems!

FIGURE 3.2: Fall in love with the problem not the solution

LOVE THE PROBLEM!

So, now that we have explained the process to you, you may be excited and keen to embark on your project – or you may wonder 'so what'? Why is Design Thinking different? Why is it important? In our view, Design Thinking is important because it ensures we focus on the end user and it helps us to love their problem, not the solution. Actually, in years to come, if you only remember a few lines from this book, we'd like you to remember this one:

'Fall in love with the problem, not the solution.'

Why is this so important? Let us have a look at a real example from industry.

In this example, the end user was a young child in a hospital. The problem was the medical team needed to take scans of the inside of the child's body to make a medical diagnosis. Great news! There are fantastic technology solutions which address this problem, including MRI and CT scanners.

But let's have empathy for our end user for a moment. What sort of experience do you think the sterile looking room with the MRI or CT scanner, the narrow tube and noise of the scanner will provide for a young child? Experience in hospitals has shown that many young children and their parents find scanning an intimidating and, in some cases, terrifying experience. The child patient often does not remain sufficiently still on the scanner bed

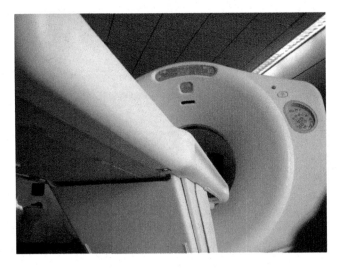

FIGURE 3.3: A sterile-looking scanner room (image courtesy of Doug Dietz)

and a second scan may be needed. This is expensive and delays diagnosis, which leads to poorer patient outcomes. Alternatively, the child patient may need to be sedated, which comes with its own risks and issues.

A design engineer working for GE Healthcare, Doug Dietz, identified the problem. Doug worked with hospital teams to use Design Thinking to have empathy for child patients. The result? Scanner rooms were transformed into children's adventure games. Entering the room, climbing onto the scanner bed and laying still and keeping quiet in the scanner tube (for example to hide from pirates!) were all part of the adventure.

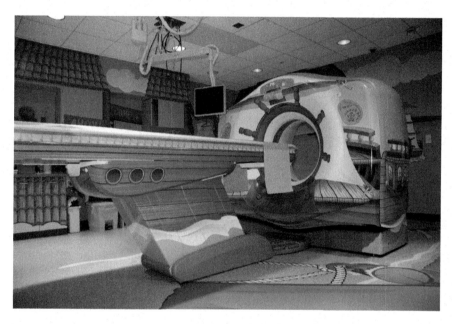

FIGURE 3.4: The scanner room redesigned as an adventure game (image courtesy of Doug Dietz)

The result? Happier child patients, much higher success rates of first-time scans, less sedation, reduced costs and improved patient outcomes (Dietz, 2012).

This all came about from the use of Design Thinking to love the problem, not the solution, and from Doug and his team having empathy with and understanding the needs of their end users, as well as the sponsors funding their solution. Today GE Healtcare has a range of different set-ups in its 'Adventure Series' that aims to improve the experience of children as patients. Doug Dietz has done a great TED Talk on this project, which we highly recommend watching. And, even better than that, Doug has provided the interview below to share his experience with us, exclusively for this book.

EXPERT

EMPATHY IN DESIGN THINKING

Doug Dietz now runs his own innovation and Design Thinking consultancy. In his previous role at GE Healthcare, he designed the Adventure Series, reimagining MRI scanner rooms and other medical imaging devices to transform the experience of child patients. He's also a Design Thinking coach at Stanford's D-School, focused on human-centred design.

1. YOUR REAL-LIFE STORY OF REDESIGNING THE MRI SCANNER ROOM FOR CHILD PATIENTS IS A GREAT EXAMPLE OF DESIGN THINKING IN ACTION. THE SOLUTION IS SO POWERFUL BECAUSE IT'S BUILT BY GENERATING EMPATHY FOR CHILD PATIENTS. WHY DO YOU THINK EMPATHY IS SUCH AN IMPORTANT ASPECT OF DESIGN THINKING?

For me, empathy is key to Design Thinking. Think of it as like lining up a set of dominoes, with empathy being the first domino. If you get the empathy right, things will start moving and, before long, all the dominoes will fall in place.

A lot of times, we see companies with cool technologies looking for a problem to solve, but for me innovation starts with generating empathy for the users. Take the MRI scanner and wider GE Healthcare Adventure Series. When we started working on this, hospital environments seemed to have stayed the same forever. Developing empathy for the medical staff, young patients and families set me on a different path. I began to think much less about the cool technology and much more about people's experience of using it. There's no substitute for witnessing and observing people and generating empathy. This allows us to identify unmet needs and desires that we didn't even know existed.

On a project, having empathy really helps. I've been in meetings when someone has said 'Nurse Sue wouldn't like that', and they really know this, because they've generated so much empathy for her. I had another colleague, and I love this story, who had a picture of the key user for their project. He printed out the picture, glued it onto some cardboard and placed it in a chair at every meeting, so even though the user wasn't there, the team always maintained their empathy for her. As I said, empathy's really key for Design Thinking.

2. HOW DID YOU GENERATE EMPATHY FOR THE CHILDREN AND THE FAMILIES USING THE MRI SCANNER ROOM?

I talk about this in my TED Talk [note by the authors: we provide a link to that at the end of this interview]. It all started when I did a site visit and saw the families struggling. This was a real 'A-ha!' moment for me. Up until then, I'd been focused on the technology and the technologists using it. I realised I'd missed the bigger picture.

We went back and began talking to the families. We spent a lot of time listening to and engaging patient advisory boards with child patients at paediatric hospitals. For instance, I remember talking to one little boy (he was about eight years old) about what would help him have a much better experience in hospital. He used to call me 'Designer Doug'. The boy looked up at me and said, 'Designer Doug, I've had three MRI scans this week'. I thought, 'Oh my gosh, here's the best designer for what we need right in front of me. He understands the procedures better than I do and I designed the darn things'. It was his input that started us off down the track of creating the pirate adventure.

We also spent time at children's museums and observed families going through the experience, which was educational but also safe and fun. There was a magic to that, which we drew upon, but the most powerful input was working directly with the children in the hospitals. If you can create an environment where the child is the protagonist in the story, the hero in the journey, you have set a different stage for the experience.

3. WHAT OTHER APPROACHES HAVE YOU USED TO GENERATE EMPATHY FOR END USERS?

I try to carry out observational research as best I can – to actually get out there with the users, but this isn't always easy. For instance, during the Covid pandemic we were working with a family, a mother and her son in Canada, but we couldn't physically visit

(Continued)

them to generate empathy. The project focused on infusion pumps, which the patient wears around their waist to receive continuous medication 24/7 for 28 days.

We worked remotely and talked to the family but the thing that got me was when the little boy said, 'When I wear the pump at night, it's really hard to sleep. Here, let me show you'. He handed his iPad to his mum, and she followed him so we could see what he was doing. He went into his bedroom and lay down on his bed, placing the pump on a chair. He then showed us what happened when he rolled over and the struggles he was having. It was a powerful moment. We weren't there with him, but we gained a lot of empathy.

4. MANY OF THE PEOPLE READING THIS BOOK WILL BE QUITE NEW TO USING DESIGN THINKING TO ADDRESS INNOVATION CHALLENGES. WHAT ADVICE WOULD YOU GIVE TO THEM?

Design Thinking is such a great way to find a problem that's worth solving. Think of the kick-off as a discovery phase. You're not really sure where you're going, you might not even have defined the problem you're trying to solve. You may feel you're surrounded by creative chaos, but my advice is don't be afraid of this ambiguity. Embrace it! Something's going to come out of all this, and when it does, you'll say 'Oh, my gosh!'

IDEO used to state, 'fail early and fail often, to succeed sooner'. I changed this to 'learn early, learn cheap'. To me, it's about doing some very early ideation and quickly creating a very rough prototype. Test your thinking early on in the process with a simple prototype, even a storyboard. You'll learn so much from the feedback, your team's progress will go vertical. Keep improving and keep getting more feedback. It's so much better than the big reveal at the end when you lift the sheet and it's not quite what people wanted.

TOP TIP

Get out from behind your desk. Sometimes it can feel uncomfortable to talk to strangers about their emotions and feelings and do things you're not used to, but that's where the magic and the richness lie.

There are many other examples like Doug's which you could look up online or that are described in Design Thinking books. Have a look at the further resources section at the end of the chapter.

REFLECTION POINT: DESIGN THINKING

Reflecting on the information above, think about a 'solution' – a product, service, app, webpage or something else you've used – which has given you a poor user experience. Consider the following questions. Make a note of your answers in the space provided and/or in your journal.

1. WHAT WAS THE PROBLEM WITH THIS SOLUTION?

2. WAS THE SOLUTION DEVELOPED WITH EMPATHY FOR AND A FOCUS ON THE NEEDS OF THE END USER?

(Continued)

3. HOW DO YOU THINK THE SOLUTION COULD HAVE BEEN DEVELOPED DIFFERENTLY?

TEAMWORK

Having established the definition, process and key principles of Design Thinking, what are the other concepts you should be aware of? There are three more Design Thinking principles we want to introduce to you which are all related to the fact that Design Thinking is about working in a team.

In our experience it is true, **teamwork makes the dream work!**

- **Diversity:**
  - In general, diverse teams generate a wider range of thinking and ideas and create better innovation outcomes than groups of people with similar mindsets and cultural backgrounds.
  - Another advantage of diversity is the bringing together of different knowledge sets. For example, a specialist in a specific business unit may have an idea which a business analyst can add to, and an IT specialist can further develop. The resulting idea is likely to be something quite different and better than any of them could have developed individually. For the same reason, we now see more and more inter-disciplinary research projects addressing the grand challenges of our time.
- **Divergence and convergence:**
  - Many Design Thinking techniques deliberately instruct teams to diverge when developing their thinking and input. By diverging we mean that for a moment the team does not work as a collective but rather each team member works individually for a while. This ensures that unique inputs are gathered from everyone in the team.
  - After the team has diverged, many Design Thinking techniques instruct the team members to get back together and converge: they review, explore and analyse their

individual inputs, and combine and build on them if appropriate. The team then collaborates to agree on the best ideas or other outcomes to work collectively on.

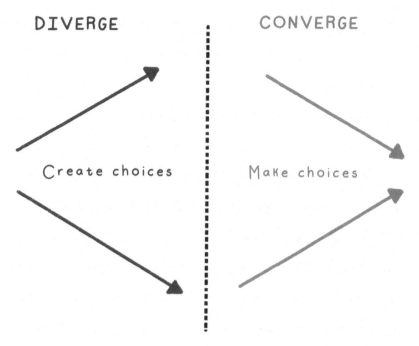

FIGURE 3.5: Design Thinking encourages us to diverge and converge

- **Playbacks:**
  - Playbacks are an important feature of Design Thinking. What do we mean by playback? A playback involves the listening or watching of something that was previously recorded. In Design Thinking the term is used for a demonstration of an outcome. Once a team has undergone a set of activities, playbacks can be used to summarise outcomes and brief the team, other teams, end users, sponsors and other stakeholders – to get everyone up to speed on progress, gain feedback and/or agree actions, decisions and priorities.

DESIGN THINKING PRACTICE

Now that you've heard a little more about Design Thinking, we're going to return to the challenge we discussed earlier. We still have the same 'end user' we need to create an innovation for. The end user is a 75-year-old person with limited mobility who lives in their own house and wants to enjoy fresh flowers at home.

In the starter exercise, we jumped very and much too quickly into a solution, by asking you to 'Design a vase with fresh flowers in it' for the end user to enjoy in their home, rather than developing any empathy for the end user. See what we did there? Of course, if we weren't writing in a book, we should really wish to spend some time observing and speaking to them about what they really want and need. As we can't do this, we should at least consider what we do know – the end user is 75 years old, has limited mobility, lives in their own house and wants to enjoy fresh flowers at home.

EXERCISE: DESIGN WITH EMPATHY

Let's reframe the challenge. We'd like you to 'Design a solution for the end user to enjoy flowers in their home' – because, from what we know, that's what they really want – we just assumed before that the best solution was a vase.

Take a few minutes out... Develop ideas of how the end user could enjoy flowers in their home. Remember, focus on the end user's perspective. Have empathy for them – if you were a 75-year-old person with mobility issues, how might you like to enjoy flowers in your home? Be creative, attempt to look at the problem from different angles. Try to come up with a few different ideas.

Select one of your ideas, describe it in a few words or sentences and/or create a sketch in the space below. Again, it doesn't need to be very detailed or elaborate.

REFLECTION POINT: THE IMPORTANCE OF EMPATHY

Reflect on the different approaches and outcomes from the two exercises.

- How different is your new idea to the vase?
- Do you think the end user can derive more enjoyment from it?

Make a note of your answers in the space provided and/or in your journal. If you know fellow students or others using this book, compare notes on what each of you have created. One of you might even come up with an idea for a brand new business. We've used this exercise many times and seen some fantastic ideas we'd never have thought of, including some very interesting ideas which had real commercial potential.

TEAMING

While we hope that you have found this exercise useful, we also acknowledge that Design Thinking works best in a team. However, working in a team is not always easy and requires good communication and collaboration skills. As highlighted by Amy Edmondson, Professor at Harvard Business School, 'teaming is a verb. It is a dynamic activity, not a bounded, static entity. It is largely determined by the mindset and practices of teamwork' (Edmondson, 2012). She also emphasises that in today's world we rarely work in stable teams over a long period of time. Instead, we work in and with different teams on different tasks, which is why she advocates talking about 'teaming' rather than teams.

Effective collaboration with team members, wider stakeholders and others is a key employability skill. This is because virtually all activities in a work environment, apart from small or mundane ones, require some level of team working. A 'team' may need to collaborate to deliver a business process, work together to deliver a set of tasks or, as in the context of this book, deliver a project. A team may consist of colleagues from the same business unit, colleagues from different business units and/or people from one or more organisations. Equally, student teams may include students from one course, from multiple courses, schools, colleges and/or universities. We should remember that each member of a team is an individual, with different strengths and weaknesses, knowledge, experience and personality traits.

This diversity can be a huge benefit. When the team members work together successfully and combine their strengths to achieve a common goal, more often than not, the output will outweigh what the team members could have achieved by working individually. In Design Thinking we usually try to work in diverse teams – so we try to have a good mix of people, if possible, ideally with different backgrounds and areas of expertise. A recommendation you will often see repeated in the related literature is to recruit *T-shaped people* (Brown, 2009). No, you do need to start looking for slim individuals with wide shoulders! In this context, T-shaped means that someone has a depth of knowledge in a given field but is also able to reach out and connect with others in meaningful cross-disciplinary collaborations in many other areas.

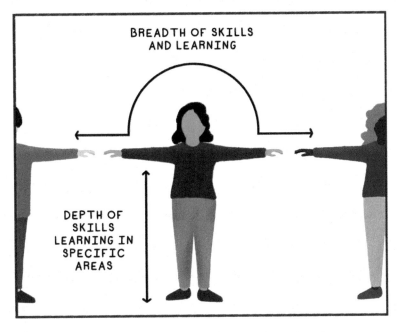

BREADTH OF SKILLS
AND LEARNING

DEPTH OF
SKILLS
LEARNING IN
SPECIFIC
AREAS

FIGURE 3.6: T-shaped person

For this project or any future ones, you may or may not have a choice about who you will work with. You may know the other team members quite well or not at all. You may have been assigned to a team, or you may have to recruit others to join your project. No matter whether you will have a say in the selection of your team or not, you have always one choice: What type of team member *you* will be. We often forget this – in particular, when we grow frustrated with others (and this happens in most teams at some point). If individual team members can't, don't or won't work well together, the outcome is likely to be poor and it's unlikely the team will achieve its full objectives. If this occurs, individual team members may blame each other but the whole team will have failed. The failure will reflect on everyone in the team, particularly any team members who didn't actively participate and collaborate in the team's activities. That's why pausing to reflect is a critical learning stage.

Why are we pointing this out here? We hope this book will make you a better team player than you are now and help you to discover your ability to work with others as a 'T-shaped person' – even if you are convinced that you are already a high-performing individual and hence would be better off running your project by yourself.

Why is being a good team worker so important? Because we want you to do well and we want your team to succeed. It is also because many of the most desired graduate employers look for this – a T-shaped person with great collaboration skills! Besides, remember 'Joy's Law' about the smartest people working somewhere else. In order to find and collaborate with the smartest people, you will need to be able to engage with them. This requires a professional attitude and the right skills – which can be learnt but also to some degree require a level of experience and practice. This is where the skill areas we have focused on coincide – can you see now, the value to you of developing them all? Please share your thoughts with us on our LinkedIn group.

DESIGN THINKING ONLINE

We often get asked whether Design Thinking can be done online. The answer is an emphatic 'Yes'. We anticipate you may be one of the readers who may, out of choice or through necessity, wish to work in this way, at least at times.

Although traditionally Design Thinking techniques have often been undertaken by co-located teams working together in a physical space, we can also carry them out very effectively online. For example, we can make use of specialist collaboration tools. Such an approach is frequently used by geographically dispersed teams, for example those working in large countries or in multi-national organisations. The Covid-19 pandemic also drove many additional collaboration activities to run online. For example, we have moved some of our Design Thinking teaching and learning activities to run virtually.

The team activities described in this book make reference to working together in a room AND using online tools. In the online materials accompanying this book, we have included facilitation guides for online and face-to-face workshops, in which we provide practical guidance, describe the resources needed and provide related checklists that will all help you to run the activities smoothly.

In addition, we have created a template using the MURAL tool covering many of the activities included in the book. If using MURAL, this template can be used to give you a fast start.

You can find more information on this template – as well as links to a practice MURAL and a fully populated sample MURAL – in our facilitation guide for online workshops. If running online but not using MURAL, you can still use the templates to create your own versions using tools such as Miro and so on.

Remember, working online is different. It does require some additional thinking and planning. Having said this, it also offers some fantastic opportunities. As we've seen, Design Thinking thrives on diversity. By working online, we can reach out to a much greater number of diverse individuals and teams to collaborate and work with.

EXPERT

LEARNING ABOUT DESIGN THINKING

You have already met Tony Morgan – he is one of the authors of this book! Before his academic career, Tony worked for many years in leading innovation roles in IBM. This is why Lena Jaspersen (the other co-author) interviews him here about his experiences of learning about Design Thinking.

1. WHERE DID YOU FIRST LEARN ABOUT DESIGN THINKING?

A number of years ago, when I worked at IBM, the company rolled out a huge programme of staff training on the practical use of Design Thinking based techniques and approaches. I was involved due to my Innovation Leadership role. As well as encouraging my team to use Design Thinking, I began training other teams to use Design Thinking too. It was a lot of fun but also hugely useful when working internally and with IBM clients.

2. YOU'VE HAD A LOT OF EXPERIENCE SINCE THEN TEACHING DESIGN THINKING – AT IBM AS WELL AS IN THE UNIVERSITY. IN YOUR VIEW, WHAT IS THE BEST WAY TO LEARN DESIGN THINKING?

Definitely by doing it. It's always good to read about things, but there's no substitute for practical experience. The more Design Thinking activities you engage with, the better you'll get at them. I like to teach Design Thinking by encouraging students and companies to use these techniques to address real challenges, research problems, generate empathy for end users, generate diverse ideas and prototypes and so on.

The great thing about most of the techniques is how intuitive they are. Once you've been through them two or three times, they become second nature. You really do begin to care more about your end users and fall in love with their problems, not just your ideas and solutions. Of course, as covered elsewhere in this book, facilitation is important too, and to become a good facilitator you need to gain experience of using the techniques first-hand.

3. WHAT IS THE ROLE OF TEAMWORK IN DESIGN THINKING?

Teamwork is vital. I think it centres around the three underlying concepts of diversity, divergence and convergence. Diverse teams really do generate wider ideas and better outcomes.

My favourite innovation projects at IBM were always the ones where we combined the unconstrained thinking of new graduates, interns and apprentices with experienced technology people and business experts. Using Design Thinking, they always created better solutions than any one group could have achieved on their own.

And, of course, Design Thinking techniques deliberately flex between diverging and converging. When we diverge, we ensure we get the unique and diverse individual inputs of every member of the team and, when we converge, we come back together and utilise the combined power of the team. It's powerful stuff.

(Continued)

4. CAN YOU GIVE ME AN EXAMPLE?

One of my favourite Design Thinking projects at IBM was with an online retailer. They had a challenge with their in-bound supply chain. They sold a huge range of goods and with so many orders and suppliers, it was difficult to see the wood from the trees, which orders risked being late, which needed to be followed up, which needed to be prioritised due to the impact on revenue and sales and so on. All the information was there but it was spread across so many places, it took a huge amount of time and effort to identify and extrapolate.

It was a tricky problem to solve. We jointly agreed to run a Design Thinking project. As well as IBM technology experts, we introduced a small team of interns. We facilitated a series of Design Thinking activities with the retailer's business experts as the end users of the supply chain systems to understand their real problems. What a day that was! I don't think I've ever learned so much in such a short space of time.

A small number of ideas were selected, and the intern team began developing them, working with the technology experts and business users. The overall team had different ages, genders, specialities, levels of experience, countries of origin, you name it. I can't give any details of the specific innovative solution developed, but everybody loved it and I think everybody saw how the positive outcome was closely linked to the diversity, divergence, convergence and collaboration of the team.

TOP TIP

I probably can't say 'fall in love with the problem, not the solution' as that's covered elsewhere! As this is the case, I'll focus on empathy. Generate empathy for your end users and really care about them. You're also going to need empathy for your sponsor and other key stakeholders but, don't forget, generate empathy for your teammates too. Design Thinking is a team game. You're going to succeed or fail together.

CONCLUSION

Some critics have described Design Thinking as 'just' a toolbox of activities. You won't be surprised to read that we do not agree with this position. While it is true that Design Thinking has a focus on practice and is more about doing than it is about some grand theory, we should not forget that in order to work with a designer toolbox to create great success, it needs both *knowledge* and *skill* (Johansson-Sköldberg et al., 2013). Design Thinking is ultimately rooted in a perspective that focuses our thinking on usage and the end user, and on understanding their problems rather than jumping at a solution. It encourages us to be creative but not for the sake of being creative; and it requires teamwork.

This chapter has introduced you to Design Thinking and has set out what it involves. We have explained where Design Thinking comes from, the process around which it unfolds and its underlying principles. We have given you a practical example and invited you to have a little go yourself at 'user-centric design' (albeit in a rather modest way).

You have likely found out from your course or module who your teammates are, or are in the process of doing so. It is time to embark on your project! How will we do this? That is what the next chapter is all about.

KEY LEARNING POINTS

- Design thinking is an iterative process or approach for creatively solving problems.
- In Design Thinking particular emphasis is placed upon: a) addressing the needs of the people who will be using the solution; b) thoroughly understanding the problem or opportunity being addressed; and c) working in diverse teams.
- The different methods and techniques associated with Design Thinking can be used in isolation or in combination. When they're used in combination, they form the Design Thinking process, which comprises five stages: empathising, defining, ideating, prototyping and testing.
- Design Thinking is about falling in love with a problem and not your solution for it.
- Design Thinking is also about working in a team, where members sometimes diverge and develop their own ideas and inputs and then converge when they share ('playback'), collaborate and decide about a common way forward.
- Design Thinking can help you to learn how to work as a 'T-shaped person' which means using your expertise constructively when collaborating with others.

- Teamwork makes the dream work – but this only works when you adopt a professional attitude and team spirit.
- Design Thinking activities can effectively be delivered face-to-face and online.

ACTION POINTS

☐ Please complete the reflection points and exercises.
☐ We strongly recommend you review a number of the further resources below to find out more about Design Thinking and about working in an effective team.

EXERCISE

Please complete the mini quiz below.

1. What was the key tip in this chapter?

   a. Fall in love with the problem.

   b. Fall in love with the solution.

2. Design Thinking is best described as a...

   a. Technology-centred approach.

   b. Human-centred approach.

   c. Solution-centred approach.

3. Which of the three concepts are used in many Design Thinking techniques?

   a. Ideas, invention, innovation.

   b. Technology, applications, platforms.

   c. Diversity, divergence, convergence.

4. The best way to learn about Design Thinking is by...

   a. Reading this chapter.

b. Doing it.

c. Observing a workshop.

Note: Sample answers for this exercise are available online.

FURTHER RESOURCES

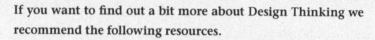

If you want to find out a bit more about Design Thinking we recommend the following resources.

IBM has some great Design Thinking resources you should have a look at: **www.ibm.com/design/thinking/**
And so do IDEO (**https://designthinking.ideo.com/**) and Google (**https://designsprintkit.withgoogle.com/**).

We also recommend the Interaction Design Foundation:

www.interaction-design.org/literature/topics/design-thinking

The following article is a classic:

Brown, T. 2008. Design Thinking. *Harvard Business Review*. June, 84–92.

If you like the article above, you can also have a look at his book:

Brown, T. 2009. *Change by Design: How Design Thinking Transforms Organizations and Inspires Innovation*. New York: HarperCollins.

We recommend watching Doug Dietz' TED talk on the MRI scanner example we introduced in this chapter:

Dietz, D. 2012. *Transforming Healthcare for Children and their Families*. TEDxSanJoseCA.

They are many examples of Design Thinking on the internet but if you prefer to read a book, we recommend this one:

Liedtka, J., King, A., & Bennett, K. 2013. *Solving Problems with Design Thinking: Ten Stories of What Works*. New York: Columbia University Press.

Another useful resource on Design Thinking teams:

Dam, R.F., & Siang, T.Y. 2020. *Design Thinking: Select the Right Team Members and Start Facilitating*. Interaction Design Foundation.

You may also want to have a look at the following video where Amy Edmondson explains 'Teaming':

www.youtube.com/watch?v=sZZHkqIY0Fo

LOVING THE PROBLEM

Chapter contents

Goals

- To learn how to form an effective innovation team.

- To discover ways of approaching an innovation challenge.

- To find out about methods for researching innovation challenges.

- To find out how to conduct an interview with an industry expert.

INTRODUCTION

In this chapter, you finally embark on your innovation project. You will decide (or find out about) your challenge and learn what you can do to form an effective team to tackle that challenge. We also cover the first stages of undertaking research on an innovation challenge, both by conducting some research online and through interviewing a relevant industry expert. When you have reached the end of the chapter you will have identified issues and opportunities that you may wish to address, so that in Chapter 5 you will shift from understanding the problem to thinking about ideas and solutions.

As we said in the previous chapter, Design Thinking is about *falling in love with the problem* and not the solution. Therefore, the initial stages of problem definition are really important! In this chapter, we provide you with seven sample innovation challenges to address. If you're using this book in conjunction with a course or module, it's likely you've already been assigned to a team and your team has been given a challenge to address by your instructors. Some instructors may decide to adopt some of the challenges in the book and/or create new ones.

If you're using the book independently, you can select which challenge to address or create a new challenge yourself using a similar format as used for the examples. If you'd like to work in a team (this is our strong recommendation), you can round up some teammates or use our LinkedIn group to connect with other students in a similar situation.

We appreciate that most of us prefer to pick our own challenges and teammates. This said, in most graduate jobs you often do not get to select your tasks, nor your team. Being able to work with people you don't know (or, worse, you do know and don't like) requires skills and experience. Working on a project or a topic you do not know much about or are not very interested in can also appear more difficult than working on something you care about.

The chances are that your next job will present you with some challenges and colleagues you are not keen to deal with. That is the bad news. The good news is that **Design Thinking can be a very powerful way of helping diverse teams to click, while at the same time requiring you to empathise with potential users**.

When we empathise with someone and see the world from their perspective, we often find the problems they face more important and much more interesting. You may have already noticed this when you worked on the flower challenge in the previous chapter. So, when you do not get to pick your challenge or team, you are just as likely, if not more so, to benefit from the experience of doing this project. By the time you have finished this chapter and the next chapter, you will feel much more excited about your project. You may even have fallen in love – with the problem!

CREATING AN EFFECTIVE TEAM

Let us start with the team. For Design Thinking challenges we usually recommend four to eight members per team. This allows for diversity but is still a team size that makes it relatively easy to get organised. We have already talked a lot about the importance of teaming in the last chapter, and by now you should have been assigned to (or be in the process of joining or putting together) a team for your project.

Once you know who is in your team, the next task is to build the team so that you can collaborate effectively. Many people associate 'team-building' with awkward encounters and silly games. Don't worry, some ice breakers make us cringe too! But it is part of professional life to learn how to overcome reservations and engage with others. We recommend taking the initiative and making the most of it. Moreover, creating an effective team involves a lot more than this! Below we include a list of recommendations – sometimes we call them 'ground rules' – for initial and ongoing team activities that have been drawn from a range of industry sources and experts, based upon their practical experience of working across many teams and projects.

1. **Set and agree common goals and objectives:**
   a. At the outset, the team members should discuss, agree and write down the common objective(s) of the team, in relation to the project. The objective(s) may initially be set by a sponsor or another key stakeholder. Even so, the team members should review and ensure that everyone buys into the objective(s). From then on, the team should work collectively towards the objective(s).
   b. It will be useful to refer back to the objective(s) regularly to ensure the team remains on track and hasn't inadvertently been diverted.
   c. Due to specific circumstances, the objective(s) may change over time, but the team should collectively agree to this, and then work together towards achieving the new objective(s).
   d. Individual team members may also set additional personal objective(s), e.g., to gain experience in a specific knowledge area, perhaps to address a wider career objective. Personal objectives should not conflict with the team's overall objective(s). It's useful to share your personal objectives with the team, so that other team members are aware of them and, if appropriate, can assist with their achievement.

2. **Have empathy for and support the other team members:**
   a. One of the key concepts of Design Thinking is empathy for the end user. Equally, we need to demonstrate empathy for our teammates, understand what's important to them and, at times, consider how we can take action to help them.

b. Successful delivery of the team's common goal will be based upon the collective strength of the team. Egos must be set aside.

c. If one or more teammates struggle, the others should support them for the benefit of the team and to enable delivery of the team's overall objective(s).

3. **Agree to act professionally:**

   a. Whether the team is working on a credit-bearing course or module or not, team members should act professionally at all times. This is important. How will you develop the skills needed to be a great professional if you do not act like one?

   b. Examples include the timely attendance of scheduled lectures, workshops and team meetings, active participation in team activities and completing allocated tasks on time.

   c. When attendance or progress isn't possible, issues should be highlighted in advance. Help or support from teaching staff or teammates, should be requested, if and as appropriate. Knowing when to ask for help is a skill in itself, and an important one. You can expect to be treated professionally and with empathy.

4. **Make good use of the team's diversity:**

   a. Each team member brings different strengths and weaknesses, knowledge, experience and their own personality to the team.

   b. The team should seek to understand what these are (e.g., during kick-off activities and through experience gained from working together) and make use of this knowledge to support delivery of the team's objectives.

   c. Sometimes, team members may collaborate towards improving another team member's capabilities; for example, if a teammate is struggling or seeks to achieve a personal objective.

5. Hold effective face-to-face and online meetings – we'll return to this in Chapter 6.

6. Plan and manage the team's activities – we'll return to this in Chapter 6.

In the further resources section at the end of the chapter, we have also included a useful article by Rikke Friis Dam and Teo Yu Siang on team building for Design Thinking.

REFLECTION POINT: WORKING IN A TEAM

Self-awareness is important and an awareness of your own strengths and concerns is very useful, as it will help you to shape your personal contributions to the team. Reflecting on the information above, consider the following questions. Make a note of your answers in the space provided and/or in your journal.

1. WHAT STRENGTHS DO YOU THINK YOU CAN PERSONALLY BRING TO THE TEAM? THESE MAY INCLUDE SKILLS, EXPERIENCE AND/OR PERSONALITY TRAITS.

2. WHAT AREAS OF CONCERN DO YOU HAVE ABOUT WORKING IN THE TEAM? THESE MAY INCLUDE SKILL AREAS YOU WISH TO IMPROVE ON AND/OR PERSONAL CONCERNS.

There are a number of things teams can do (beyond adhering to the recommendations above) to accelerate positive dynamics, and yes, this takes us back to icebreaker territory!

1. **Hold a social event**: We won't cover this in too much detail here, because we think you'll know what to do, but here are a few ideas just in case.

    a. A social event can be a great way to introduce team members to each other. The event could take the form of a lunchtime meeting, evening out or other activity. It's important to consider the needs of all team members before proposing an event. For example, some team members may wish to avoid alcohol or have childcare commitments and so on. All team members should be encouraged to introduce themselves to each other, ask questions about the others and discuss topics of personal interest, rather than just talk about the project.

    b. If working online, you can still organise a virtual event, you'll just need to be a little more creative. Don't sit in silence, staring at each other on the screen, but avoid cringeworthy icebreakers too. Some people like 'Home Treasure Hunts' (asking team

FIGURE 4.1: Breaking the ice

members to find interesting items around their home). Or you could organise a quiz, where each team member sets a round of questions. Different formats can be fun – one of our favourites is to re-enact famous scenes from movies. How would you mime the Titanic sinking? Even online, you have options and, in our experience, getting to know each other a bit more from the outset is time well spent.

2. **Create a team name and team video**: Something which we often do with our students is ask them to create a short video as part of the team's kick-off activities.

   a. We have included instructions for doing this below.

   b. We know a small number of students may consider this to be a rather 'awkward' activity but our experience has shown, once the task has been completed, the vast majority of students (even the reluctant ones) recognise the benefit and find it an engaging and fun way to begin to get to know their teammates! And as we'll see in Chapter 6, use of video is also a key communication skill.

TEAM ACTIVITY: CREATE A TEAM VIDEO

It's best to do this once you've been assigned your innovation challenge.

Each team member should generate one or more ideas for team names – these can be linked to the challenge, and some might be humorous, but keep it professional!

Review the ideas and vote to select a team name (you can always change the name later). Using your preferred device and software, create a short team video as follows:

- Open with your team's name. Have each team member introduce themselves. Close by discussing how you'll work together on the project.
- Depending on the team's size, we recommend keeping the length down to just a couple of minutes.
- You are welcome to use props, music, credits and so on. Be creative – but don't spend too much time refining the video. Save time and energy for the actual project!

If you decide to create a team video while working remotely, the following video will give you some hints and tips of how best to do this: **www.youtube.com/watch?v=cD-Sytv2YFkM.**

Share your video with the wider class. In our own module, we play the videos when students arrive in next week's class. Humour and good production values are always well received!

INNOVATION CHALLENGES

An innovation challenge for a project may be defined as a brief statement that defines a problem or opportunity in context. Ideally, an innovation challenge should be broad enough to allow for a range of different responses and ideas. For example, the challenge to design a vase was perhaps a rather narrow one, and it turned out to be much better to focus on the needs of an 75 year old person wishing to enjoy flowers in their home. On the opposite end of the spectrum, there are challenges that are so broad and complex that it can be difficult to know where to start! While Design Thinking offers a range of useful methods to work on such 'wicked problems' (see below for more on this concept), you may want to choose something less overwhelming for your first project. We recommend that courses and modules adopt a similar approach as shown in the examples below.

In contrast to more elaborate design briefs, innovation challenges rarely include long lists of specifications and requirements. Why is this so? As a user-centred approach, Design Thinking assumes that we do not know the full extent of the problem before we start working on it, and that we have to do some research, and understand more about the problems and experiences of those involved, in order to identify relevant requirements.

You'll usually be assigned an innovation challenge to address by your instructors. We've also included seven sample challenges below. If you have decided to develop your own challenge, we suggest that you still have a closer look at these to determine how the task of defining a challenge can be approached. Often, challenges come from organisations, as many graduate innovation projects involve industry partners. While such engagement is invaluable for the development of a useful project and quality outcomes, we suggest that all challenges are anonymised, rather than include the name of a real-world organisation. This inspires more blue-sky thinking and by and large removes the need for complex commercial agreements on confidentiality, intellectual property rights and so on.

SAMPLE CHALLENGES

1. HEALTHCARE CHALLENGE

- You are the innovation team for a national health care provider.
- A tiered range of healthcare services is provided free of charge for patients. The cost of delivery rises across the tiers from:
    - self-service online advice (lowest cost)
    - telephone helpline
    - doctor's surgery
    - accident & emergency department in hospitals (highest cost).
- Many patients use the higher cost tiers for minor ailments when they could have used the lower cost tiers and received a faster service.
- You also face the issue of an aging population with more complex health issues.
- Your challenge is to develop a solution which will address one or more of the issues described above.
- Your team must generate an idea to address the challenge, develop a prototype solution, articulate the business value and pitch the prototype, business value and wow factor to your sponsor (Healthcare Innovation Director Laura Wound) and a panel of industry experts.

2. BANKING CHALLENGE

- You are the innovation team for a retail bank.
- The average age of the bank's customers is increasing.
- The bank wishes to sell more banking services to existing customers and attract more young professional customers.
- Your challenge is to develop a solution which will address one or more of the issues described above.

- Your team must generate an idea to address the challenge, develop a prototype solution, articulate the business value and pitch the prototype, business value and wow factor to your sponsor (the bank's CEO John Cash) and a panel of industry experts.

3. RETAIL CHALLENGE

- You are the innovation team for a multi-channel (shops and online) fashion retailer.
- Customer demand for fashion is constantly changing.
- The lead time between ordering garments to be made and selling them can be quite long. Often, by the time garments are ready to sell, demand has changed, and stock needs to be marked down or can't be sold at all, reducing profits and increasing environmental impact.
- Your challenge is to develop a solution which will address one or more of the issues described above.
- Your team must generate an idea to address the challenge, develop a prototype solution, articulate the business value and pitch the prototype, business value and wow factor to your sponsor (the retailer's CEO Cheryl Blouse) and a panel of industry experts.

4. LOCAL GOVERNMENT CHALLENGE

- You are the innovation team for the council of a medium-sized city.
- The Covid-19 pandemic has created economic problems and social change for the city and its citizens – some of these may persist after the pandemic, for example rising unemployment, and more people working at home may impact transport, the hospitality sector and jobs.
- The Council needs to address the climate emergency and aims to make the city carbon-neutral by in the next 8–10 years.
- There was a 'reset' caused by the pandemic – this may be an issue and/or an opportunity for the Council, local organisations and citizens to address inequality, social mobility and/or climate change.

(Continued)

- Your team must generate an idea to address the challenge, develop a prototype solution, articulate the business value and pitch the prototype, business value and wow factor to your sponsor (the Council's Innovation Committee led by Maria Mayor).

5. TRANSPORT CHALLENGE

- You are the innovation team for an NGO promoting sustainable mobility and transport solutions that align environmental, social and economic objectives.
- The needs of those who drive vehicles are often prioritised over those who walk and cycle.
- Public transport and mobility sharing programmes (such as bicycle, scooter and car sharing initiatives) often lack integration.
- As a result of the pandemic, transport patterns have changed. This may be an opportunity or challenge.
- Your team must generate an idea to address the challenge, develop a prototype solution, articulate the business value and pitch the prototype, business value and wow factor to your sponsor (the NGO's Director Billy Bike).

6. CINEMA CHALLENGE

- You are the innovation team for a cinema chain.
- In the years following the pandemic, you are under acute financial pressure at a time when many face job loss and hardship.
- Streaming, user-created content (e.g. YouTube) and new virtual reality technologies are disrupting the market.
- Your team must generate an idea to address the challenge, develop a prototype solution, articulate the business value and pitch the prototype, business value and wow factor to your sponsor (the cinema chain's CEO Fyn Film).

7. CHARITY ORGANISATION CHALLENGE

- You are the innovation team for the fundraising arm of a leading charity which supports people in the UK and overseas in times of crisis.
- The charity's funding sources include fundraising campaigns and one-off and regular donations supported by members of the public. Supporters tend to be middle aged and older people.

- Even though you are a well-known charity, you are in competition for funding with many others. Your organisation would like to attract additional funding from beyond its traditional supporter base.
- Your team must generate an idea to address this challenge, develop a prototype solution, articulate the business value and pitch the prototype, business value and wow factor to your sponsor (the charity's Fundraising Director Seymore Cash).

Note: We've used the charity organisation challenge above to create example outputs of Design Thinking and related activities included in the book. You'll see images of these examples (created using the MURAL tool) included in many chapters to give you a feel of what the output of each activity might look like. You can also have a look at the entire project MURAL using the link in this QR code.

For those of you who are working online, we've also made available an online template for carrying out many of the activities.

We've created the online template (and the example outputs mentioned above) using the MURAL tool, as this is the toolset we currently use. We suggest that you use this template to create your own project MURAL. Of course, similar online tools such as Miro can also be used for this purpose!

MORE IN-DEPTH: INNOVATION CHALLENGES AND WICKED PROBLEMS

When you read about innovation challenges, these days one often comes across the notion of 'wicked problems'. Wicked problems have nothing to do with witches! Rather they are a label used for complex problems that comprise interconnected subsets of problems (Rittel & Webber, 1973). Every wicked problem can be considered a symptom of another problem (Rittel & Webber, 1973). When you think about topics such as climate change and education design, you will quickly come to realise what this means. It is difficult or even impossible to develop an understanding of wicked problems that is independent of one's strategy for solving them (Weber & Khademian, 2008). And this is where Design

(Continued)

Thinking comes in. Because of its iterative and human-centred approach, Design Thinking is very useful when tackling ill-defined problems. If you want to find out more about wicked problems and how to address them, have a look at the further resources section at the end of this chapter.

Let's now hear the views of one leading expert on why Design Thinking is so useful for us when we're tackling complex problems.

EXPERT

TACKLING COMPLEX PROBLEMS USING DESIGN THINKING

Professor Ulrich Weinberg is the Director of the School of Design Thinking at Hasso-Plattner-Institute in Potsdam, Germany. As a leading innovator in Germany, he has many years of experience in advising companies such as SAP, Janssen, Volkswagen and Bosch in digital transformation processes. Ulrich is also the president of the Global Design Thinking Alliance, a world-wide network of institutions which promotes excellence in Design Thinking.

1. YOU HAVE WORKED WITH DESIGN THINKING FOR MORE THAN A DECADE. WHAT IS IT THAT KEEPS YOU ENGAGED AND EXCITED ABOUT DESIGN THINKING?

There are several aspects to this. Design Thinking is a truly holistic approach, perhaps even a school of thought, if you will. The dominant discourse often presents Design Thinking as a method, it focuses on processes and tools. For me, Design Thinking also builds on the much older tradition of the *Bauhaus*, and its premise of multidisciplinary teamwork and appreciation of the power of design. After all, *design* is not just about products and services but systems; think about organisational design, for example.

Design Thinking offers us some useful tools but more importantly it gives rise to a different mindset. It promotes a set of underlying values around openness, empathy and respect. David Kelley from the Stanford d.school argues Design Thinking is 'radical democracy'. By working with multidisciplinary teams in ways that are creative and user-centric, we can tackle complex problems in innovative ways. It is the experience of doing just that which intrigues me and keeps me excited.

At the HPI D-School, Design Thinking has become our way of working and learning with others. Amongst other things, we are currently working on hybrid collaboration methods for a post-pandemic world, and we are exploring the role of artificial intelligence in teamworking. So, there is a lot to be excited about. And, of course, there is no shortage of complex challenges that need addressing as a matter of urgency! When we look at climate change – or at how this pandemic has been handled – it is obvious that we need to learn how to address complex problems in new (and complex) ways. Design Thinking is the first step in the right direction, but there is a long way to go.

2. SO, IN YOUR VIEW, DESIGN THINKING IS ABOUT LEARNING HOW TO COLLABORATE BETTER?

Perhaps this is a little simplistic but yes. Design Thinking is the experience of collaborating in a different way. Different, because for centuries we have developed systems that are based on specialised silos. One ministry deals with one aspect and another with another. While this works for some things, it has also led us to create problems that cannot be addressed in this way. Our emphasis of hierarchy and competition has further impeded our ability to collaborate across disciplinary and other boundaries. Now, we have to learn how to collaborate in new ways so that we can tackle the complex problems that we ourselves have created. As of now, Design Thinking offers us the best set of instruments to do just that. And the process is scalable…

3. WHAT DO YOU MEAN BY THAT?

We can embark on a Design Thinking process for a day or for a week or for a year or even longer than that. Depending on the scope and the complexity of the problem, and on our ambitions, we can work in flexible ways – and yet the underlying mindset and process remain largely the same.

As you know, Design Thinking is an iterative process, so usually we work through several rounds or loops. [Comment from the authors: have a look at Figure 3.1 which illustrates this loop.] In practice, it can be a surprise, problem or failure that pushes us back to the

(Continued)

drawing board, so to speak. But this need not be the case. We can also decide from the very beginning to iterate a certain number of times throughout the lifecycle of a project. At the HPI School of Design, we run shorter and longer courses that involve a smaller or larger number of such iterations or loops.

TOP TIP

Knowing about iterations can also help you to focus successively. For example, you may do as much research as possible within a given timeframe, but you may still feel that there are a lot of things you don't know about your challenge. When you have planned a second loop, this can be less of a problem because you know that at the next stage, in the next loop, you will have developed a better understanding as to what key aspects you really need to know more about.

STARTING OUT

Once your team has received or agreed on the challenge, **the first step is usually to read the challenge or problem statement very carefully and to think about what the text says and does not say. With innovation challenges, causes and effects, problems and context are often far from clear.** Hence, it can be useful to ask yourself:

- Why is there a problem/opportunity?
- Who has a need?
- When and where does it occur?
- How is it being solved today? Where are the gaps?

You then may also want to consider your assumptions regarding the problem(s) and what you deem important. A deeper analysis of the challenge is the next step. At the beginning, however, it is all about reflecting about the meaning of the challenge and your own and your team's take on it.

Design Thinking includes a technique called 'Hopes and Fears' to gain an understanding of how the team feels at the beginning of an activity.

- 'Hopes' are about the positive expectations team members have.
- 'Fears' show the doubts and/or concerns team members have.

'Hopes and Fears' can therefore be used to gauge and take into account attitudes, aspirations and concerns of the team and of individual team members. These may relate to the problem or challenge as well as to working as a team or other personal or practical concerns. While this activity can be useful at different stages of a project, we often use it as a kick-off activity.

TEAM ACTIVITY: HOPES AND FEARS

You can run this activity once your innovation challenge has been agreed.

1. PREPARE TO RUN THE ACTIVITY

- Place a flip chart (it can be portrait or landscape) onto a wall or use a virtual whiteboard.
- Draw a vertical line down the centre of the page/board.
- Write 'Hopes' in marker pen at the top of the left-hand side.
- Write 'Fears' in marker pen at the top of the right-hand side.
- Alternatively, if using MURAL, you can make use of our online template to create your own project MURAL.

FIGURE 4.2: Hopes and Fears activity template

(Continued)

2. THE TEAM DIVERGES TO PROVIDE INPUT – THIS STEP SHOULD BE CARRIED OUT IN SILENCE!

- Individual team members write their personal 'Hopes' and 'Fears' about the challenge, the project and working as part of the team onto sticky notes (one point per note) and place these onto the appropriate side of the flip chart/virtual whiteboard.
  - o I hope…
  - o It would be great if we could…
  - o I'm concerned about…

3. WHEN THE TEAM MEMBERS HAVE FINISHED, THE TEAM CONVERGES TO REVIEW WHAT HAS BEEN POSTED

- Each sticky note is discussed, so that the team understands the input.
- Overlapping and linked entries can be moved into groups.
- Identify and highlight key hopes and fears (e.g., by circling or starring with a marker pen sticky notes or groups of sticky notes).
- The team can create a list of priority hopes and major fears – this can be reviewed and tracked during the project.
- Figure 4.3 shows an example of Hopes and Fears – prior to grouping and highlighting the items – from the charity organisation challenge.

4. REVIEWING HOPES AND FEARS DURING THE PROJECT

- The 'Hopes and Fears' output should be kept accessible during the project and be referred to from time to time.
- Aspirations which have been met and fears which have been addressed or mitigated can be ticked off.

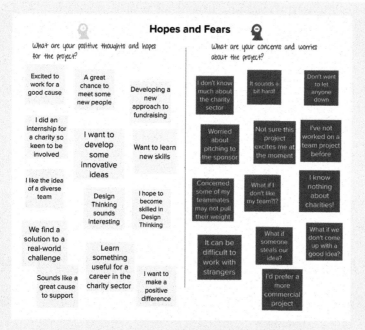

FIGURE 4.3: Hopes and Fears example

RESEARCHING YOUR CHALLENGE

Now that you are familiar with your challenge, and have explored your initial understandings, hopes and fears, it is time to start researching your challenge. The aim is to uncover as much information as possible about the challenge. The amount and level of research the team can carry out may be constrained by the description of the challenge provided, and the time and/or information available. We recommend the team carries out as much research as it realistically can, using whatever information is available.

In the era of fake news, it is also important to evaluate the quality of different sources of information.

When doing so, we suggest that you focus in particular on:

- **Authority** – Who is the author, what is the source of their authority, has the information been checked or reviewed.
- **Purpose** – Why the information was created and its audience, and how this may impede objectivity.
- **Evidence** – What evidence is provided and what is the quality of that evidence.
- **Relevance** – How is the information relevant to the project and is it applicable and recent (or might it be outdated).

It can be difficult to start researching a challenge as there are so many ways to go about it. Most teams start with openly available information on the internet, where they seek information on the organisation and/or similar organisations, the subject focus area of the challenge and so on.

It can be very useful to use templates to keep track of the research. Suggestions for two types of template – a Project Research Canvas and Problem Statement template – are outlined below.

PROJECT RESEARCH CANVAS

The first template is a Project Research Canvas for documenting and integrating the research undertaken by the different members of your team.

TEAM ACTIVITY: PROJECT RESEARCH CANVAS

This is a really useful activity to guide research activities, record the information discovered and identify gaps in your knowledge.

1. PREPARE TO RUN THE ACTIVITY

- Place a flip chart onto a wall or use a virtual whiteboard.
- Structure the chart or whiteboard into boxes or sections where you can record relevant information, as shown in Figure 4.4.
- Alternatively, if using MURAL, you can make use of our online template to create your own project MURAL if you have not done so already.

2. THE TEAM CONVERGES TO PROVIDE INPUT

- The team agrees key items which would be useful to research and uses these to populate the canvas.
- The team assigns individual team members to research specific items.
- Don't worry at this stage if the information gathered is limited or incomplete. The more information the better, but we appreciate you will have limited time to do this.

3. THE TEAM PLAYS BACK AND REVIEWS THE PROJECT RESEARCH CANVAS TEMPLATE.

- Once the team is ready, the team converges to review the findings, highlighting key learning points and remaining questions and knowledge gaps.

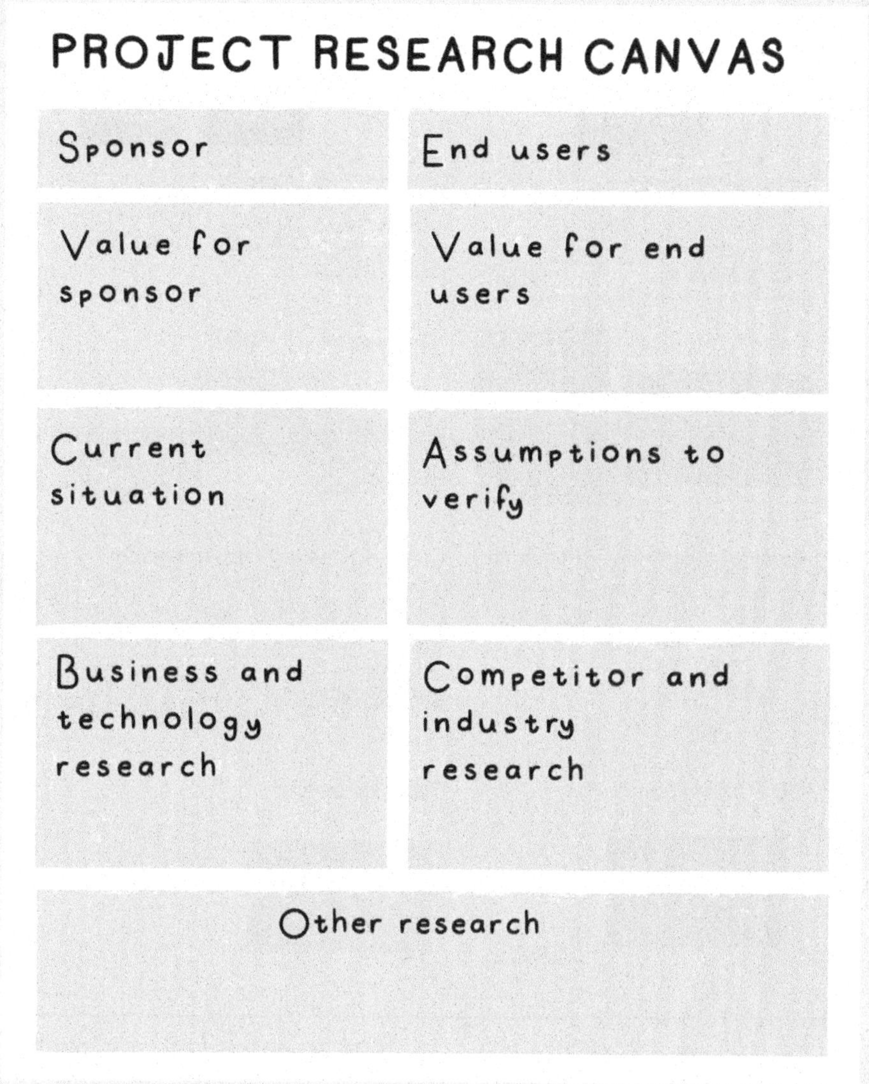

PROJECT RESEARCH CANVAS

Sponsor	End users
Value for sponsor	Value for end users
Current situation	Assumptions to verify
Business and technology research	Competitor and industry research
Other research	

FIGURE 4.4: Project Research Canvas template

- The canvas should be kept accessible to all team members throughout the duration of the project. It may be referred to from time to time as needed. The canvas can be updated as the team gathers more information.
- Figure 4.5 shows an example of an initially populated Project Research Canvas from the charity organisation challenge.

(Continued)

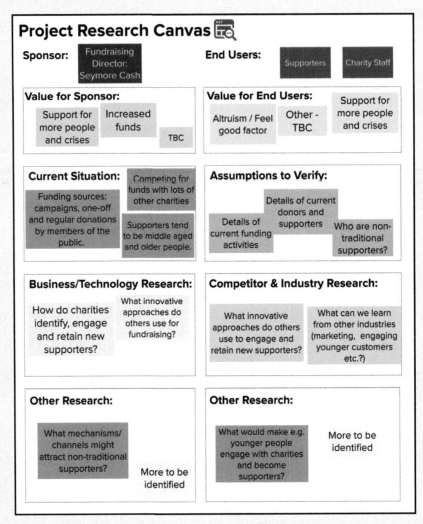

FIGURE 4.5: Project Research Canvas example

4. REVIEWING THE PROJECT RESEARCH CANVAS DURING THE PROJECT

- The Project Research Canvas output should be kept accessible during the project and be referred to from time to time.
- Additional areas may be identified and added to research and notes added on additional or updated findings.

PROBLEM STATEMENT – WHY? WHO? WHAT? WHEN? WHERE? AND HOW?

Another template which can be used to help you to integrate key insights into your innovation challenge is the problem statement. It is used by Lewrick, Link and Leifer (2020) for their useful handbook *The Design Thinking Toolbox* and focuses on understanding the problem statement around the key questions of Why? Who? What? When? Where? and How?

If you think this template will be useful and decide to use it, make sure that you keep your problem statement in line with your innovation challenge. Taken together, the Research Canvas and the Problem Statement template will help you to assemble insights gained and to evaluate them in relation to your challenge or problem.

STAKEHOLDER MAPPING

Because Design Thinking is a human-centred approach, we need to focus a bit more on the *who* and include a brief stakeholder analysis in the initial research phase. What do we mean by this? A stakeholder is someone who has an interest or concern in your challenge or problem.

Stakeholders will include **end users**, one or more **sponsors** (usually these are the people – often business executives – who have set the challenge and/or will eventually fund development, delivery and commercialisation of your ideas and solutions if they feel there is sufficient benefits) and other individuals or teams who may have stronger or weaker links to the project. In our sample challenges, we have indicated who the sponsor is.

Often, some key stakeholders may be overlooked, and their needs not taken into account. For example, Tony once worked with an organisation which was addressing issues with its in-bound supply. One specific group of people who understood the problem more than anybody else weren't initially involved in developing the solution. Once they were identified as key stakeholders, their insight was critical to the success of the final project.

In order to avoid such problems, and to ensure a human-centred approach, we suggest one more guided activity, the creation of a 'Stakeholder Map'.

TEAM ACTIVITY: STAKEHOLDER MAP

Carry out this activity to better understand the many stakeholders who may have input or involvement in your project. You may identify some you hadn't even thought of.

(Continued)

1. PREPARE TO RUN THE ACTIVITY

- Place a flip chart onto a wall or use a virtual whiteboard.
- Write 'Stakeholder Map' in marker pen at the top of the chart and 'Who are the key stakeholders for the project?'
- Alternatively, you can also complete this task on your project MURAL. Our MURAL template includes sections for each of the Design Thinking activities that we describe in this book.

2. THE TEAM NOW DIVERGES – THE NEXT STEPS SHOULD BE CARRIED OUT IN SILENCE!

- Individual team members write the names of stakeholders on sticky notes on the chart.
- You can identify stakeholders by asking yourselves **'Who has an interest or stake in the problem and/or its solution?'**
- Really think about this – there will be obvious stakeholders such as the sponsor and end users, but less obvious ones too. Don't worry if you're not sure if a stakeholder is relevant or not, add them anyway – they can easily be removed in the next step if they're not relevant.

3. WHEN THE TEAM MEMBERS HAVE FINISHED, THE TEAM CONVERGES TO REVIEW WHAT HAS BEEN PRODUCED

- Remove duplicates and group similar stakeholders together. If useful, you can colour code similar stakeholders.
- Identify, discuss and highlight key relationships between stakeholder groups.
- Figure 4.6 shows an example of a Stakeholder Map – with duplicates removed, before key relationships have been identified – from the charity organisation challenge.

Stakeholder mapping can be used to understand the problem from different perspectives.

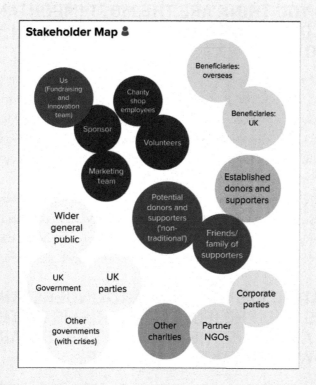

FIGURE 4.6: Stakeholder Map example

Stakeholder mapping is taken very seriously in industry, as we'll hear from our next guest interviewee, Michael Lewrick.

EXPERT

STAKEHOLDER MAPPING

Michael Lewrick is the lead author of four international bestselling books on Design Thinking. His research specialties include Design Thinking, Business Ecosystem Design & Innovation Management. He often works in cooperation with Stanford and a number of European universities.

(Continued)

1. WHO DO YOU THINK ARE THE MOST IMPORTANT STAKEHOLDERS TO ENGAGE DURING A DESIGN THINKING BASED PROJECT?

Internal and external stakeholder analysis is one of the most important elements of a Design Thinking project. The most important stakeholder is the (internal or external) 'customer' for whom a problem is to be solved. The external stakeholders also include the influencers who are close to the customer, as well as others with whom the customer interacts. Customers do not only have relationships with one set of people, company or organisation. They exist in an ecosystem.

When working on company projects, I recommend starting with an internal stakeholder map at an early stage to find out which departments, decision makers and people are relevant for the design and implementation through to market launch. The credo is to get these people involved as early as possible and to overcome any hurdles as soon as possible.

2. GENERATING EMPATHY FOR AND UNDERSTANDING END USERS AND PROJECT SPONSOR(S) IS CRITICAL TO SUCCESS. AS THIS IS THE CASE, IS IT NECESSARY TO CREATE A WIDER STAKEHOLDER MAP?

Yes, definitely. The creation of a stakeholder map is a great tool to maintain the dialogue in the team from many different perspectives. I usually introduce the concept of stakeholder maps as soon as the problem is clearly defined, and the first point of view has been obtained. Typical questions at an early stage include:

- How do the stakeholders interact with each other?
- Which internal stakeholders can help us gain access to customers and/or end users?
- Who has already solved similar problems and what were the lessons learned?
- If not already defined, who is going to be the project's sponsor?

In a later phase, typical questions include:

- Who can help us to implement the solution?
- Which budgets can be used?
- If the project is creating a new product or service, which part of the business, region or country can help us enter the market and/or launch and validate our new offering, for example by using a minimum viable product?

3. MANY STUDENTS ARE NEW TO DESIGN THINKING. WHAT HINTS AND TIPS WOULD YOU SHARE WITH THEM? THESE CAN BE RELATED TO STAKEHOLDER MAPPING AND/OR THE WIDER APPLICATION OF DESIGN THINKING TECHNIQUES.

Here are five tips for students:

1. Always begin at the beginning – Apply the Design Thinking mindset at the very start, before any direction has been set.

2. Take a human-centred approach – Investigation of the problem space should factor in human behaviour, needs and preferences.

3. Seek outside help whenever you can – Co-create with customers, other student teams and external stakeholders.

4. Try things out early and often – Use rapid experimentation and prototyping to gain feedback. Encourage your team to create simple prototypes before rushing into creating more extensive and expensive solutions.

5. Design for the cycle – Encourage the team to go through the complete design cycle, rather than just a small part of it. This will build better experience and judgment and create longer term benefits for your personal learning.

TOP TIP

I always ask myself what kind of person I am talking to before reaching out. If the internal stakeholder is the CFO of the company, he/she might be more interested in numbers. If I talk to the Strategy Team, they might be more interested in the bigger vision.

My top tip is to customise your engagement and communications to the thinking preferences of the person(s) you are engaging with. Show not only the value of the solution to the customer or user you are designing for but also the benefits related to the person you are speaking to.

Remember, in general, any feedback you can get from the stakeholders is a gift. Be grateful for the feedback and use it to improve your potential solution. Good luck!

You will note that while you research the challenge and identify the key stakeholders, your personal and team's understanding will expand and change a number of times. There can be exciting moments of discovery as well as others where research appears more of a chore. Different members of the team may develop distinct understandings and interests. It is therefore important to review outputs such as the Hopes and Fears chart, the Project Research Canvas, Problem Statement and Stakeholder Map at regular intervals and as a team. It is also helpful to be aware of your understandings and interests. The following reflection point aims to help you do this.

REFLECTION POINT: RESEARCHING THE CHALLENGE

Reflecting on the activities above, consider the following questions. Make a note of your answers in the space provided and/or in your journal.

1. WHAT INTERESTS YOU MOST ABOUT THE CHALLENGE YOU'VE SELECTED OR BEEN ASSIGNED TO?

2. WHAT AREAS AND STAKEHOLDERS WOULD YOU MOST LIKE TO EXPLORE DURING THE COURSE OF THE PROJECT?

INTERVIEWS

Doing 'desk research' online is a great way to obtain more information about an innovation challenge. However, during the research process questions may arise that are difficult to answer. Therefore, we often recommend reaching out to relevant people from industry and conducting **expert and user interviews**. Your course or module instructors will often be able to help with this, providing contact points for industry experts and/or users to interview and so on.

If you need to find your own contacts to interview, one of the easiest ways to do this is by using your own networks and/or networking tools, such as LinkedIn. You may be surprised by how often people positively respond to requests for their input. When approached proactively, carrying out expert interviews can be a very empowering experience. It is great to see that we can just approach people and ask questions, and that more often than not they are willing to share their valuable insights.

Don't forget universities and colleges usually have rules and processes for reaching out to people in industry, covering areas such as safeguarding and ethics. Always review these before reaching out and ensure you follow the correct procedures.

When contacting potential interviewees, it is very important to have empathy for them. Don't just think about what you want to know but also about their experience. How would you feel if you were approached for an interview? While many people will be happy to help and enjoy the interactions they have with you, remember they are busy people! So, the team should act courteously and professionally with the expert and make the most of the limited time they have available.

You should be well prepared, have your questions ready, perhaps even have sent them ahead of the interview (well phrased, formatted and proofread!), and check with your institution and the interviewees involved if you are required to use consent forms and so on. Again, when you work in graduate jobs later down the line, these are all skills that your employer will expect you to have developed.

TEAM ACTIVITY: EXPERT INTERVIEW

You may run this activity to gain a better understanding of the challenge you are researching and its context.

(Continued)

1. PREPARE FOR THE MEETING

- Review the assigned challenge, the Project Research Canvas and any other research carried out – identify key knowledge gaps and areas where additional insights and/or guidance would be useful.
- Create a pre-prepared interview script – this should include an introduction to the team and challenge, an introduction from the expert, a list of pre-agreed questions and a formal closing, including thanking the expert and next steps.
- Consider sending your questions ahead of the interview. If you decide to do that make sure the document looks professional and features a heading, time/date of the interview and contact details.
- Agree team roles for the meeting – e.g., who will ask the questions, who will take notes, etc.
- Agree if the meeting will be recorded – if so, agree with the expert and verify any compliance requirements and plans for storage and future deletion of the data in line with university or college policies. You may be required to use a consent form which needs to be sent to the interviewee ahead of the interview.
- Arrange the interview date and time, providing options for the industry expert. Indicate how long the interview will take. In our experience, interviews of about 30–60 minutes often work best for both sides.
- Once a timeslot is agreed, agree the approach:
  - Face-to-face meeting – Agree who will schedule the meeting and where it will be, book a room if needed and provide and/or receive details of logistics.
  - Online meeting – Agree who will schedule the meeting and the platform used; ensure participants can use and have tested the platform.
- Provide backup contact details in case of issues on the day.

2. RUN THE MEETING

- Kick-off the meeting with introductions.
- If needed, address the formalities around the use of consent forms and recording. Ensure that the interviewee has the opportunity to ask questions about the project and the interview.

- Ask the questions – listen carefully to the answers, ask additional questions if useful, ensure notes are taken and/or the session is recorded, play back answers if needed to verify understanding.
- Close the meeting by thanking the expert for their time and input. Outline how the team will use the information, keep the expert updated and any other next steps and future interactions.

3. AFTER THE MEETING

- Hold a team review of the outcome of the meeting, including any team members who couldn't be present – agree key things the team learned, identify how these are important for the challenge, identify any questions only partially or not answered and agree plans to fill any remaining knowledge gaps.
- Update the Project Research Canvas with additional information. Reflect on implications for your problem statement.
- Ensure a plan is in place for storage and future deletion of the data captured in line with university or college policies and the agreement made with the expert.

Below, we have included a list of important Dos and Don'ts for expert interviews. On YouTube and similar platforms you can find examples of good and bad research interviews. While the purpose of your research may be different from that of many qualitative researchers, rules and best practice for conducting expert interviews are similar. In our experience it is more than worthwhile to put in the time and effort needed to become a good interviewer. Why is that so? Good interviewers know how to manage a conversation, how to listen and have empathy – and retain a degree of flexibility – without losing sight of what they want to know. Conducting interviews hence helps you develop communication skills you also need when engaging with customers or clients or when negotiating with your boss.

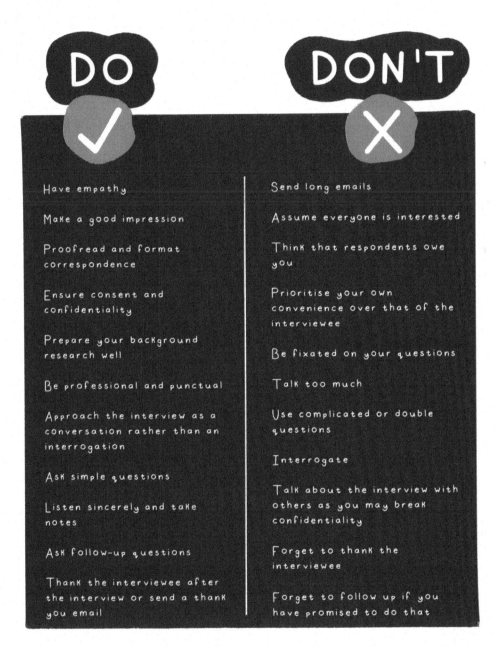

FIGURE 4.7: Expert interviews – Dos and Don'ts

REFLECTION POINT: INTERVIEWING

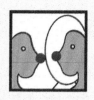

Reflecting on your interview, consider the following questions. Make a note of your answers in the space provided and/or in your journal.

1. WHAT DO YOU THINK WENT WELL, AND WHAT DID NOT?

2. WHAT WOULD YOU DO DIFFERENTLY THE NEXT TIME YOU CONDUCT AN INTERVIEW?

Expert interviews are a useful strategy for finding out more about a challenge and its context. However, experts have their own views and opinions as to what the problems are and how they should be approached. While these may be well-founded (they are the experts!), we also need to be careful not to simply adopt the views of the experts we interview. After all, we want to innovate! Going back to our example of the fun MRI scanner, we have little doubt that if they had talked only to a pediatrician or MRI expert they would have focused more on the technology rather than the way children experience it. Or if you had asked an expert on vases, you would have narrowed down even more on the shape or material of the vase rather than questioning if there were other ways in which the underlying needs of a person could be met.

Design Thinking focuses on the experiences of users. What better way of finding out about the experiences of users than to ask them directly! Although we appreciate this may not always be possible with student projects, if you can, please do engage one or more users involved in your innovation challenge.

User interviews are *interviews for empathy*. They are a great way of building empathy and understanding a challenge from the perspective of a user. While many of the practicalities of user interviews are similar to those of expert interviews, there are also important differences. User interviews focus on the user experience and usually aim to elicit detailed accounts or stories of particular events or incidents. When we ask users about their experiences, we are interested in their understandings as well as their emotions. Therefore, building rapport with the interviewee is even more important when conducting user interviews. We also pay a lot more attention to *how* something is said and to body language than we do when interviewing experts.

We also tend to capture the outcome of user interviews in a different way. Expert interviews are about facts we can add to our Project Research Canvas. They help us to further refine the problem statement in context. In contrast, user interviews help us to identify experiences and processes in the form of stories. These stories may or may not be representative of the experience of many users. The crucial point here is that they give us a view from the inside, and an understanding of the temporal dimension (i.e., what happens first and where it leads to). As we will see in the next chapters, such insights can be invaluable when we start to think about solutions.

For now, there is just one more thing to add. Interviews are not the only method that you can use to do research on your challenge. Oftentimes, innovation teams combine these with other methods that bring in a different perspective or degree of verification. Observational and participatory research methods can be particularly important here. In particular after some initial interviews, it can be great to see if users 'walk the talk'. Sometimes, users have grown so used to navigating challenges that they no longer notice them. For example, they have always had to log in three times using different passwords to access a document they need. Or coordinated their team using WhatsApp rather than the technology they should be using. Only when you start observing them will you start to pick up that such day-to-day obstacles could be part of a bigger problem (e.g., delayed response to client requests or data protection concerns).

We have not included any team activities involving observation here, in part because of time and resource constraints, but also because issues around ethics and consent are a bit more complicated when we use observation. There are some suggested readings in the further resources section below, if you want to have a look at a wider range of methods and techniques for understanding your innovation challenge.

CONCLUSION

While this chapter was all about you embarking on your project, it also covered some key employability skills. We discussed how to create an effective team and told you about ground rules for good teamwork. You learnt about some team activities that can help a team to get going. We encouraged you to reflect on your experiences of teamwork and to consider how you may be able to improve your skills in an area that is so key to most graduate jobs.

We also had a closer look at innovation challenges and how to approach them. In our experience, it can be difficult not to jump from the challenge into ideation straight away and instead research a challenge first. If you felt impatient at times rest assured – the time for creative thinking has now come, and you will soon see that the hard work will have paid off. Moreover, research skills, and the organisational and communication skills needed to conduct good expert and user interviews are also key employability skills. The Dos and Don'ts list could be used for a job interview as well as a research interview!

KEY LEARNING POINTS

- Design Thinking activities help teams to break the ice and facilitate effective teamwork.
- All teamwork should start with agreeing some ground rules.
- An innovation challenge is a brief statement that defines a problem or opportunity in context.
- No matter how broad or narrow, an innovation challenge requires further research and interpretation in order to understand the underlying problem or opportunity more fully and identify relevant requirements.
- With innovation challenges, causes and effects, problems and context are often far from clear. Researching an innovation challenge may involve a lot of desk-based research as well as observations or interviews. It is important to evaluate the quality of different sources of information.
- Stakeholder mapping can help to understand the problem from different perspectives.

- When engaging with experts or stakeholders it is of pivotal importance to have empathy and act courteously and professionally.
- Expert interviews are a useful strategy for finding out more about a challenge and its context. User interviews help to develop empathy with users.
- Good interview skills are important for many graduate jobs.

ACTION POINTS

☐ Agree with your team some ground rules for teamwork. The recommendations above may provide a good starting point.

☐ Decide on the team name and how you want to collaborate in terms of when, where and how. It can be very useful to have a regular meeting set up and agree what communication channels you will use.

☐ When reading a new challenge, ask yourself: Why is there a problem/opportunity? Who has a need? When and where does it occur? How is it being solved today? Where are the gaps?

☐ Run the team activities and make sure to keep and regularly review and update the outputs (Hopes and Fears, Project Research Canvas, Problem Statement and Stakeholder Map).

☐ Please complete the reflection points and the short exercise below.

EXERCISE

1. Make a list of key things you should consider when preparing to interview someone (such as a sponsor, industry expert or end user) for a project.

FURTHER RESOURCES

The following book provides an overview of a wide range of Design Thinking methods:

Lewrick, M., Link, P., & Leifer, L. 2020. *The Design Thinking Toolbox*. Hoboken, NJ: Wiley.

A useful article on Design Thinking teams:

Dam, R.F., & Siang, T.Y. 2020. *Design Thinking: Select the Right Team Members and Start Facilitating.* Interaction Design Foundation.

Find out about the Global Design Thinking Alliance:

https://gdta.org

Have a look at this seminal article on wicked problems and Design Thinking:

Buchanan, R. 1992. Wicked problems in Design Thinking. *Design Issues*, 8(2), 5–21.

Two more practical accounts of wicked problems and how to solve them:

de Almeida Kumlien, A.C., & Coughlan, P. 2018. Wicked problems and how to solve them. *The Conversation*, 18 October. and

Ashton, R. 2012. How do you tackle a 'wicked' issue? *The Guardian*, 8 June.

A useful website with more guidance on stakeholder mapping:

www.smaply.com/blog/stakeholdermaps

There are a lot of resources on how to conduct interviews! We recommend this book on research interviewing you may have in your library:

Kvale, S., & Brinkmann, S. 2014. *InterViews: Learning the Craft of Qualitative Research Interviewing.* 3rd edn. Thousand Oaks, CA: SAGE.

We also recommend the following resource on 'how to conduct user interviews' more specifically:

www.interaction-design.org/literature/article/how-to-conduct-user-interviews

Finally, this website provides some useful recommendations on how to conduct Design Thinking interviews:

https://webdesign.tutsplus.com/articles/techniques-of-empathy-interviews-in-design-thinking--cms-31219

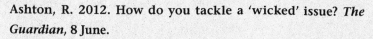

IDEA
GENERATION

Chapter contents

Goals

- To reflect on how ideas can be generated and where they often come from.
- To deepen your understanding of the challenge and the needs of end users.
- To identify pain points and opportunities.
- To generate and quickly prioritise ideas.
- To learn how to use Design Thinking techniques for deepening your understanding, ideation and idea selection.

INTRODUCTION

So far, you've learned about innovation and Design Thinking, formed a team, received a challenge and kicked off research. At this stage, you may well be wondering when we'll be getting to the more exciting stuff like generating ideas and solutions. The answer is soon, and in this chapter, but not quite yet.

If we're really going to live by the mantra of *'Love the problem, not the solution'*, there are a couple of things we need to do first. For one thing, we need to develop a better understanding of the needs of those we're creating our solutions for! While we have already done some research, our thinking is still mainly focused on our own and/or some experts' understanding of the challenge. But in most cases, it is not (just) us or the expert we're innovating for! So, in this chapter, we'll tell you about some methods for developing empathy with end users. When we understand the current experience of our end users, we are in a much better position to identify pain points and opportunities. This understanding also enables us to generate wider value. As you are about to discover, having empathy is not just an important skill for leading a good life, it's also a very important employability skill.

Generating ideas is about having empathy, but it's also about creativity and communication. Design Thinking is well known for enabling teams to develop creative ideas. As you'll see, this is important but so is the ability to select the right idea. And again, there are some great Design Thinking techniques for doing just that.

As Design Thinking is best understood by doing it, in this chapter, you will do a lot of Design Thinking work with your team! We'll walk you through two Design Thinking workshops – by the end of which you'll have generated a diverse set of ideas and selected one or more ideas to focus on for the rest of the book.

For now, however, we'll focus on Phase 1, the idea generation phase of the innovation management process.

GENERATING IDEAS

DIFFERENT APPROACHES TO GENERATING IDEAS

Let us start by having a closer look at the ways in which ideas can be generated and where organisations frequently get them from.

Two major approaches for organisations to generate new ideas are called *knowledge push* and *need (or market) pull* (Bessant & Tidd, 2015).

Knowledge push happens when a new concept or technology is created, for example during research and development, rather than as a response to a need for a specific solution to address a problem or opportunity. Once the concept or technology has been created, an organisation may decide they want to verify how they can practically exploit this to create value.

Touch screen technology was created by the UK Royal Radar Establishment in the 1960s. In the 1980s Hewlett Packard were looking for ideas to exploit this technology and created the first touch screen computer. The touch screen computer was really a technology push idea. More recently, when IBM developed its initial 'Watson' artificial intelligence technology, it ran a large internal competition to find real-world industry problems which the Watson technology could solve. IBM then used these to take the technology to market.

In contrast, **need or market pull** occurs when an organisation seeks to create innovations which will address the problems, challenges and/or opportunities of their customers, employees or partners. It is more commonly used to drive innovation than knowledge push in most organisations. Here, our thinking does not focus on finding a problem for a new solution to address, but on developing ideas and solutions to solve existing problems and/or opportunities! In the context of technology, fingerprint-based access to smartphones is an example of a market pull generated idea. The solution was developed as a direct response to customer needs for simplified authentication and not having to always remember a password.

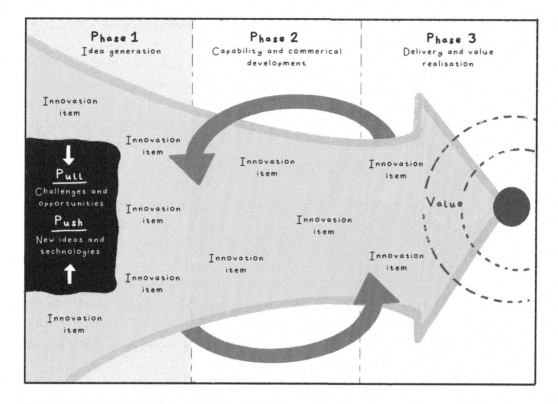

FIGURE 5.1: Push and pull in Phase 1 of the innovation management process

Different 'markets' sometimes pull in different ways. In the public sector, one example is the need to simplify forms and improve processes for engaging with government agencies. Whilst such solutions may involve new technologies, the starting point isn't the technology, but the need to respond to complaints about duplication and bureaucracy and poorly designed forms which lead to mistakes and inaccurate data.

WHERE DO THE BEST IDEAS COME FROM?

Ideas for innovation may have many different sources. For example, they can arise by accident. The microwave was created as a result of an accident at a defence company where a chocolate bar had melted in someone's pocket. Ideas can also arise from day-to-day observations. For example, the Pritt Stick was developed because a scientist working for a glue company observed a woman applying lipstick and wondered if the lipstick tube could become a great new vehicle for applying glue (Bessant & Tidd, 2015)!

Often, companies turn to so-called lead users. There are people who not only face a challenge but also have a proactive attitude towards addressing it. For example, Ted Golesworthy, a boiler engineer with a terminal heart condition, developed a new heart valve which has saved his life and that of many others (Golesworthy, 2011, see further resources below).

Industry reports, such as Boston Consulting Group's annual Innovation Index of the most innovative companies in the world, show the companies who innovate most successfully generate ideas from a wide range of sources. For example, in 2016, the Boston Consulting Group report highlighted sources of ideas included internal sources and employees, customers (including customer complaints), competitor analysis, strategic partnerships, innovation incubators, suppliers and business partners, external firms and social media.

But there's not a one size fits all model here. Each organisation needs to determine the best sources of ideas for their own context, depending on their size, industry, sector, strengths and weaknesses and so on. You may remember that we already discussed this when we introduced the concept of open innovation in Chapter 2, and the different types of inside-out and outside-in open innovation. As we noted there, and re-emphasise here, organisations need to ensure they have ways of identifying and progressing the best ideas from their own key sources – so that they can eventually deliver and get value from them. Can you still recall the six innovation enablers we introduced in Chapter 2?

MORE IN-DEPTH: WHAT ABOUT THE ROLE OF CREATIVITY?

Creativity or 'the use of imagination and new ideas' is key to any innovation project. Whilst some people are more creative, for others creativity is a skill that can be learnt and managed. It is also a skill that, in times of automation and artificial intelligence, has become even more valued. Usually, we distinguish between creativity at an individual level (how creative a person is has been the subject of much research) and at a group level (how to foster the creativity of teams or entire organisations).

Creativity is often described as a complex and messy process (De Bono, 1992). Because creativity is deemed to be so important, there are thousands of books about how to develop your creativity or that of your organisation and use it to great effect. Similarly, there is no shortage of guidelines and rules for managing creativity. Robert I. Sutton's (2001) 'weird' rules of creativity are a case in point (see further resources section at the end of the chapter). Amongst other things, he advises to 'reward success and failure – punish inaction; [...] take your past successes – and forget them; [and] ignore people who have solved the exact problem you face' (p. 97). While such rules can help organisations to become more creative, they also have pitfalls when it comes to innovation. After all, innovation is about 'making new ideas real, so that they can create value' (Kastelle, 2014). So, what is possible (rather than fantasy), is an important consideration – as is the need to understand how the application of a new idea (however creative and marvellous it may be) creates value. Tim Kastelle has recorded a great TED Talk on 'making ideas real', which we recommend watching to get a deeper understanding of this issue.

APPLYING DESIGN THINKING TECHNIQUES TO THE CHALLENGE

For now, let us focus on how to be creative, whilst not losing sight of the need to create actual value *for someone*. And this 'someone' is key here.

Deciding what is a real opportunity and what is fantasy has a lot to do with understanding the needs, thoughts, emotions and motivations of end users. Remember, it's the end users who will ultimately use any innovative solution you develop – not you! And this is where Design Thinking comes in. We want you to be creative and to develop extraordinary ideas, even crazy ideas, but we also want you to do that based on a deeper understanding of the problem from the perspective of those who have a need. This is why Design Thinking often emphasises *pull* over *push*. And this is why Design Thinking involves some great activities which aim at creative thinking and ideation – often it is even described as a methodology for 'unleashing creativity' – but only *after* one has had a closer look at the problem from the perspective of those experiencing it.

As you will see, in this chapter we do both. First, we'll explain to you some of the basics of how to run a Design Thinking workshop. In the next section, we'll walk you through a workshop that enables you to better understand your challenge from the perspective of those experiencing it. We're going to identify users' issues or 'pain points' and we're going to find opportunities to intervene and add value for them, and for the sponsor and the organisation we're delivering the innovation for. In the final section of this chapter, we'll finally guide you through a second workshop that is all about idea generation, prioritisation and selection.

PREPARING FOR THE DESIGN THINKING WORKSHOPS

In this chapter, we walk you through six different Design Thinking activities, so you and your team will be busy! We have structured the activities into two different workshops. You can do everything in one day – but it will be intense. And if you do it online, you may be suffering from 'Zoom fatigue' by the end of it. So, if you decide to do it all in a single workshop, ensure you schedule sufficient breaks to maintain the team's energy levels!

If the workshop is to be held face to face, the activities can be run in two workshops, or combined into a single workshop if desired. You'll need a room with plenty of wall space and flip charts, marker pens, sticky notes and Sharpie-style pens as detailed in our facilitation guide which you can download from our companion website.

There is also a second guide that details how to run these workshops online, where we recommend combining a video conferencing tool such as Zoom with an online workshop collaboration platform such as MURAL. And, of course, if using MURAL, you can make use of our MURAL template.

Figure 5.2 provides an overview of the six selected Design Thinking activities. The first workshop is all about generating empathy for the end users and deepening your understanding of the problem. The second is about idea generation, prioritisation and selection. As shown by the figure below, the second workshop builds on and is framed by insights obtained in the first. At the end of these workshops, you will have created some great ideas and selected one or two to be developed further.

We include time estimates for each technique to provide a level of guidance, but please do bear in mind the time needed may vary widely, depending on factors such as face-to-face or online working, the complexity of the challenge, the number of team members, experience levels of the team and so on. However, experience shows it can be helpful to put some time pressure on to keep the ball rolling, so to speak. It's often preferable to have a few busy, even

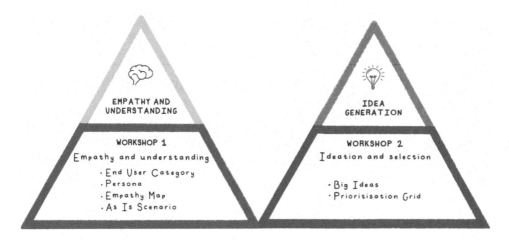

FIGURE 5.2: Idea generation workshops and activities

a little hectic, periods of activity followed by proper breaks rather than long slowly paced sessions that seem to last forever. This is why we recommend sticking to the time estimates for each activity but do give yourself the flexibility to extend a session if necessary.

All of the Design Thinking techniques we use in this chapter make use of a combination of 'diverge' and 'converge' based approaches. Remember, *diverge* means that you temporarily break up the team and *work individually* so that you get the most diverse input. It's really important that you stick to this and that you do not talk when diverging. Be assured, whenever you diverge, you will have a *converge* activity afterwards, where the team will get together to review and discuss what the team members have done. You then can share your great ideas, ask questions and, most importantly, find out about the amazing insights and ideas of your teammates.

Let's now get the views of one of our experts on why working in diverse teams is so important.

EXPERT

WHY WE NEED WEQ

We introduced Professor Ulrich Weinberg of the HPI School of Design in Chapter 4. Here, Ullrich shares his thoughts on the importance of multidisciplinary teams

(Continued)

for idea generation and why IQ (intelligence quotient) and EQ (emotional quotient) are not enough to succeed in the world of tomorrow.

1. WHY IS WORKING IN DIVERSE TEAMS SO IMPORTANT FOR IDEA GENERATION?

 Multidisciplinary teams bring into dialogue completely different people and ideas. In this way, they enable creative network thinking and idea generation, in particular when they include different subject experts as well as users.

Think about the pandemic, for example. What would have happened if we had asked a teacher, a General Practitioner or an entrepreneur struggling with pandemic related supply chain issues to join a task force that generates ideas for how to respond to the situation? Chances are that the public response and our experience of this pandemic would have been quite different. At the present time, however, we still tend to work (and think!) in specialist silos.

Moreover, creating a multidisciplinary team by itself is not always enough. We also need team members who have empathy and who are willing and able to collaborate with others…

2. SO WE ARE NOT ALL NATURAL TEAM PLAYERS?

I think we are – but then we are trained to compete rather than collaborate. Think about our education system. We evaluate individual performance. We focus on competition (who is the best or worst in class) rather than on teamwork. Many students experience team-based teaching as an obstacle to personal success. And this is a huge problem!

3. EVERY YEAR, WE HAVE SOME STUDENTS WHO ARE VERY KEEN TO LEAD WITH THEIR IDEAS AND ARE THEN FRUSTRATED WHEN OTHERS DO NOT ACCEPT THEIR LEADERSHIP OR FAIL TO MEET THEIR EXPECTATIONS IN SOME OTHER WAY. I SUPPOSE THIS ALSO SHOWS THAT THE FOCUS IS OFTEN ON THE INDIVIDUAL TEAM MEMBER AND WHAT THEY PUT IN, DECIDE OR GET OUT RATHER THAN THE TEAM AS A WHOLE…

Exactly! But at the end of the day, it is often the strength of the team that is key. A study of contemporary trends found that they all had at their heart a collaborative orientation: sharing economy, social entrepreneurship, co-creation, open-source… need I say more?

Many employers have understood the importance of teaming and have started changing the ways they operate... but they struggle to recruit good team players. Those who excel at this often prefer to do their own thing!

We really need a paradigm shift in education. I am involved in a related initiative called the WeQ Foundation. The idea is that we need more than just IQ and EQ. We need *WeQ*, an orientation to the common good and a clear commitment to teamworking as a work attitude. And we need new ways to train and assess WeQ. We are in the early stages of finding out how to do this.

TOP TIP

Use Design Thinking to discover new ways of thinking, living and working. One Design Thinking project can already show you a lot about your ability to create something meaningful in collaboration with others. Often, this experience triggers a sense of empowerment and entrepreneurial spirit. Don't fight it or, worse, forget it – but do something with it!

One last piece of advice for now.

When you're asked to converge *really do collaborate* and engage with your team. Sometimes this can be hard because you may not want to listen, or you don't like some of the contributions from other team members – or you feel it takes a great deal of patience to listen to them. These things can happen to everyone! If they happen to you, remember that this is also training in employability skills, and how important teaming is for most graduate jobs. Use this as an opportunity to step back a bit, observe yourself as a 'team player' and reflect on *how you can listen better*, as well as make it easy for others to listen to you! It might be worth having a look at the ground rules for teamwork we introduced in the previous chapter. The chances are that you'll spend a lot of your life involved in teamwork throughout both your career and wider life. As you are about to see, Design Thinking activities can provide a brilliant opportunity to get better at this and enjoy yourself in the process!

FACILITATING DESIGN THINKING WORKSHOPS

Experience shows one common success factor for Design Thinking workshops is having a good facilitator. The facilitator will set up the room or online tools, agree the objectives with the attendees, direct activities, manage the timing and ensure playbacks to review progress and agree actions, etc.

Generally during modules, the teaching staff will facilitate workshops. If you're working independently of a module or if you don't have a facilitator for any other reason, we recommend you pre-agree a named member of the team to facilitate each workshop or activity. It will be good practice to rotate this role, so all team members take a turn and gain experience from facilitating the team. Remember, the facilitator is a key member of your team – so show them empathy and support them!

There are some very useful resources available on facilitating Design Thinking workshops – have a look at the further resources section at the end of the chapter for more information. In Chapter 6, we will have a closer look at the communication and collaboration skills needed for effective teamwork.

WORKSHOP 1 – EMPATHY AND UNDERSTANDING

In industry, if a team is working on a change or innovation project, the team usually spends a certain amount of time gathering information about their end users. For example, team members may interview the end users (as mentioned in the previous chapter), shadow them or ask them to complete questionnaires or surveys.

Often, the end users are directly involved in Design Thinking activities, such as the ones you're about to carry out. We appreciate it's unlikely this is going to be possible for the purposes of a student project – unless you decide your end users are students or some other group that you can easily engage with! No matter whether or not you have the opportunity to do some research directly with your end users, we ask you to 'keep yourselves in their shoes' at all times. Think about what's important to them – and not about what's important to you.

END USER CATEGORIES

Just like students, end users are people. They're not all the same! To help us better understand different sets of end users, we break them down into 'End User Categories'. Each category represents a different set of end users who each share some common characteristics.

The categories can consist of internal employees, customers and/or third parties. For example, categories for a retail project might include:

- Retail employees: Checkout Operator, Store Manager, Warehouse Worker, Call Centre Agent, Delivery Driver, etc.
- Retail customers: Student Customer, Young Professional Customer, Parent with Children Customer, Retired Customer, etc.
- Third parties: Supplier Manager, Regulator, etc.

As you can see, the list can be quite long! You may or may not have identified all these in your Stakeholder Map. Don't worry though, for your project we'll only want you to focus in detail on one or two categories.

TEAM ACTIVITY: END USER CATEGORIES – ESTIMATED TIME 15 MINUTES

Carry out this step to identify the various categories of end users in the scope of the project.

1. PREPARE TO RUN THE ACTIVITY

- Place a flip chart onto a wall or use a virtual whiteboard.
- Write 'End User Categories' in marker pen at the top of the page.
- Alternatively, you can also complete this task on your project MURAL. Our MURAL template includes sections for each of the Design Thinking activities that we describe in this book.

2. THE TEAM DIVERGES TO PROVIDE INPUT – THIS STEP SHOULD BE CARRIED OUT IN SILENCE!

- Individual team members identify categories of end users affected by the challenge and write these onto sticky notes (one point per note) and place these onto the flip chart/virtual whiteboard.
- There's an obvious crossover with Stakeholder Mapping here, so it's useful to refer to the Stakeholder Map when doing this but it's also important not to be limited by it – team members may identify some new categories too.

3. WHEN THE TEAM MEMBERS HAVE FINISHED, THE TEAM CONVERGES TO REVIEW WHAT HAS BEEN POSTED

- Remove duplicates and group similar stakeholders together. If useful, you can colour code similar categories.

(Continued)

- Identify, discuss and highlight key categories the team would like to focus on.
- The team agrees one or two primary categories to focus on – these will be the ones of most relevance to the project.
- Note: Many projects will select a number of categories to focus on, but for the purposes of your project you only wish to focus on a small number.
- The figure below shows an example of an End User Categories chart – with duplicates removed and similar categories colour coded – from the example charity organisation challenge (using the MURAL tool).

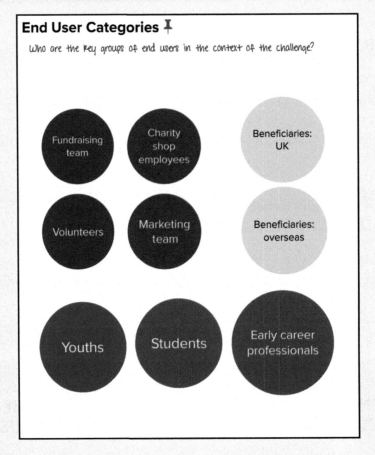

FIGURE 5.3: End User Categories example

The output of the activity is agreement on one or two End User Categories to focus on in the next steps.

END USER PERSONA

We're now going to develop a better understanding of the end users in our selected category or categories – by creating an 'End User Persona'.

An 'End User Persona' is a typical end user within the selected category, in the context of the challenge.

We use Personas to develop a deeper level of understanding and empathy for a given category of end users. It can be difficult to have empathy with a 'type', it is much easier to empathise with someone who has got a name, a job, a hairstyle, a hobby, a family – and an aging dog. (They don't always have to have a dog!)

The guided activity below should be carried out to create at least one End User Persona. The activity can be repeated as needed for additional End User Personas.

Most of the student projects we support typically develop one or two End User Personas. Sometimes, during the project, a team will realise they need to change and focus on a different End User Persona. If this happens to you, simply loop back to this step. Design Thinking is iterative, after all.

TEAM ACTIVITY: END USER PERSONA – ESTIMATED TIME 20 MINUTES FOR ONE PERSONA

Carry out this step to identify one or more end users to generate empathy for and focus on.

1. PREPARE TO RUN THE ACTIVITY

- Place a flip chart onto a wall or use a virtual whiteboard.
- Create an End User Persona template as shown in Figure 5.4.

(Continued)

- Alternatively, if you are using our MURAL template, just click on the section 'End User Persona 1'.

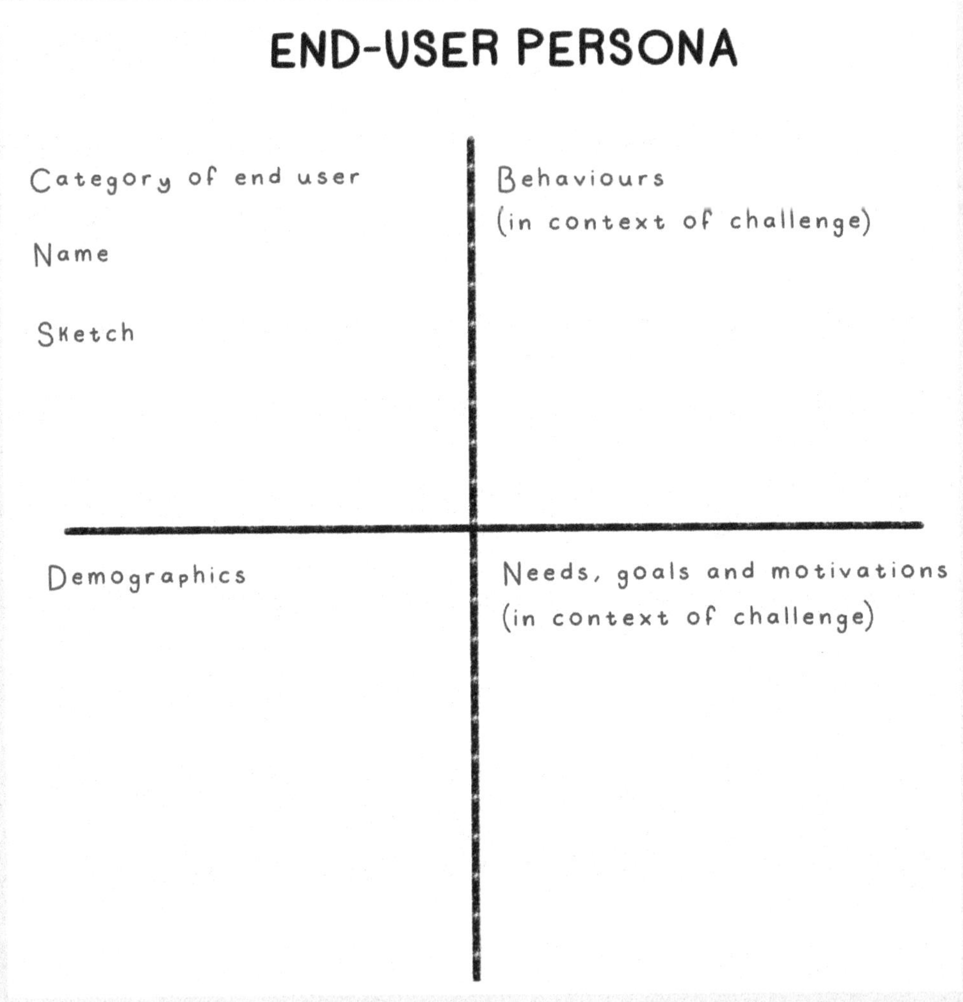

END-USER PERSONA

Category of end user   Behaviours
                              (in context of challenge)

Name

Sketch

Demographics   Needs, goals and motivations
                              (in context of challenge)

FIGURE 5.4: End User Persona template

- Note: the fields can be tailored as needed depending on the challenge and the specific End User. Remember, this is all about generating empathy for your selected end user, in the specific context of your challenge.

2. THE TEAM NOW CONVERGES TO POPULATE THE END USER PERSONA

- Assign a scribe to write down the points agreed by the team.
- The team agrees an End User Persona to focus on – select a typical end user from one of the End User Categories you agreed to focus on.
- The team discusses each field of the End User Persona template. For example, give the End User Persona a name, begin to get to know them, build up their profile in the context of the assigned challenge.
- One thing we recommend including is a picture of your End User Persona. We appreciate that not all of us have amazing drawing skills but even a fairly quick sketch based on a stickman can become a powerful anchor for understanding and empathy. When working online, it is often more practical to use an image or photo.
- You may remember Doug Dietz in Chapter 3 mentioning 'Nurse Sue' and how another user's picture was placed in a chair during meetings! These were End User Personas.
- Figure 5.5 shows an example of an End User Persona from the charity organisation challenge (again using MURAL).

3. THE TEAM REVIEWS AND PLAYS BACK KEY FINDINGS ABOUT THE END USER PERSONA

- Once the team is ready, the team reviews the populated End User Persona, highlighting key learning points.

4. MAINTAIN AND UPDATE THE END USER PERSONA

- The End User Persona should be kept accessible during the project and be referred to from time to time as needed.
- The End User Persona can also be updated over time as the team gathers more knowledge.

The exercise can be repeated, if desired, to create additional End User Personas. The output of the activity is one or more completed End User Persona templates.

(Continued)

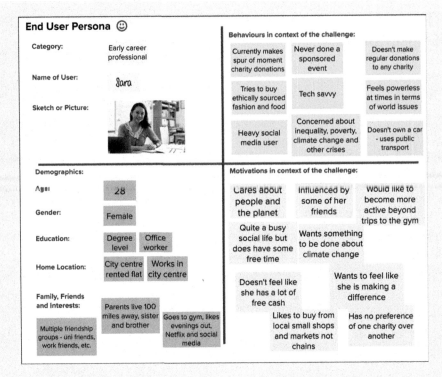

FIGURE 5.5: End User Persona example

EMPATHY MAP

Now, that we've built one or more End User Personas, it's time to develop a deeper level of understanding of each Persona *in the context of the challenge*. This will enable you to develop even greater empathy for the end users and to (re)focus attention on the challenge.

The Empathy Map shows the End User Persona's **current experience of the challenge**:

- **Does** – What activities does the user currently carry out related to the challenge.
- **Says** – What does the user currently say about the challenge.
- **Thinks** – What does the user currently think about the challenge.
- **Feels** – What does the user currently feel about the challenge – the input here tends to be based on emotions, typically only one or two words – excited, very worried, apathetic and so on.

The guided activity below should be carried out to create an Empathy Map for each selected End User Persona.

TEAM ACTIVITY: EMPATHY MAP – ESTIMATED TIME 25 MINUTES FOR ONE EMPATHY MAP

Carry out this activity to generate a deeper understanding of what's important to your selected End User Persona(s).

1. PREPARE TO RUN THE ACTIVITY

- Place a flip chart onto a wall or use a virtual whiteboard.
- Create an Empathy Map as shown in Figure 5.6, but without the questions.
- Alternatively, if using MURAL, you can make use of our online template.

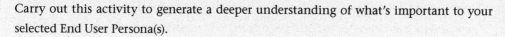

FIGURE 5.6: Empathy Map template

- As a final preparation step place the name and image of your selected end user into the centre of the Empathy Map.

(Continued)

2. THE TEAM DIVERGES TO PROVIDE INPUT – THIS STEP SHOULD BE CARRIED OUT IN SILENCE!

- Individual team members identify and write down on sticky notes (one point per note) what the selected end user does, says, thinks and feels in the context of the challenge and uses the sticky notes to populate the flip chart/virtual whiteboard.
- As you do this, remember to really generate empathy for the end user.
- Think about what is important to them, rather than to you. What would they really do, say, think and feel in the context of the challenge?
- Sometimes, it can be really useful to have a look at lists of universal feelings and needs as a source of inspiration. See further resources section for details.

3. WHEN THE TEAM MEMBERS HAVE FINISHED, THE TEAM CONVERGES TO REVIEW THE EMPATHY MAP

- Remove duplicates and group similar points together.
- Review each sticky note and highlight key learning points. What is really important to the end user? What did you discover that surprises you?
- Think about how you can verify your findings. It may not always be possible, but are there one or more end users you can verify the key points with? Or even better than that, can you repeat the activity with real end users providing the input?
- Figure 5.7 shows an example of a populated Empathy Map after duplicates have been removed, again based upon the charity organisation challenge and created using MURAL.

4. MAINTAIN AND UPDATE THE EMPATHY MAP

- The Empathy Map should be kept accessible during the project and be referred to from time to time as needed.
- The Empathy Map can also be updated over time as the team gathers more knowledge.

The exercise can be repeated, if desired, to create additional Empathy Maps. The output of the activity is one or more completed Empathy Map templates.

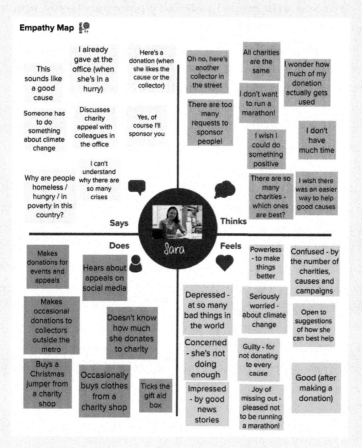

FIGURE 5.7: Empathy Map example

IDENTIFYING PAIN POINTS AND OPPORTUNITIES

You've now begun to understand and develop empathy for your end users. The next step is to narrow down even further and understand their current end user experience in one or more key areas related to the challenge. To do this we can develop one or more *As Is Scenario* maps.

An As Is Scenario map centres on a set of activities the End User Persona currently undergoes related to the challenge. While an Empathy Map explores the experience of end users in wider or more general terms, an As Is Scenario focuses on a specific chain of events. For example, if the end user is a patient it may focus on what happens when the patient visits the doctor. Or if the end user is a doctor, it may be the process the doctor follows to hold a patient consultation.

We use As Is Scenario maps to identify pain points and opportunities. **Pain points** are moments where things are difficult, or even go pear-shaped, for our poor Persona. For example, when the patient who calls his or her doctor ends up being placed on hold and listening to some dreadful interpretation of Mozart. Or the moment the doctor realises that completing the form takes much longer than the time scheduled for the appointment. In contrast, **opportunities** are about moments where we can intervene and add value. These opportunities are hence not just about the user but also about the sponsor. For example, depending on whether your sponsor is an executive in an IT company or the manager of a group of general practice doctors, the opportunities you identify when examining the above scenarios may differ. In the first instance, you may focus on the potential of technology-enabled interventions, whereas in the second instance you may think about opportunities in terms of the (re-)organisation of workflows.

Usually, it's helpful to create one Scenario map for each major set of activities an End User Persona undertakes in relation to the challenge. For a large project, there may be many scenarios. For your project, we recommend you focus on just one or two.

The guided activity below should be carried out to create one or more As Is Scenarios. You may find the creation of As Is Scenarios can be more challenging than of, say, Empathy Maps. This is because you need to decide on a particular issue and moment of time when the challenge becomes relevant for the end user but also when there may be an opportunity for an intervention of interest to the sponsor.

TEAM ACTIVITY: AS IS SCENARIO – ESTIMATED TIME 30 MINUTES

Carry out this activity to generate an understanding of the end user's current experience, pain points and opportunities for improvement.

1. AGREE WHICH END USER SCENARIO(S) TO FOCUS ON

- The team converges to agree one or more Scenarios to focus on.
- Each selected Scenario must be relevant for the challenge and centre around one of the team's selected End User Personas.

2. PREPARE TO RUN THE ACTIVITY

- Place a flip chart onto a wall or use a virtual whiteboard.
- Create an As Is Scenario template as shown in Figure 5.8.
- Alternatively, if using MURAL, you can make use of our online template.

AS IS SCENARIO

Steps or phases

Thinking

Doing

Feeling
(emotions)

FIGURE 5.8: As Is Scenario template

3. POPULATE THE AS IS SCENARIO

- The team **converges** to break the Scenario down into a series of high-level steps and adds these steps to the top row of the template.
- The team **diverges** to document the current user experience, by describing what the End User Persona **does, thinks and feels** during each step.
- All team members must provide their own individual inputs using sticky notes to populate **does, thinks and feels** activities.
- Note: This should be a silent activity, with no discussion, to ensure all team members participate without influence from the others.
- The figure below shows an example of a populated As Is Scenario from the charity organisation challenge.

(Continued)

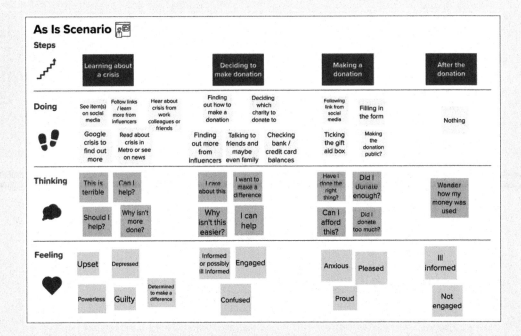

4. WHEN THE TEAM MEMBERS HAVE FINISHED, THE TEAM CONVERGES TO REVIEW THE AS IS SCENARIO

- Remove duplicates and group similar points together.
- Review each sticky note and highlight key learning points by circing or starring key findings. Highlight the end user's primary pain points. Highlight opportunities for new solutions to improve end user experience or introduce other beneficial changes.

5. MAINTAIN AND UPDATE THE AS IS SCENARIO

- The As Is Scenario should be kept accessible during the project and be referred to from time to time as needed.
- The As Is Scenario can also be updated over time as the team gathers more knowledge.

The exercise can be repeated, if desired, to create additional As Is Scenarios. The output of the activity is one or more completed As Is Scenario templates.

REFLECTION POINT: UNDERSTANDING END USERS

Reflecting on the activities above to better understand end users, consider the following questions. Make a note of your answers in the space provided and/or in your journal.

1. WHAT IS MOST IMPORTANT TO YOUR SELECTED END USER PERSONA(S) IN THE CONTEXT OF THE CHALLENGE?

2. WHAT DO YOU THINK MOTIVATES THE END USER PERSONA(S) IN THE CONTEXT OF THE CHALLENGE (POSITIVELY AND/OR NEGATIVELY)?

3. WHAT AS IS SCENARIO(S) HAVE YOU CHOSEN, AND WHY?

(Continued)

4. WHAT HAVE YOU TAKEN AWAY FROM THE ANALYSIS OF PAIN POINTS AND OPPORTUNITIES?

WORKSHOP 2 – IDEA GENERATION

By now, you will have developed an in-depth understanding and interpretation of your innovation challenge. You have done your homework and researched the context of the challenge and what problems it entails. You have also explored your challenge on a micro-level by really thinking through what it means to those experiencing it. You have identified key situations, pain points and opportunities. Now, finally, we're going to generate some new ideas.

You may decide to ask why it has taken quite so long to get to this stage. Well, the answer's simple and we hope you know it by now. Yes, we have to 'love the problem, not the solution'.

By carrying out research, thinking about the stakeholders, understanding and developing empathy for the end users and finally identifying pain points and opportunities, you should know a lot more about the challenge area than when you started!

But before we get to the workshop activities, we'll ask another expert to share their views – this time on ideation.

EXPERT

IDEATION

Ian Smith is a technology and innovation leader. As senior IT and Innovation Architect, Ian delivered many challenging projects for IBM before starting his own consultancy. Ian teaches and facilitates Design Thinking workshops for a variety of clients and industries.

1. WHAT DRIVES IDEATION IN DESIGN THINKING?

You really need to find the right user and invest in deeply understanding them and their situation, using tools like personas and empathy maps to document what you learn. You then move to examine what they are actually doing when they are doing the work and solving the problems that you want to help them with. Document these findings using scenario maps. This understanding will help you to narrow down the challenge, and make it more specific. This is a crucial but often difficult step to take.

Sometimes, it can feel like we are losing time doing the scenario maps. I think that time is usually well invested. Scenario maps are such a powerful tool for identifying pain points!

To drive ideation, this is what you need more than anything else, you need accurate opportunities and pain points that genuinely apply to selected end users.

2. BUT HOW DO WE KNOW THAT THE PAIN POINTS WE HAVE IDENTIFIED ARE THE RIGHT ONES?

This takes us back to the importance of empathy and user involvement. Empathy can go a long way in scenario development – but of course the more we know about our end users, the better. We should play back our findings to our users, as we go, and it can also be really helpful to do more user interviews or see if we can observe the users as well. Sometimes, important pain points are not identified as such because users have accepted them as something that cannot be changed. When we observe them and ask questions, we

(Continued)

often come across key issues that previously had been overlooked. It can also be useful to ask users what they spend their time on. Answers to this question can help us to identify opportunities where important gains could be made.

Of course, sometimes it can be difficult to engage with end users, in particular when teaching and learning Design Thinking. This said, there are often more opportunities than one thinks, in particular these days where social media makes it much easier to find and engage with users online. The importance of engaging with the users that you want to help cannot be overstated – the best time to discover you are working on the wrong problem is right at the beginning, when you can change direction at minimal cost and inconvenience.

TOP TIP

Make sure that you have identified the right personas and accurate pain points before you embark on the ideation process. If you can, validate the pain points by engaging with actual users.

IDEA GENERATION

It is now time to have some fun and generate new ideas. To quote many people's favourite historical inventor and innovator Thomas Edison (who needs Elon Musk!):

'To have a great idea, have a lot of them.'
– attributed to Thomas Edison (Clegg, 1996, p. 20)

With these words, Edison was very much in line with modern-day Design Thinking.

We need to *diverge* to generate many diverse ideas and *converge* to select the best one(s) to focus on. Big thanks to Thomas Edison for being so on message.

In the guided activity below, we're going to focus on a Design Thinking technique called Big Ideas. To make this most effective, there's a question we'd like you to consider first. What sort of ideas do you think a similar group of people are most likely to come up with? If your answer is 'similar ones', we agree. To address this challenge, we believe the best approach is diversity. This is one of the reasons why we always try to work in and with diverse teams. We can generate diversity by involving and engaging people from different courses and faculties, different age groups, different genders, different countries, people with different life experiences and different cultural backgrounds and so on.

The second tip is don't forget to use the knowledge you've already learned from everything you've done so far. That's why you did it! And do try to take a wider perspective too. For example, what can you learn from what's happening in parallel challenges in other industries?

Have you got all that? Right, let's have some fun.

The guided activity below should be carried out to generate a diverse set of ideas.

TEAM ACTIVITY: BIG IDEAS – ESTIMATED TIME 20 MINUTES

Carry out this activity to generate a diverse set of ideas for addressing the challenge.

1. PREPARE TO RUN THE ACTIVITY

- Place a flip chart onto a wall or use a virtual whiteboard.
- Write 'Big Ideas' in marker pen at the top of the page.
- Alternatively, if using MURAL, you can make use of our online template.

2. THE TEAM DIVERGES TO GENERATE IDEAS – THIS STEP SHOULD BE CARRIED OUT IN SILENCE!

- Individual team members write their ideas onto sticky notes (one idea per note) – and uses the sticky notes to populate the flip chart/virtual whiteboard.
  - Don't write too much – a phrase or one sentence summary will be enough.
  - Bring in your knowledge of everything done to date – review the challenge, the Project Research Canvas and associated research, End User Persona(s), Empathy Map(s), As Is Scenario(s) and wider thinking.
  - Each team member should create as many ideas as possible.
  - Each team member should attempt to come up with at least one 'wild card' idea – 'wouldn't it be great if we could do that', 'it will never work but', etc. Often, when reviewed and discussed some of these ideas can be transformed into something very feasible of high value.

(Continued)

- Figure 5.10 shows an example of a populated Big Ideas template from the charity organisation challenge.

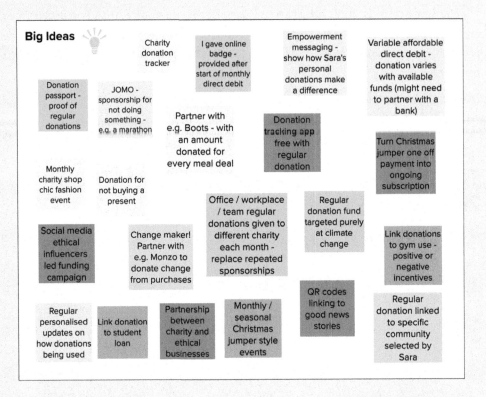

FIGURE 5.10: Big Ideas example

The output of the activity is a populated Big Ideas template, (hopefully!) packed full, with a great set of diverse ideas targeted at addressing the challenge.

IDEA PRIORITISATION

If you've taken Thomas Edison's advice, your Big Ideas template will now be filled with many diverse ideas. If so, you've done a good job, but at this stage you may feel like you have too many ideas, perhaps it is even a bit overwhelming. How can we quickly review so many different ideas?

Thankfully, Design Thinking has some nifty techniques for reviewing ideas. The one we use here is called the Prioritisation Grid, and it's simple and easy to use.

The Prioritisation Grid is a simple chart with two axes:

- **Value** – In the vertical axis we consider the relative **value or impact** of the ideas.

- ○ In Design Thinking, it's most usual to consider the value from the end user perspective.
- ○ But it's equally easy for us consider the value to the sponsor and the organisation (e.g., what the cost savings will be, how much revenue will we generate, what's the relative impact on customer satisfaction, how will patient outcomes improve and so on).
- ○ The team should hence decide how they define value and whether they want to consider the value for the end users or for the sponsor.
- **Feasibility** – In the horizontal axis we consider how feasible the idea will be to deliver.
  - ○ Feasibility can be rated by one or a combination of measures (time, cost, ease of doing and so on).

Your team needs to decide how you wish to measure feasibility. One thing we recommend you take into account is just how feasible the selected ideas will be for your student project. Don't forget, you'll need to create some form of prototype and be able to articulate the value in the time available to you.

You may now be thinking, come on, how are we going to know the value or the feasibility at this stage? The truth is you won't know in detail, but you should have a decent idea of the likely value and feasibility of one idea relative to another. We're not asking you to put numbers down here – simply to rate which ideas you think are likely to be of greater value and more feasible than others.

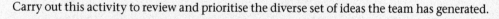

TEAM ACTIVITY: PRIORITISATION GRID – ESTIMATED TIME 40–60 MINUTES

Carry out this activity to review and prioritise the diverse set of ideas the team has generated.

1. PREPARE TO RUN THE ACTIVITY

- Take a photograph or make a copy of the Big Ideas template.
- Create a Prioritisation Grid template as shown in Figure 5.11 – the curved lines in the template are optional.
- Key facilitation tip – place the Prioritisation Grid next to the Big Ideas chart.
- Alternatively, if using MURAL, you can make use of our online template.

(Continued)

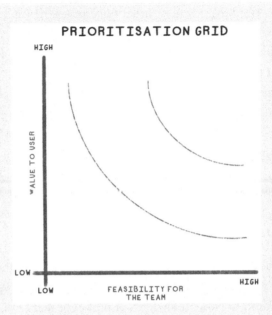

FIGURE 5.11: Prioritisation Grid template

2. THE TEAM CONVERGES TO REVIEW THE IDEAS AND POPULATE THE PRIORITISATION GRID

- The team reviews the ideas on the Big Ideas template.
- Duplicates can be removed and similar ideas grouped together (note: this action can be carried out by a member of the team beforehand, for example in a break, or as part of a team activity).
- Each idea or group of ideas is placed in an agreed position on the Prioritisation Grid, until all ideas have been reviewed.
  - The team discusses the relative value and feasibility of each idea and uses this to agree where to place the idea.
  - Don't worry at this stage about the exact value and feasibility – the idea here is to make a quick assessment. Ideas selected for follow up will be reviewed in more detail later.
  - As additional ideas are placed upon the grid, the team may decide to move some of the ideas already placed.
- Key facilitation tip: This activity can sometimes take a long time – you may need to hurry the discussion on a bit at times to ensure you get around to reviewing all the ideas.

3. THE TEAM CONVERGES TO SELECT WHICH IDEA(S) TO FOLLOW UP AND REVIEW IN MORE DETAIL AFTER THE WORKSHOP

- The team reviews the populated Prioritisation Grid and selects one idea or a linked group of ideas to focus on.
- When selecting the idea to take forward, in addition to the value the team should consider the feasibility for use in your module and/or this book. Factors to consider may include:
  a. Will the idea address the challenge, or part of the challenge, set?
  b. Will the idea provide value for your selected end user persona(s)? If not, you will likely need to create a new end user persona for the relevant end user category.
  c. Is it feasible to develop the idea whilst progressing through the module and/or book – will you be able to create at least a paper-based prototype and articulate the value of the idea?
- Figure 5.12 shows an example of a populated Big Ideas template from the charity organisation challenge.

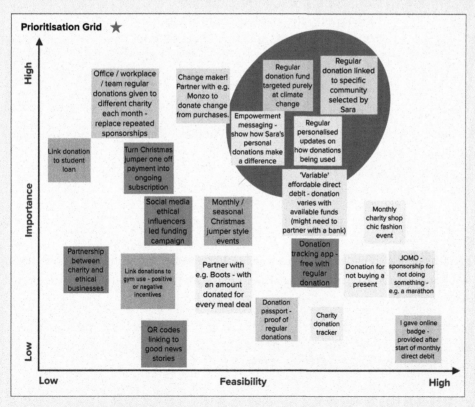

FIGURE 5.12: Prioritisation Grid example

(Continued)

4. THE TEAM CONVERGES TO DOCUMENT A SUMMARY OF THE SELECTED IDEA

- Figure 5.13 shows an example of a populated Idea Description from the charity organisation challenge.

Idea Description

Change makes change

New monthly 'affordable' donation option targeted at people like Sara.

Sara can select a specific type of community she wants to support and can access personalised updates highlighting the positive difference her contributions are making to real people in the community.

FIGURE 5.13: Idea Description example

The output of the activity is a populated Prioritisation Grid and a documented summary of a selected idea or linked groups of ideas.

REFLECTION POINT: IDEA GENERATION

Reflecting on the activities above to generate and prioritise diverse ideas, consider the following questions. Make a note of your answers in the space provided and/or in your journal.

1. WHAT WAS YOUR PERSONAL EXPERIENCE (POSITIVE AND NEGATIVE) OF USING THE BIG IDEAS AND PRIORITISATION GRID ACTIVITIES?

2. HOW DO YOU FEEL ABOUT THE IDEA THE TEAM HAS SELECTED?

3. WHAT CAN YOU DO DIFFERENTLY NEXT TIME TO IMPROVE YOUR EXPERIENCE AND/OR THE OUTCOME?

CONCLUSION

You've now reached a significant milestone in your project. You've engaged with and researched the challenge, developed empathy for and an understanding of the needs of end users, you've identified pain points and opportunities, and finally you've generated and prioritised a diverse set of ideas.

Congratulations! You've learned through experience by engaging in a number of important Design Thinking techniques. Of course, we don't expect you to be an expert at this stage, but you've made a great start. The more you reflect on and repeat these activities, the more of an expert you'll become. You will find that these methods are surprisingly versatile. For example, a Persona and Empathy Map can help you to prepare for job applications. Why? Because it helps to look at the application process from the perspective of the person who is hiring. Big Ideas and Prioritisation Grid are also useful for identifying suitable topics for dissertation projects. Perhaps even more importantly, a number of our previous students have fed back to us just how much they have benefited from these techniques when embarking on graduate trainings and jobs. Some students, for example, have told us they have used techniques such as End User Personas, Empathy Maps and so on to better understand and meet the needs of their customers, in established companies but also when creating their own start-ups.

During this chapter, you have also collaborated and communicated with your team. You have practised divergence and convergence techniques, as well as communication skills. When you considered pain points and opportunities, you had to take into consideration the needs of the user as well as the interest of the sponsor. This is a really important aspect of commercial awareness, which you have further practised when reviewing the value and feasibility of the ideas generated.

Now that you have shortlisted your ideas, perhaps have even selected one, it is time to consider how best to communicate your idea. Communication skills are also important for good teamwork, so let's have a closer look at them before we take the project to the next phase: capability and commercial development, which are the topics of Chapters 7 and 8.

KEY LEARNING POINTS

- Ideas can be generated in a number of different ways and from a wide range of sources. Two major approaches for organisations to generate new ideas are called knowledge push and needs (or market) pull.
- Developing an understanding of end users and their current experiences is critical for successful idea generation.
- An 'End User Persona' (for short: Persona) is a typical end user within a selected category, in the context of the challenge. Personas enable us to develop a deeper level of understanding and empathy for a given category of end users.
- Design Thinking provides a set of structured activities to understand end users and have empathy with them, to identify pain points and opportunities and to generate and prioritise ideas.
- A good facilitator is often a critical success factor for Design Thinking and many other workshop-based activities.

- An As Is Scenario map centres on a set of activities the end user currently undergoes related to the challenge, and enables the identification of both pain points and opportunities.
- Design Thinking activities are a brilliant opportunity to get better at teamwork and enjoy yourself in the process!

ACTION POINTS

☐ Run the two Design Thinking workshops.

☐ Make sure that you document and keep copies of *all the outputs* you produce, and that you keep them in a place where all team members can access them (for example, save pictures and/or screenshots in a shared folder). If using a tool like MURAL or Miro also make regular backup copies of your work.

☐ Please complete the reflection points and exercises.

EXERCISE

1. Below we list some of the Design Thinking activities you have now tried out. We would like you to bring these into the correct running order by numbering them and write one to two sentences describing what each activity aims to do. If you want to use these methods in other contexts it is really helpful to have a clear understanding of what they are about!

Activity	Order (1–8)	Objectives
As Is Scenario		
Persona		
End User Categories		
Big Ideas		

Activity	Order (1–8)	Objectives
Empathy Map		
Stakeholder Map		
Prioritisation Grid		
Hopes and Fears		

Note: Sample answers for this exercise are available online – but try to have a go at answering this first.

FURTHER RESOURCES

Tim Kastelle's talk on making ideals real is a powerful reminder that innovation is not just about ideas:

Kastelle, T. 2014. *Making Ideas Real*. TEDxUQ 2014.

Ted Golesworthy's story is not just moving but also a great example of lead user innovation:

Golesworthy, T. 2011. *How I Repaired My Own Heart*. TEDxKrakov October.

If you want to find out a bit more about Design Thinking we recommend the following resources.

IBM has some great Design Thinking resources you should have a look at (**www.ibm.com/design/thinking/**), as do IDEO (**https://designthinking.ideo.com/**) and Google (**https://designsprintkit.withgoogle.com/**).

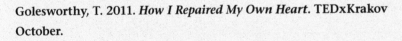

We also recommend the Interaction Design Foundation:

www.interaction-design.org/literature/topics/design-thinking

The Center for Nonviolent Communication has put together two useful lists of universal needs and emotions that can be really useful for developing empathy:

1. Needs Inventory (**www.cnvc.org/training/resource/needs-inventory**)

2. Feelings Inventory (**www.cnvc.org/training/resource/feelings-inventory**)

If you are interested in Design Thinking and innovation in public services, this is an interesting report with some insightful examples:

Liedka, J., & Salzman, R. 2018. *Applying Design Thinking to Public Service Delivery.*

If you want to read more about creativity, we can recommend the following rules of creativity (even if you may take them with a pinch of salt):

Sutton, R.I. 2001. The weird rules of creativity. *Harvard Business Review*, 79(8), 94–103.

If you are interested in a book on how to organise creativity, the following book by one of the founders of Pixar might of interest:

Catmull, E., & Wallace, A. (2014). *Creativity, Inc: Overcoming the Unseen Forces that Stand in the Way of True Inspiration.* London: Transworld Publishers.

Two useful resources about how to facilitate Design Thinking workshops:

Bid, J. 2019. *Design Facilitation: The Secret Sauce of Great Designers.*

and

Voltage Control. 2019. *Design Thinking Facilitator Guide: A Crash Course in the Basics.*

If you are keen to find out about alternative Design Thinking techniques for understanding and ideation, we recommend having a look at the following handbook:

Lewrick, M., Link, P., & Leifer, L. 2020. *The Design Thinking Toolbox*. Hoboken, NJ: Wiley.

The following book showcases some great brainstorming activities for teams:

Gray, D., Brown, S., & Macanufo, J. 2010. *Gamestorming*. Sebastopol, CA: O'Reilly Media, Inc.

COMMUNICATION
SKILLS

Chapter contents

Goals

- To understand the importance of communication.
- To examine why, how and who we communicate with.
- To apply empathy and active listening in our communications.
- To explore the benefits of storytelling.
- To learn about useful communication skills for team-based projects.

INTRODUCTION

This chapter is all about communication skills. The ability to communicate effectively with different audiences and in different situations is a key skill in almost every job – and in human relationships more generally! Therefore, communication skills are key to professional success as well as personal fulfilment.

Multiple studies have identified significant gaps between what employers want and expect from their graduate recruits in this area and what graduates initially provide (Jackson, 2010). Considering this, it is surprising that many degree programmes only focus on a narrow set of written communication skills and formal presentations, when the ability to run effective meetings, conduct interviews, provide briefings and engage via different online platforms (all with their own written and tacit rules) is so central to many graduate jobs today.

Communication is hugely important for innovation too. Earlier in the book, we shared our favourite catchphrase: 'Fall in love with the problem, not the solution'. We also have a second favourite mantra:

You can have the best idea in the world, but if you can't communicate its value it will go nowhere.

In order to succeed, we need to communicate our ideas, solutions and their value very clearly and positively to multiple stakeholders. First, we need to communicate with other team members, and the importance of good team communication cannot be underestimated. Second, we also communicate as a team – to stakeholders such as our end users and the sponsor(s) funding the project.

As we consider communication skills to be such an important area, we've dedicated two chapters to it. Developing and delivering a compelling innovation 'pitch' is a critical success factor for many innovation activities and projects. As this is the case, Chapter 10 will focus purely on that topic.

In this chapter, we examine a wider set of communication methods and skills, including key employability skills for developing an effective team-based innovation project. We have sandwiched this chapter in between two Design Thinking chapters to give you an opportunity to step back and review your teamwork so far. What has worked or has not worked? How can you improve? Before you develop your idea further, you want to be sure that you have all the skills needed for your team to succeed. The same applies to your graduate career.

Often, we do not really teach professional communication and collaboration skills at university. The way teaching and assessment is organised does not really lend itself to it. We believe this is a shame as we cannot expect graduates to know how best to communicate in a team or run effective meetings if we do not give them much of an opportunity to learn such skills. Some of these skills are straightforward, such as the importance of preparing for a meeting. Others are rather implicit and take more time to develop such as active listening. Because we communicate all the time, yet rarely think or talk about communication skills, it makes all the more sense to have a closer look at this area. After all, you will need these skills throughout the three stages of the innovation management process – and well beyond.

WHY DO WE COMMUNICATE?

Before we proceed any further, we'd like you to take a step back and ask yourself a few questions. We know it is early for a reflection point, but we think it's useful to have a closer look at this before we get into the chapter's more detailed content. Please don't read ahead to find a model answer! Simply provide a quick and honest response to the questions below.

REFLECTION POINT: WHY DO WE COMMUNICATE?

Before we examine communication skills in more detail, we'd like you to reflect on your existing views and knowledge. Make a note of your answers in the space provided and/or in your journal.

1. WHY DO WE COMMUNICATE WITH OTHERS?

(Continued)

2. WHAT BENEFITS DO YOU THINK WE GET FROM COMMUNICATING WITH OTHERS?

3. WHAT BENEFITS MIGHT OTHERS GET FROM COMMUNICATING WITH US?

At the most fundamental level, we communicate in order to share information with – and receive information from – others. The use of the word 'others' is important. Communication, after all, is an interactive activity, which involves multiple parties. If you shout something loudly where there's nobody to hear you, you're not really communicating.

The involvement of others adds a level of complexity to our communications. It increases the possibility that something might go wrong. Have you ever said something, or sent a message, and the other person didn't understand what you meant, or what you asked them to do? Maybe they didn't even reply or ended up causing an issue by taking the wrong actions. How did you feel? Frustrated, not listened to, perhaps even angry? How many times have you been spoken to, or received a message or email, and got the 'wrong end of the stick'? Perhaps you misunderstood something. Maybe you or the sender became angry or upset. You may then have responded in haste, possibly making things worse. No worries, everyone has done this at some point… even communication experts have! This said, we can all learn from such experiences and seek to do better in the future.

And this takes us to the other end of the spectrum – moments when we communicate effectively. When we share ideas, experiences or feelings with ease.

Effective communication helps us to deliver what we want to achieve as well as ensure we get the right help and support. Everyone knows how good it can feel to be understood. When others communicate effectively with us, or we take time to verify their points, we can receive and process some very useful information. If necessary, we might need to take action. If someone shouts, 'Look out!' and you avoid being knocked down by a speeding car, you've been involved in a very effective communication!

A warning like this is of course straightforward. However, more often than not we communicate about much more complex matters both in our private lives and at work. We often find ourselves in situations where – like in the infamous Facebook relationship status – things are 'complicated'. How can we best deal with this? In our view, the first step is to make sure that we tailor our communications in order to engage with others, no matter if we are taking part in a job interview, planning a Valentine's date, drafting a newsletter or wanting to convince our boss of a new initiative.

To communicate effectively, we need to pay attention to the needs and wants of the other person or persons we're communicating with.

We need to understand where they are coming from, what is important to them, what motivates them – and not just think and care about what we want or need. Therefore, communication skills are all about active listening and engagement. Even when we present in front of a huge audience, we are 'listening out' for signs of engagement! The importance of listening and empathy may appear to be a rather banal point to make but in our experience it is not. You would be surprised how many graduates write applications focusing on their own motivations and expectations rather than those of the recruiter! So, we will return to this point later in this chapter.

HOW DO WE COMMUNICATE?

At work, most of us communicate in different ways and use different methods of communication. We provide an overview of some in Figure 6.1, but we're sure you can probably think of a few more.

Each of these methods of communication comes with its own nuances. The key factors include:

- **Type of engagement** – Face-to-face communications enable us to read the facial expressions and body language of the people we're communicating with, but we can't do this if we're communicating electronically by email, text or messaging app.

FIGURE 6.1: Methods of communication

- **Level of interactivity** – If you're having a one-to-one conversation, it should be possible to ask questions, listen and respond to the answers, but if you're writing a report for others to read, there may be no interactivity at all, at least in the short term.
- **Number of people** – When working with a small group, it's possible to engage and ask open questions; when running an event for 200 people, a better engagement approach may be to run a poll using closed questions with a limited number of possible answers.
- **Time** – It makes a difference if we are communicating at the same time (e.g., in a live meeting – we call this synchronous communication) or if we put something out for others to respond in their own time (i.e., asynchronous communication).

Two additional very important factors we should always consider are:

- **Audience** and our **relationship with that audience** – If you find yourself having a conversation in an elevator, it's likely you'll handle the communication differently depending on whether it's a personal friend or a senior executive of your company.
- **Wider context** – When meeting a friend in an official meeting you will engage in a different way than when you meet socially.

This long list shows that in today's work environment, we all need to be communication experts to a degree. There are many nuances to consider! We also know that there are different written and tacit rules for all of these different types of communication, and that these can vary across cultures. For example, we have international students who send us emails addressing us as 'Dear Honourable Professor Dr' and others that start with 'Hi' followed by an anonymous request that does not even include a signature. Different organisations have different routines and practices. Whereas some will expect you to mainly communicate via email, others value meetings or use of a messaging app. There may also be unwritten rules as to what kind of issues will be raised via a message and how and what is required in an email or call.

Part of becoming a successful graduate is about:

- **selecting the method of communication most appropriate for each problem and context**
- **learning the rules that apply**
- **developing the right skills to communicate effectively *in your environment*.**

This is not a matter of personal character ('I am a direct person') or preference ('I am not keen on unnecessary small talk') but one of professionalism! As such, having the right communication skills is a key enabler for professional success.

WHO DO WE COMMUNICATE WITH DURING AN INNOVATION PROJECT?

If we ask this question too widely, we could end up with a very long list, so we've limited our thinking here to communications during an innovation and/or other team-based project, such as the one you're currently working on. In this context, we usually communicate with:

- **Team members**: Arguably, communication within your team will take up most of your time and energy. It usually involves different forms of communication and is a key enabler for successful collaboration, innovation management and goal achievement. Good team communication makes teamwork more enjoyable, and that's important, too! Given the importance of teaming for most graduate jobs, we have dedicated an entire section below just on the topic of communication in teams.

- **End users**: As discussed in Chapters 2–4, in order to innovate successfully we need to discover what people *actually need*. So, in a way, being able to communicate with end users in ways that are both engaging and effective is key for any innovation project.

- **Sponsor(s)**: Similarly, there are few innovation projects that can go ahead without the approval of sponsors. Communication with sponsors can evolve around a pitch but many projects also involve more continued communication, and the preparation of briefings. End users and sponsors have different motivations and communication needs. It is important to be aware of these and to respect them.

- **Experts**: Often, we consult not just with one but with multiple experts on business, market, technology, finance, policy and other matters. The expert interview we discussed in Chapter 4 is a great starting point but often not the only form of communication we use with experts. Written correspondence can also be very important.

- **Other stakeholders**: Depending on the project, there may be other relevant stakeholders in the wider context that we need to talk to. For example, let's think back to the example with the MRI scanner for children, which we introduced in Chapter 3. Here, it was of crucial importance not just to talk to the children themselves but also to their parents and the medical professionals involved.

ACTIVE LISTENING AND EMPATHY

You'll remember we used the word 'empathy' a lot when we introduced many of our Design Thinking techniques. **Empathy is about understanding and being sensitive to the needs, feelings and experiences of others.**

This makes it a key technique for enabling successful communication. To communicate successfully, we do need to understand the needs, concerns and motivations of those we're communicating with. If we do this, our communications will be much more effective.

Don't worry, we're not suggesting you create an Empathy Map for every person you plan to have a meeting with! But we are advising you to *actively listen* to what others are telling you. Whenever possible, you should take account of the other person's tone of voice (or written words), facial expression and body language. These can be just as important as the words themselves.

If someone takes an opposite point of view to us, one option is to disagree loudly with them and ignore what you don't understand. We think a better option though is to find out why they've taken that position and react accordingly. How do we recommend that you do this?

You can make a great start at improving your ability to communicate by doing three simple things:

1. **Ask questions** – In particular open questions – and use these to discover and tease out information from the other person(s). It also offers them a great opportunity to share additional information with you, information which they think is important.

2. **Actively listen** – It's great to ask questions but you really do have to listen to the answers! When you ask a question, concentrate on actively listening to what the other person is saying. Sometimes, we are tempted to prepare our response or counter argument and not listen properly. We are stuck in our own head. Make an effort to understand the real meaning behind their words and, if necessary, ask supplemental questions to find out more.

3. **Be mindful** – When listening, it is important to pick up on and be mindful of others' points of view, their motivations, needs and problems. Often, we miscommunicate because we operate within different frames of reference or have different needs and objectives.

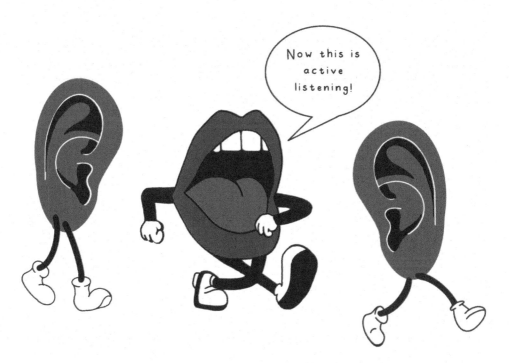

FIGURE 6.2: Active listening involves two ears and one mouth

ACTIVE LISTENING

Active listening is a key technique, and it's one we could all do with more of. We love the adage 'two ears and one mouth' – because most of us would benefit from listening twice as much as we talk!

Have a look below at our list of Dos and Don'ts of active listening. Can you recognise some of these from your own experience? Think back to a recent situation where you felt misunderstood or not listened to. What was the problem? What negative practices (Don'ts) played a role in this?

DO ✓

Pay full attention

Have empathy

Listen to answers

Keep eye contact

Put away distractions

Shut down your internal dialogue

Ask questions to clarify

Show that you are listening: verbally and body language

Defer judgement

Allow the speaker to finish

Provide feedback respectfully

Learn to recognise active listening

DON'T ✗

Be stuck in your own mind

Interrupt or rush the speaker

Become distracted

Plan your reply rather than listen

Top the story ('this reminds me of...')

Miss the big picture

Ignore what you don't like or don't understand

Offer unsolicited advice or solutions

Be defensive

React too emotionally

FIGURE 6.3: Top tips for active listening

TEAM ACTIVITY: ACTIVE LISTENING – ESTIMATED TIME ABOUT 30 MINUTES

You can do this activity with your team members but also in another group setting. It is a great opportunity to practise active listening and engage in team building at the same time!

1. You start by forming pairs, ideally pairing up team members who don't know each other very well.

2. In pairs, you interview each other about one of the best days of your life. What happened? What made the day so special? Decide who begins and conduct the interview for about ten minutes. Pay close attention to how you listen/experience being listened to.

3. Swap roles and repeat the exercise for about another ten minutes.

4. Meet as a team. Each team member provides a summary of what they have learnt about the other's special day. Make an effort to really show that you have listened and understood.

5. Debrief as a team and/or reflect on your learning below.

REFLECTION POINT: ACTIVE LISTENING

Make a note of your answers in the space provided and/or in your journal. You can reflect on the team exercise, or you can use another conversation to practise active listening (chances are your conversation partner may be delighted to have another conversation).

1. HOW DID IT FEEL TO REALLY LISTEN?

2. WAS IT DIFFICULT? WERE YOU TEMPTED TO FALL BACK TO SOME OF THE PRACTICES LISTED UNDER 'ACTIVE LISTING DON'TS' IN FIGURE 6.3 ABOVE?

3. LOOKING AT THE DOS LISTED IN THE ABOVE FIGURE – WHAT COULD YOU DO EVEN BETTER NEXT TIME?

THE IMPORTANCE OF EMPATHY

Now that we have discussed active listening, let us return to the important point of empathy. Active listening is the (very important) first step. The next step is to be mindful what you have heard (and not heard) and empathise with those you want to communicate with. This may sound to you like an unconventional thing to do. It is not. Let us give you a real-life example.

During his time at IBM, Tony was the Innovation Leader of the Global Technology Services unit in the UK. One day, his boss changed jobs and was replaced by a new IBM Vice President, who Tony had never met. This happened a number of years ago now, in the early days of cloud computing. Tony worked in a different location to the new Vice President and wasn't due to meet him for several weeks. Tony wanted to welcome his new boss, who was called Andrew. Most of all, Tony wanted to speak to Andrew about his concerns about the rise of cloud computing and the implications for the business.

Tony sent a message to Andrew using the company's messaging app.

Tony: Hi Andrew, congratulations on the new job.

Andrew gave a polite reply.

Andrew: Hi Tony – thanks.

Tony followed this up with what he really wanted to talk about.

Tony: I think it would be useful for us to have a quick chat about cloud computing.

Andrew replied a few minutes later.

Andrew: Cloud computing? No, not interested.

This placed Tony in real a dilemma! Andrew was his new boss; he was important to Tony's career and it appeared they'd got off to a bad start. Tony wondered whether to wait and raise the topic again when they would meet in a few weeks' time or attempt to recover the situation there and then.

Tony reflected on the situation. He decided what had been missing from his earlier message was empathy for Andrew's point of view. Tony took a step back and tried to understand what was important to his new boss. Andrew was new in his role and was sure to be very busy. Even though Andrew was in charge of the Technology Services unit, his job was to manage it, not to understand key technology trends. That was part of Tony's job! Andrew might be less concerned about particular technologies than the things he was measured on – financial metrics, customer satisfaction and so on.

Tony wrote out another message.

Tony: Actually, what I really wanted to speak to you about was a threat to our revenue, but one we could turn into a really big opportunity to grow our business and profits.

Andrew replied immediately.

Andrew: You learn quickly! When do you want to talk?

Tony's career was saved! Andrew and Tony got on very well after that, with Andrew eventually supporting Tony's application for promotion.

The above is a true story! Pephaps the key lesson learned from this successful communication was that Tony generated empathy for Andrew's point of view. In a way, he 'actively listened' to Andrew's reply – even if there were only a few written words on a messenger app for him to 'listen' to.

The example above shows, **it is really important to consider the motivations and needs of those we wish to engage with, and to be mindful of these in our communications**. This also relates to the methods of communications we use and how we apply them. Sometimes, it can be difficult to strike a good balance between being polite and being too wordy. We communicate in different ways when we write a message, email or letter. But whatever we do, we want to make sure the other feels respected. Sometimes such respect can be shown by a friendly comment or by wishing someone a nice weekend. Sometimes, it is about communicating in a more minimalist style, knowing the other person has little time to engage with us. Active listening and empathy go a long way in enabling successful communication.

EXPERT

COMMUNICATION SKILLS

Kat Owens is a Senior UX Researcher in the technology industry. She is an experienced innovator, who loves using Design Thinking to identify user frustrations and transform insights into action.

1. WHY DO YOU THINK COMMUNICATION AND COMMUNICATIONS SKILLS ARE IMPORTANT?

Communication is essentially a conversation using different forms; there are always at least two people involved! A major part of communication is about developing a shared understanding. This is absolutely crucial, as it enables us to break down many of the barriers which may exist between ourselves and others.

Good communication skills promote knowledge and encourage learning. When we effectively communicate, both we and the people around us gain something.

Every business, every single organisation, relies on communication. Without good communication, you are unlikely to have a very good business, so it's a critical enabler of business success.

2. CAN YOU GIVE US AN EXAMPLE?

Sure. This morning I had a call with my team, because we're planning to share some new research results with the wider business, which they haven't seen before. Actually, it's quite dramatic feedback, if that's the right word. There may be some major implications, so it's really important we get our message right, and communicate in the right way.

I started working on our communication at 8 am this morning, and I wanted to test it with the team as early as possible, so we had an online meeting at 11 am. This was great because I got some really useful early feedback, which was very helpful and constructive.

(Continued)

I can now see a much clearer picture of how we should present this information, in a way which is most likely to achieve both impact and action.

Practising is great too, because it helps us to build both our competence and confidence in the way we communicate.

3. DO YOU THINK STUDENTS HAVE OPPORTUNITIES TO IMPROVE THEIR COMMUNICATION SKILLS?

Absolutely. You have a real opportunity when you are a student to reach out to a wide range of people to test out and practise your communication skills.

I think one of the scary things when you first join a business is you suddenly realise there are so many people you don't know. In fact, it's like your first day at university, when there are lots of new people and so many things you don't know.

Start with those close to you like your house mates and friends. Practise your communications, ask for some honest feedback and offer to give them some feedback on something, too. This sounds pretty formal, but it doesn't have to be. A chat over a coffee, bouncing ideas off each other, can be a huge step forward.

If you've been given a task and you know of people who have some knowledge in the area, approach them. First communications are good skills to develop in themselves. Most people will be happy to help you out. Ask them questions and listen to what they've got to say. Listen to how they interpret the problem, or the project, or assignment brief, and use the information they share with you to your advantage.

4. WHAT ARE YOUR VIEWS ON ACTIVE LISTENING?

I think this is a key area, which is often overlooked, or at least one we typically don't spend enough time on. When focusing on communication, often people think it's about producing something. It's an email, it's a report, it's a presentation and so on. It's some kind of output.

But the thing is it's actually more important to listen. If I don't listen, I can't do my job properly. And I think that's true of communication in general.

Imagine being asked to speak at a conference where you don't know anything about the theme and you have to present something to a group of strangers. How on earth are you going to know whether what you're communicating to them is useful and valuable? You're not going to know that unless you ask, and you listen, and understand what the audience is looking for.

Once they've spoken and you've listened to them, repeat back to the person what you've learned, and ask them to validate it, so you can verify whether what you understood is actually what they meant.

It can be a lot harder than it sounds, but it's really important.

TOP TIP

Learn more about active listening, and then put it into practice. See the difference it makes to your communications, and to your professional and personal relationships.

REFLECTION POINT: COMMUNICATIONS SKILLS

We'd like you to reflect on what you've already learned in this area. Make a note of your answers in the space provided and/or in your journal.

1. WHO HAVE YOU COMMUNICATED WITH WHILE WORKING ON YOUR PROJECT SO FAR (TEAMMATES, OTHER STAKEHOLDERS, ETC.)?

2. WHAT METHODS OF COMMUNICATION HAVE YOU USED WHILE WORKING ON YOUR PROJECT SO FAR (CONVERSATIONS, FACE-TO-FACE AND/OR ONLINE MEETINGS, MESSAGING APPS, EMAIL, ETC.)?

(Continued)

3. HAVE YOU ACTIVELY LISTENED AND SHOWED EMPATHY FOR OTHERS WHEN COMMUNICATING WHILE WORKING ON YOUR PROJECT SO FAR?

4. IF YOU ANSWERED 'NO' TO THE PREVIOUS QUESTION, PLEASE HIGHLIGHT EXAMPLES WHEN YOU HAVEN'T DONE THIS AND WHAT THE IMPLICATIONS MIGHT BE.

5. WHICH METHODS (E.G., MEETINGS, PRESENTATIONS, WRITTEN REPORTS, ETC.) AND TECHNIQUES (E.G., EMPATHY, ACTIVE LISTENING, STORYTELLING) RELATED TO COMMUNICATION SKILLS WOULD YOU LIKE TO FURTHER DEVELOP AND/OR IMPROVE? REFER TO THE LIST YOU MAKE WHEN WORKING ON YOUR PROJECT AND UNDERTAKING WIDER ACTIVITIES. SEEK LEARNING OPPORTUNITIES TO DEVELOP THE ITEMS THROUGH PRACTICAL EXPERIENCE AND FURTHER READING AND RESEARCH.

STORYTELLING

Empathy and listening are important enabling techniques, but sometimes we need to persuade others to make note of what we're telling them. We want them to be as excited about our ideas, solutions and innovations as we are. One of the best techniques to help us do this is to tell stories. You may have noticed that we have just told you one such story. The true story of Tony's first encounter with the new IBM Vice President. We included this story because we think that it helps to illustrate a point – and is more fun than just ploughing through lists of 'Dos and Don'ts' (although these can be useful too!).

When we work with our students on storytelling skills, we often have a few students who consider stories as being something a little immature, to be used with children but not for business. We believe they are wrong. In fact, storytelling is used every day in many organisations; and not just for advertising and marketing, but also to share ideas and solutions in ways that make them more real and personal to us. Many people in industry are huge advocates of storytelling. When Steve Jobs was the leader of Apple, he said:

'The most powerful person in the world is the storyteller' (as cited in Higbey, 2013).

Why did he say this? Well, **good stories have impact. They are meaningful and memorable, in ways that lines of figures and statistics aren't. Good stories draw people in and engage them.**

They make us care about what we've been told, and crucially remember it afterwards. When Apple began launching new products, Steve Jobs brought them to life – not by saying the new iPhone has got a five-inch screen, a 128 megapixel camera and so on – but by telling stories of how real people could use the iPhone to change their lives.

Steve Jobs and other industry leaders know there are two basic ways for sharing knowledge with others:

1. We can push information out to people using facts and figures and so on.
2. We can draw people in by telling them an engaging story, which makes them care about the people involved, and ultimately the solutions which are helping them.

Being able to tell effective human-centred stories about our ideas and solutions can have a huge impact, particularly when compared to reeling off a dull list of facts and figures.

Well-designed and well-told stories often have a huge impact in the business environment. Human-centred stories make us care about the people in them. They show how their problems are solved – and we remember them for a long time afterwards.

Dave Byrne (Global Head of Brand Safety & Industry Relations at TikTok) has published a blog about the Steve Jobs quote, and how Steve learnt about storytelling. You can access this piece using the QR code. We think it makes for a useful and engaging read. Why? Because it tells an interesting story!

WHAT'S IN A GOOD STORY?

Virtually every book, every film, every TV series, every scene and humorous anecdote has three main aspects – characters, a setting and a plot.

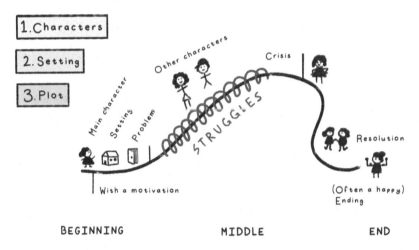

FIGURE 6.4: Elements of a good story

Figure 6.4 shows **the key elements of a good story**. All good stories have a specific set of characters that engage in something in a specific setting. The characters have a goal or motivation that is recognised by the audience, yet they struggle to meet their goal. Usually they face some problem, risk or conflict in their pursuit, which intensifies until they hit a crisis point – the climax of the story. Agency or rescue drive towards a resolution. This can be an open or a closed ending but importantly it needs to be one that provides a connection back to the beginning. Something has changed after all!

To sum up, a story has a beginning, a middle section that builds up to a climax, and an end. Usually, it evolves around a tension between a problem or conflict and its resolution. There are different templates and methods for creating stories in this way. We explain one in the textbox below.

MORE IN-DEPTH: STORY STRUCTURE

One of the most prominent models of reflective learning is Gibbs' Reflective Cycle. In his book *Learning by Doing*, Gibbs (1988) presented learning as a cyclic process involving six steps, as illustrated below.

Let's take a look at an example from industry. Pixar are the makers of well-known movies like *Toy Story* and *Finding Nemo*. The company is famed for the way it engages audiences by telling great stories. One of Pixar's key tips is to focus on the structure of the story. For example, watch this short video on YouTube. It's from a series of videos where Pixar share how they bring their stories to life: **www.youtube.com/watch?v=bKrCKg9ggVI.**

As you can see in the video, even a short story (or a corny joke!) needs a structure. In this example, there are characters (the mushroom, the barman and the girls dancing), a setting (the disco) and a plot – which leads up to the joke's punchline.

Pixar is a very interesting example because almost every Pixar movie uses the same simple structure, the so called 'story spine' (Adams, 2007). The story spine was originally a technique for jump-starting improvisational theatre, but it is a very versatile technique. Figure 6.5 provides an overview of the main steps of a story spine.

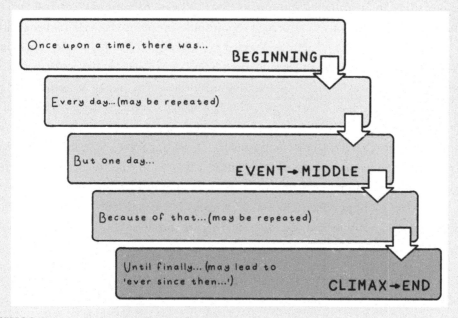

FIGURE 6.5: Story spine (based on Adams, 2007)

We're not suggesting all of your stories follow the story spine structure, but we do think it's a great example of using stories, with a set structure, to bring something to life. We have included an exercise on story spines in the exercise section at the end of this chapter.

In the next chapter on idea validation and development, we encourage you to develop a story that communicates your selected innovation idea using the Design Thinking storyboarding technique. This will give you a great opportunity to apply what you have now learnt about storytelling. Your storyboard will then help you with the transition to prototyping as well as feature in your innovation pitch. Hold onto that thought until we get to Chapter 10 about presentations and pitches!

COMMUNICATING AND COLLABORATING IN TEAMS

Design Thinking suggests that diverse teams will create better solutions than a group of similar people (Liedtka & Salzman, 2018). This is why when we run Design Thinking workshops with students or external partners, we usually pay a lot of attention to team composition. While working in a diverse team can deliver better results, most people prefer to work with others that are similar to them; that are from their own little 'Facebook bubble' so to speak. At university in particular, students often have only limited contact and interaction with students from other schools or faculties. They frequently select friendship groups, and mix with other students, of a similar nature and background as themselves. Having an opportunity to work, study and collaborate with others from a diverse background is a great way to enhance collaboration skills. More of such opportunities are needed because most graduates are thrown into the deep end and are expected to work on projects with people from many different teams, departments and organisations from Day 1. Ideally at that point, they need some well-developed skills for communicating and collaborating in diverse teams.

Working in a diverse group of people can be challenging. Sometimes, there may be cultural differences. For example, some cultures tend to be more reserved than others. Even in the same culture, there are often many different personalities in a team. Some people in the team may be gregarious and (perhaps at times overly) talkative, while some people may be introverts, and/or want to really think something through before sharing their opinion and engaging.

So, how do we most effectively work as a team, collaborate and communicate with each other? A lot of hints and tips for doing this are spread right throughout the book. They include:

- **Creating an effective team** – In Chapter 4, we highlighted a number of items in this area, including agreeing common goals and objectives, having a kick-off social event, creating a team video and acting professionally.
- **Design Thinking** – Many of the techniques you're using in multiple chapters of this book are designed to get the most from working in a diverse team. In some activities we **diverge** to encourage everyone's individual involvement. Usually, after this we **converge** to bring everyone back together and utilise the power of the team.
- **Empathy and active listening** – As highlighted earlier in this chapter, we'd like you to focus on applying these techniques with your teammates during the rest of your project to better understand and engage with their challenges, concerns and opinions. When you do this, reflect afterwards on the difference it makes. And, of course, check that they're showing empathy for and listening to you, too!
- **Facilitation, chairing and planning of activities** – A good workshop facilitator or meeting chairperson will ensure the whole team provides input and that discussions

and activities aren't dominated by just one or two extroverted team members. Planning the team's activities is also a key activity. We examine this area in more detail below.

HOLDING EFFECTIVE MEETINGS

No doubt, you have already had several meetings with your teammates during your project. You can also look back at prior experiences with teamwork in different settings. Reflecting on this, chances are you can remember some very well-managed meetings as well as a few very badly run meetings. Paying attention to how and why we experienced these meetings as good or bad is the first step to improving our ability to hold effective meetings. It really is as simple as that!

EXERCISE: ANALYSING A BAD MEETING

1. FOLLOW THE QR CODE AND WATCH THE YOUTUBE VIDEO OF A MEETING. TAKE SOME NOTES ON WHY YOU THINK THE MEETING IS RUN BADLY.

2. HAVE A DISCUSSION WITH YOUR TEAM. HAVE YOU ALL PICKED UP ON THE SAME POINTS? HOW COULD SOME OF THESE PROBLEMS HAVE BEEN AVOIDED?

Sample answers for this exercise are available online.

Drawing on our own experience of many years of meetings, we have drawn up a list of recommendations that will enable you to hold professional and effective meetings. You'll see as much of the 'magic' comes from preparing for the meeting as well as running and attending it. We've provided recommendations for both the chairperson leading the meeting and the attendees taking part in it. We appreciate that some of these practices may come across as a bit over the top in some informal settings. However, in our experience it is always worthwhile sticking to them. When offered the chance to decide, most people prefer to have a professional meeting and then spend their time on something worthwhile rather than being stuck in a long meeting that does not go anywhere.

Recommendations for holding effective meetings:

- **Preparation (chairperson):**
  - O Set clear objectives.
  - O Set a clear agenda – including who will lead on specific agenda items.
  - O Set the timing for the meeting and agenda items.
  - O Document any pre-meeting actions (e.g., read specific reports, etc.).
  - O Verify who should attend – if someone won't add value and it won't be a good use of their time, don't invite them…
  - O Find the best date, time and method (face to face or online) for the meeting.
  - O Book a room or set up the online meeting if required.
  - O Send a calendar invitation with the room or online meeting details, the objectives, timed agenda and any pre-meeting actions to the attendees.

- **Preparation (attendee):**
  - O Review invitation, objectives agenda and agenda.
  - O Accept meeting invitation.
  - O Action any pre-meeting actions (e.g., read specific reports, etc.).

- **Run the meeting (chairperson):**
  - O Open the meeting on time!
  - O Ensure attendees have arrived and welcome them – have empathy for attendees.
  - O Play back the objectives and agenda.
  - O Set out any rules or constraints – e.g., the meeting will run on time!
  - O Take notes or ensure that one of the other attendees agrees to do this.
  - O For each agenda item – introduce the item, assign people to cover items, if necessary ensure input from quieter team members, agree and document actions.
  - O Manage timing – it's good to stick to the agreed timings, but sometimes you may need to be flexible if something is particularly important.
  - O At end of the main agenda, ask if there is any other business.

- ○ The final point on the agenda should be to play back actions and next steps – so that the whole team is on board.
- ○ Thank attendees and close the meeting.
- **Attend the meeting (attendee):**
  - ○ Attend the meeting on time!
  - ○ For each agenda item provide input as appropriate – have empathy for chairperson and other attendees.
  - ○ Agree actions and accept ownership of actions as appropriate.
  - ○ Take notes.
- **After the meeting (chairperson and attendees):**
  - ○ Follow up on actions and report on progress as required.

We considered writing a separate guide for face-to-face meetings and online meetings, but in the end, we decided that the vast majority of activities are the same whichever medium is used. However, here are some specific extra tips for online meetings:

- As part of preparation, ensure attendees have tested the technology platform if it is new to them – so you don't spend the first 30 minutes on the tech rather than the agenda.
- Set rules about cameras and microphones – we prefer microphones on mute unless someone is talking and camera on unless there's a connectivity issue.
- Verify attendee engagement – particularly if not all cameras are on – it's useful for the chairperson to include occasional polls or questions to ensure the attendees remain engaged.
- If it's a long meeting, include regular short breaks (at least every 30–40 minutes) to maintain focus and reduce screen-fatigue.

For the duration of your project, **we recommend that each team member takes a turn at setting up and running a meeting whether you conduct your meetings online or face to face.**

REFLECTION POINT: HOLDING EFFECTIVE MEETINGS

Please use this textbox to document your learning after previous or future meetings with your team. Make a note of your answers in the space provided and/or in your journal.

1. CONSIDER THE PREPARATION OF THE MEETINGS. WHAT WORKED? WHAT DID NOT WORK?

(Continued)

2. WERE THE MEETINGS WELL RUN? WHAT WORKED? WHAT DID NOT WORK?

3. WHAT WERE THE MEETINGS' OBJECTIVES, AND DID YOU MEET THEM? IF NOT, WHY NOT?

PLANNING TEAM ACTIVITIES

Most of the recommendations we make above also apply to the running of wider team activities, including Design Thinking workshops. Again, good preparation is key. It is usually worthwhile to have a detailed schedule that provides an overview of:

- the activities and their objectives
- how long they are expected to take
- whom they involve and in what way
- what resources are needed.

When preparing, do not forget to build in time for breaks as well as some contingency time. Plan your team activities with your audience in mind. Empathy is key here as well as an initial effort to consult with those involved. In your current situation you may be safe to assume that you and your team members have a shared interest. When you prepare meetings and activities for others, this may not always be the case (see Chapter 11 for a powerful example of a training programme where this went wrong).

FIGURE 6.6: 'Teamwork makes the dream work'

WHEN THINGS GO WRONG...

When we run meetings and activities, we sometimes find ourselves in a situation where we feel that things are not going well, and where we witness poor teamwork and unhelpful team dynamics. For example, we may face a long and awkward silence, or we can see that some team members do not fully engage. If this happens, it is often the best strategy to ask some friendly questions and invite feedback that can help you to understand why this is the case. Facilitators with little experience often focus so much on the execution of their plan that they sometimes fail to pick up dissonances. Instead of being frustrated and increasingly forceful it is usually better to involve attendees in a joint attempt to make the planned activity or meeting more interesting or meaningful.

Another source of problems is negative team dynamics. These may arise from team members lacking commitment, clarity or agreement as to the objectives and their respective roles. Sometimes we have team members that dominate others, often unintentionally. This can be difficult to avoid – yet it still needs to be addressed. In the interview below, Professor Jeanne Liedtka recommends the use of a 'conversation guardian' who moderates a discussion ensuring that everyone is heard. In our experience this can be very useful. She also reminds us how the twin principles underlying Design Thinking – divergence and convergence – can also help us to reign in such problems.

EXPERT

FACILITATING DESIGN THINKING WORKSHOPS

Jeanne Liedtka is United Technologies Corporation Professor of Business Administration at the University of Virginia. She works on Design Thinking, innovation and leading growth in industry as well as the government and social sector. Jeanne has recently co-authored a new book: *Experiencing Design: The Innovator's Journey.*

1. WHAT IS THE BEST WAY TO MANAGE TEAM DYNAMICS WHEN FACILITATING DESIGN THINKING ACTIVITIES?

In Design Thinking, we usually work with diverse teams. There are many types of diversity: diversity in roles or expertise but also gender, race, age, culture and personality. Understanding diversity is key for managing team dynamics. For example, we can have team members who have a lot of confidence and risk steamrolling everyone else. While they may not be a good consensus builder, they are very comfortable taking actions. These people tend to get frustrated with more conscientious team members who feel less comfortable stepping into the unknown and want to verify assumptions and assess the situation more carefully. I think we have all witnessed such dynamics at some point or another.

As a facilitator we can step in and intervene. For example, I am usually quite explicit about turn taking. Sometimes, I appoint a conversation guardian and tell everyone in the team that this person's job is to ensure everyone has the opportunity to be heard respectfully. If this doesn't happen, the guardian has to call it out. But intervention is often not the best way to manage unhelpful team dynamics. It is much better to avoid such problems by strengthening the self-awareness of your team members.

WHAT DO YOU MEAN BY THAT?

If you understand yourself better and how you work, this can help you a lot when you work in a team! When someone is self-aware, they make the effort to understand others and their differences. They are more likely to be open to recognising issues and disagreements.

They understand that different ways of working aren't failures or inadequacies – they're just differences! People then begin to appreciate that these differences, the diversity of minds, actually contributes to success.

I often work with personal assessment tools such as DiSC that focus on different personality traits, in this case **d**ominance, **i**nfluence, **s**teadiness and **c**onscientiousness (Sugerman, 2009). It can be really helpful for team members to reflect on what personality profile they have got, and what the implications are for teamwork and engagement. For example, dominant drivers need to be careful that they don't run over everybody else in the team. They need to recognise they're more comfortable working without data than a lot of other people in the team. So ideally, as a facilitator, we need to give each member of the team such self-awareness, rather than always acting to intervene. Where we can't do that, say perhaps we don't have the time, we need to be sensitive to people's differences, prompt and encourage the team.

The beauty of Design Thinking is the open and inclusive nature of it, which allows each participant to contribute. The key principles of divergence and convergence built into Design Thinking also help us with that. When we diverge, we stop talking and ask everybody to provide their own input. It revolutionises the brainstorming process and the range of ideas generated is so much richer. When we converge, we may still have to moderate the discussion but at least we can be sure that everyone has had a chance to contribute.

2. WHAT WOULD YOU SAY ARE THE BIGGEST DIFFERENCES BETWEEN RUNNING DESIGN THINKING ACTIVITIES ONLINE AND IN A PHYSICAL ROOM?

Moving Design Thinking online can enable us to work with even more diverse teams. At the same time, it requires more structure because as facilitators we can't sense the pulse of the group in the same way. While breakout rooms can work really well, they change the way we interact with the teams involved. We can't be everywhere at the same time! When I'm running face-to-face workshops, even with a big room and many tables, it's much easier to see where my help may be needed. Because of this we also need to build in more safeguards so that the conversation doesn't run into common problems like debates or someone dominating.

On the plus side, one of the wonderful things about Design Thinking is that it lends itself more to virtual work than many other processes and techniques. Rather than being overwhelmed with a project or challenge, we ask students or business teams to deal with activities in a structured way, one activity at a time.

(Continued)

TOP TIP

I don't think there is anything more powerful than self-awareness. Design Thinking looks to build co-creation and co-ownership into solutions in advance rather than trying to sell them after the fact. I think the same is true for differences within a team. If we try to intervene after the fact, it's likely to be sub-optimal.

We think the point on self-awareness is a great one. Empathy and self-awareness go hand in hand. Without empathy one cannot really have self-awareness and vice versa. Often, when we plan and attend meetings, we focus on what others are doing, what they should (or should not) be doing. However, we cannot change our fellow teammates. A slightly bossy peer may have a stronger need for structure, control and drive. Another might be more perfectionist, spotting problems everywhere to avoid failure, thereby paralysing the whole process.

 We cannot change the personality traits of our team members. What we can change, however, is *how we respond* to them. Stepping back and thinking about what kind of a team member we are, and what problems and opportunities this may create for others, can really help us to improve our communication skills. Now, imagine if you all do this in a team! You do not have to pay for a personality test or strength assessment to do that (though sometimes these can help). Reflecting on and discussing your similarities and differences, your hopes and fears for the project (remember, in Chapter 4, we did an exercise on this) and the team dynamics they all give rise to can be very helpful. Try to organise such discussions around strengths and how they can complement each other rather than weaknesses.

This takes us to the last question. What if communication breaks down? What can you do when you are stuck with a truly dysfunctional team? In our own experience, no team is destined to be dysfunctional. Usually, there is always a way to re-engage. Activities promoting joint goal setting, active listening, self-awareness and empathy are always helpful – active listening in particular! By listening, asking questions and feeding back what you have taken away you may be able to pinpoint misunderstandings. Maintaining a professional attitude and focusing on what you can do (as opposed to what you want others to do) also helps. With good communication skills, chances are most of your teamwork will be productive as well as enjoyable. If that is not a good reason to hone your skills in this area, what is?

CONCLUSION

We communicate to share information with – and receive information from – others. We do this in many ways and with many different stakeholders. Communication is a critical skill area for an innovation project, for employability and for life.

You've already communicated in different ways with multiple stakeholders in your project. We've focused on a range of considerations for communication skills in this chapter, building upon many of the things you've already learned. You've explored how empathy, active listening and storytelling are all powerful techniques for improving your communications with others, and reviewed our recommendations for enhanced teaming, collaboration and communication with your teammates, including preparing for and running more effective meetings and activities.

We'd like you now to reflect on your learning from this chapter and apply it during the remaining chapters and in the final stages of your project. Remember, 'You can have the best idea in the world, but if you can't communicate the value, it will go nowhere'. We'll return to this theme in Chapter 10 when you'll develop your innovation pitch-style presentation.

KEY LEARNING POINTS

- We communicate to share and receive information, and to influence others.
- We communicate with many different stakeholders.
- We communicate using many different methods. Each of us will have preferences for particular methods and differing requirements for skills development.
- Empathy and active listening are key enabling techniques for successful communication.
- Storytelling is a powerful technique for engaging people and getting them to care about and want to use and/or buy our ideas and solutions.
- Effective teaming, collaboration and communication are key enablers for our innovation projects. They help us to engage, support and achieve success with the diverse members of our team, and wider stakeholders.
- Being able to plan and hold an effective meeting is a key employability skill. For the duration of your project, we recommend that each team member takes a turn at setting up and running a meeting whether you conduct your meetings online or face to face.

- Self-awareness enhances your ability to collaborate.
- We cannot change the personality traits of our team members. What we can change, however, is how *we* respond to them.

ACTION POINTS

- ☐ Please complete the reflection points and exercises.
- ☐ Use self-awareness, empathy and active listening with your teammates and other stakeholders on your project.
- ☐ Tailor the way you run meetings and activities to use the recommendations included in this chapter.
- ☐ Use reflective learning to enhance your communication and collaboration skills on a continuous basis.

EXERCISE

APPLYING THE STORY SPINE

Think back to one of the popular Pixar films, such as *Finding Nemo*. Can you apply the story spine?

Complete below. You can look up a sample solution for *Finding Nemo* in the exercise solutions.

1. Once upon a time there was...
2. Every day...
3. One day...
4. Because of that...
5. Because of that...
6. Until finally...

FURTHER RESOURCES

A thought-provoking article on how managers often shut down their employees despite their best intentions:

Detert, J., & Burris, E. 2016. Can your employees really speak freely? Despite their best intentions, managers tend to shut people down. *Harvard Business Review*, 94(1–2), 80–97.

A handbook on teamwork with useful guidance on collaboration and communication skills:

Levin, P. 2005. *Successful Teamwork! For Undergraduates and Taught Postgraduates Working on Group Projects*. Maidenhead: Open University Press.

Many organisations use internal social tools such as messenger apps to great success, but as the following article shows often they could be more strategic about what tools they use and for what – perhaps a great opportunity for an innovation project?

Leonardi, P., & Neeley, T. 2017. What managers need to know about social tools: Avoid the common pitfalls so that your organization can collaborate, learn, and innovate. *Harvard Business Review*, 95(6), 118–126.

GCFLearnFree.org offers some great resources around professional communication skills including a short guide on instant messanging etiquette and some tips on how to overcome phone anxiety:

GCF Golbal. 2021. *Instant Messaging Etiquette.*

Effective speaking in spontaneous situations is less talked about but very important for professional (and personal!) development:

Abrahams, M. 2014. *Think Fast, Talk Smart: Communication Techniques.*

A clear and hands-on guide to how to write a formal email:

Wikihow. 2021. *How to Write a Formal Email.*

For those of you who want to find out more about storytelling in the context of business and management have a look at:

Biesenbach, R. 2018. *Unleash the Power of Storytelling.* Evanston, IL: Eastlawn Media.

Although we don't cover this in detail in this chapter, how you write is of course really important for effective communication and the development of your professional career. One of the best-known style guides for the English language is the following and we recommend everyone to have a look at it:

Strunk, W., & White, E.B. 1999. *The Elements of Style.* 4th edn. London: Allyn and Bacon.

IDEA VALIDATION AND DEVELOPMENT

Chapter contents

Goals

- To validate, stretch and develop your selected idea(s).

- To develop an understanding of the 'who, what and wow!' of your idea(s).

- To storyboard your ideas and steer prototype development.

- To develop prototype solutions to demonstrate, communicate and gain feedback on your ideas.

INTRODUCTION

Congratulations once again for generating and selecting an idea, or group of ideas, to focus on. The previous chapter provided a lot of guidance on communication as well as some activities, which we hope you enjoyed. Now, it is time to apply this learning! In this chapter, we'll show you how to validate, stretch, develop, demonstrate and communicate the idea you selected at the end of the idea generation workshop (in Chapter 5). You'll gain practical experience in using additional Design Thinking techniques and carry out some non-Design Thinking techniques too. The final part of the chapter focuses on prototype development. Don't worry! You don't have to be a designer, engineer or an application developer to create a prototype. There are many different kinds of prototypes, and anyone can do it.

By the end of this chapter, you'll have developed a level of capability, which will allow you to demonstrate and communicate the solution you've developed from your idea. When you combine this with the output from the following chapter, focused on commercial awareness and value, you'll be ready to begin developing a compelling pitch to gain support and investment, in order to make your solution real by funding further development, delivery and commercialisation.

This chapter hence focuses on the capability development aspect of the second phase of our simple innovation management process.

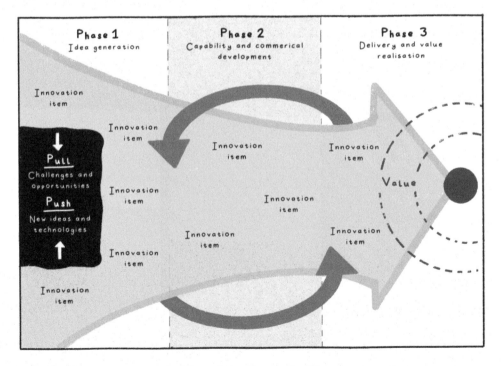

FIGURE 7.1: Phase 2 of the innovation management process

VALIDATING IDEAS

Often when we've created a new idea, it's useful to spend some time analysing it. It is important to determine what else we now need to know and to get an honest opinion from every team member about what they think about the idea. A term that is often used in the context of Design Thinking is the notion of 'stretching' an idea. This may sound strange – how can we stretch an idea like a muscle or a piece of rubber? What is implied here is that we thoroughly examine and test the idea, and that we pull it in different directions to see where this takes us, where the boundaries are, and what it means for value creation and feasibility. After all, before we put in more work and develop a prototype, we want to see if we can improve the idea and verify its value and feasibility.

THE SIX THINKING HATS TECHNIQUE

One of the best techniques for doing this is called the 'Six Thinking Hats'. The approach was originally devised by Edward de Bono who came up with the concept of lateral thinking and developed some techniques for using it (see the further resources section at the end of the chapter for more information). Although it's not technically a Design Thinking technique, the 'Six Thinking Hats' technique is very useful in this context. We sometimes omit the Six Thinking Hats technique when working under more severe time constraints (for example in ten-credit modules) – but it's so good that we didn't want to omit it from this book.

We all have our own preferences and personality traits. Some people are more creative than others. Some are naturally optimistic and see the bright side of things. Others (and we're sure you'll know examples!) are generally a bit gloomier and tend to see problems. Some people just wish to see numbers and statistics. The Six Thinking Hats technique enables us to look at a specific problem, solution or (as in our case) an idea in different ways and from different viewpoints. By doing this, you can use the collective power of your team to analyse, validate and improve the idea you've selected. In a Six Thinking Hats workshop, team members pretend to wear different coloured hats. Each coloured hat represents a different style of thinking, as shown in Figure 7.2.

The team cycles through and everyone 'wears' each hat one at a time. The hats can be used in different sequences. We recommend for the purpose of idea stretching and validation you stick to the order we suggest below.

The hats can also be used at different times during a project. You may also devise a seventh hat if you feel it could be helpful (plus it would allow for a nice impression of the seven dwarfs...).

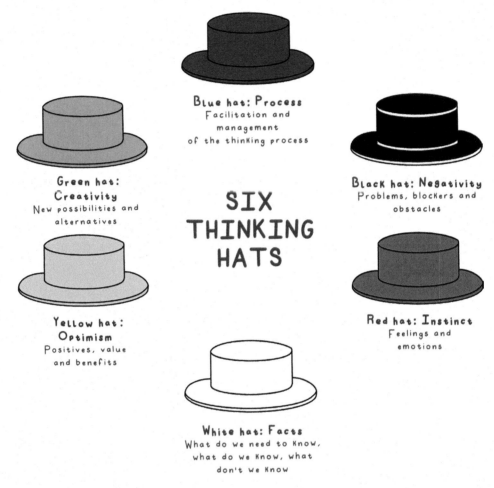

FIGURE 7.2: The Six Thinking Hats

TEAM ACTIVITY: SIX THINKING HATS – ESTIMATED TIME 60–120 MINUTES

The workshop can be run face-to-face or online. If the workshop is to be held face to face, you'll need a room with chairs and a table and a flip chart and marker pen to capture actions and notes where everyone can see them. If the workshop is to be run online, you'll need a video conferencing tool and an online whiteboard or other capability for on-screen sharing of actions and notes.

We have included the Blue Hat at the beginning and at the end of the workshop to enable the team to agree the approach at the beginning, and for the team to play back findings and agree actions at the end. We also recommend a team member is assigned to wear the Blue Hat and act as the facilitator during the whole workshop. This person should manage the timing and ensure notes and actions are captured.

1. BLUE HAT – PROCESS

- The team agrees the approach for the workshop – for example:
  - The objective is to validate, stretch and develop the team's idea.
  - All team members will wear the same colour hat during each step, apart from the nominated facilitator, who will wear the Blue Hat throughout.
  - When wearing a specific colour hat, the team will only focus on that hat. For example, when wearing the Yellow (optimism) hat, there will be no negativity (save that for when you're wearing the Black Hat!).
  - The team agrees to stick to the time limits created for each step to ensure sufficient time for a playback as the final step.
- The team reviews the current description of the team's idea to ensure everyone is on the same page.

2. GREEN HAT – CREATIVITY

- Team members focus only on creativity, addressing questions such as those listed below:
  - How can the idea be changed, built upon stretched and/or improved?
  - Are there any alternative or linked ideas which may be even better?
- At the end of the Green Hat activity, if the team feels the idea should be changed, write down a description of the updated idea – and focus on the updated idea in the following steps.

3. BLACK HAT – NEGATIVITY

- Team members focus only on negativity, addressing questions such as those listed below (if there are problems with the idea, it's better to uncover these now and know about them):
  - What is wrong with the idea? Why might it not work?
  - What are the weak points of the idea?
  - What are the obstacles which may reduce the feasibility of the idea?
- At the end of the Black Hat activity, agree and document key issues.

(Continued)

- Note: Some people really enjoy wearing the black hat – if you're one of them, please do make sure you take it off before starting the next step!

4. YELLOW HAT – OPTIMISM

- Team members focus only on optimism, addressing questions such as those listed below:
  o What is good about the idea?
  o How can the team positively address key issues raised by the Black Hat?
  o What are the value and benefits of the idea? Who will receive these?
- At the end of the Yellow Hat activity, agree and document the points, particularly on addressing issues and identifying value and benefits.

5. RED HAT – INSTINCT

- Team members focus only on emotions:
  o Each team member **diverges** to write down how they emotionally feel about the idea – using short words and phrases only – e.g., Excited, Optimistic, High Value, Apathetic, Bored, Worried it Will Fail, No Value and so on.
  o Each team member shares what they have written in turn.
  o Team members **converge** to discuss the team's inputs to check whether there is a consensus.
  o If yes and it is positive, the team can move on to the next hat.
  o If yes and it is negative, the team should review how to address the concerns raised.
  o If no, the team should review how to address the concerns raised.
- At the end of the Red Hat activity, agree and document actions to address concerns raised if needed.

6. WHITE HAT – FACTS

- Team members focus only on data and information, addressing questions such as those listed below:
  o What do we need to know to progress the idea?
  o What do we need to do to understand the value and feasibility?
  o What do we already know?
  o What don't we know? What information is missing? How can we address the gaps?
- At the end of the White Hat activity, agree and document actions required to gather missing information.

7. BLUE HAT – PROCESS

- The team plays back the workshop findings.
- The team agrees and assigns actions, with priorities.

The output of this activity will be an updated description of the idea, if appropriate, and an agreed set of assigned actions, with priorities.

We hope you enjoyed using the Six Thinking Hats technique. This is a great way to analyse and improve your ideas. Of course, if at all possible, you'll wish to validate your ideas with your end users too. Here, Ian Smith shares his views on why this is so important.

EXPERT

VALIDATING IDEAS

We introduced Ian Smith in Chapter 5 where we discussed the role of scenarios in ideation. Here, Ian shares his thoughts on validating ideas.

1. STUDENTS OFTEN ASK US WHY IT IS SO IMPORTANT TO VALIDATE OUR IDEAS. USUALLY, WE HAVE DONE QUITE A BIT OF RESEARCH BEFORE WE GET TO THIS STAGE...

That is true, and yet ideation usually involves a leap. Therefore, empathy and user involvement are key throughout the Design Thinking process. Remember, you are not the end user (at least not most of the time). Often, we think that we know what the problem is until we talk to the people who really experience the problem on a daily basis.

While we try to see the challenge from the perspective of the end user, we will always make assumptions when doing so, and some of these may be wrong. When we verify ideas, we try to make ourselves aware of these assumptions. I usually write down my thoughts

(Continued)

about a given idea so that I become more aware of my assumptions. Reflective writing also helps us to play back our ideas to ourselves or our team.

2. WHAT ABOUT INVOLVING USERS?

Ideally, we want to verify our ideas and assumptions with actual end users. We can do this by playing back our work to end users, and there are plenty of other activities that can be done to reinforce this. For example, we may do some related observations, focusing on aspects that are particularly relevant for our idea, and that we may not have paid much attention to before. Such observations can be in the workplace or augmented; for example, we can track remotely how someone uses a certain software. Or we conduct a user interview to confirm our key assumptions. But we must be very careful to avoid leading the interviewee.

It's really important to expose your ideas and thinking to end users and other stakeholders. For example, after doing some initial research, I sometimes tell a client that I am going to write down what I have grasped, even though I know that there are plenty of gaps and errors. I then invite them to have a look at it with me, so that they can set me straight.

3. THAT IS SUCH A USEFUL APPROACH! HOWEVER, SOMETIMES USERS CAN ALSO GET IT WRONG...

Yes, you are right. What somebody thinks happens may not always match with what actually happens. This is why it can be useful to engage with a range of users, engaging them in different ways – and why we often work with several personas and scenarios. Sometimes, an innovation project can also trigger a collaborative dynamic amongst users.

4. CAN YOU GIVE ME AN EXAMPLE?

Yes of course. Once I asked an account team that I was training at IBM if they would like to work on a real problem for the customer that they served. They agreed and we worked with the client to identify a suitable problem. It turned out that there was an issue around their timesheet system. Everyone hated filling in their timesheets, and staff felt put off by the tedious procedure. We created some personas, including a project manager and a finance manager, drawing on a user interview I had conducted. The client was enthusiastic about solving this problem, and some staff from the related areas actually took part in the training.

This led to a major discovery where the people who had complained about the timesheets suddenly realised that the information they had provided saved the company hundreds of thousands of pounds in tax each year, mainly because it helped them to differentiate between R&D and operational spending. It was also revealed that the level of detail of the information being recorded was much greater than required. This discovery changed the perception of some of the users. While we were still able to improve the process of filing the timesheets in significant ways, the main breakthrough in this project had come from people learning from each other about what they do and why.

TOP TIP

When validating ideas, playbacks with early prototypes can also be very useful. Paper prototypes can be very valuable, and there are many platforms that allow you to produce a good digital mockup. I have been using Figma but there are many others.

DESIGN THINKING HILLS: 'WHO, WHAT AND WOW!'

As part of validating our idea, it's useful to be able to identify and articulate which end users will benefit, what the idea will enable them to do and what is different or exciting about this.

The Design Thinking activity 'Hills' allows you to do this, as Hills describe what your users will be able to do in the future, once your idea has been developed and implemented.

Why are they called Hills? We like to think of a Hills as being about how your team might one day be able to conquer the summit of a hill or high mountain – to do this you need to know **who** will be climbing up the mountain, **what** you need to do to climb it and what you might see from the top which will make you say **wow!**

Hills are structured as follows:

- **Who** – A specific user or a group of users.
- **What** – What the user(s) will be able to do.
- **Wow** – Why this is different or exciting.

Placed together, the three parts of the Hill form a sentence. Here's an example:

- **Who** – An online shopper.
- **What** – Can find the best matching garment in our online store.
- **Wow** – By uploading an image from any device, anywhere, any time.

As a sentence, the above Hill reads – 'An online shopper can find the best matching garment in our online store by uploading an image from any device, anywhere, anytime'.

Hills can help us to identify key requirements for what the solution created from our idea should be able to do. It's very useful to create one or more Hills before building a prototype and/or selecting a specific solution or technology.

TEAM ACTIVITY: HILLS – ESTIMATED TIME 30 MINUTES

Carry out this step to create Who-What-Wow Hills for your idea.

1. PREPARE TO RUN THE ACTIVITY

- Place a flip chart onto a wall or use a virtual whiteboard.
- Write 'Hills' in marker pen at the top of the page and three columns marked Who, What and Wow to create a Hills template as shown in Figure 7.3.

HILL

WHO	WHAT	WOW

FIGURE 7.3: Hills template

- Alternatively, if using MURAL, you can make use of our online template.

2. THE TEAM DIVERGES TO PROVIDE INPUT – THIS STEP SHOULD BE CARRIED OUT IN SILENCE!

- Individual team members write and place a number of separate sticky notes into the 'Who', 'What' and 'Wow' columns – content should highlight the following:
  - **Who** – The groups of end users who will use your solution.
  - **What** – What these users will be able to do once the solution is in place.
  - **Wow** – What will be different or exciting about this.

3. WHEN THE TEAM MEMBERS HAVE FINISHED, THE TEAM CONVERGES TO REVIEW AND CREATE ONE OR MORE AGREED HILLS FOR YOUR IDEA

- The team converges to review the Hill inputs, removing duplicates and linking together the Who, What and Wow elements to create sentences which meaningfully describe what your idea and solution will deliver.
- Figure 7.4 shows an example of a completed Hill from the example charity organisation challenge (created using MURAL).

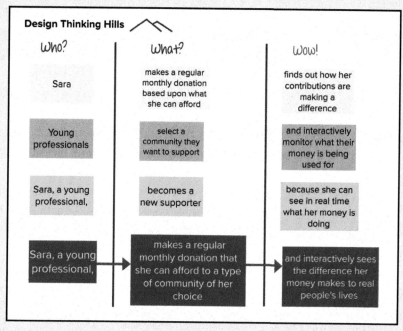

FIGURE 7.4: Hills example

The output of the activity is agreement of one or more Hills for your idea, to be used as input during the next steps.

Because 'Hills' are so effective in documenting ideas and related requirements at the most fundamental level, they are often used in 'agile' application development projects to input into specific development cycles (these are sometimes known as 'sprints').

MORE IN-DEPTH: AGILE, WATERFALL AND DESIGN THINKING

You may or may not be familiar with the term 'agile'. Chances are you have already come across it but are not sure what it means in the context of Design Thinking.

Both agile and waterfall stand for different ways of managing change. Traditionally, project management was often based on a 'waterfall' style approach where a project begins by agreeing a set of requirements. The remainder of the project is then planned out as a series of sequential steps or phases. Any changes to the requirements along the way will need to be formally managed. For example, the target dates may have to be moved and/or additional resources may be required if the project hits unforeseen problems.

There are many advantages to a waterfall-based approach. For example, because the requirements are fixed and formally managed, it is relatively easy to envisage and plan out what the project will deliver. It's also easier to contract out aspects of the work. You can say to someone, 'if you deliver this component, we will pay you this amount of money'. However, a waterfall approach also has disadvantages. These include limitations to flexibility, innovation and creativity during the project. For large lengthy projects we may find what is delivered in the end is no longer what is needed (even though that's what was asked for at the beginning!).

'Agile' approaches were developed to address these disadvantages. In general, agile is used as a term to describe a more iterative approach to project management. Instead of focusing the project on a set of pre-designed phases with the majority of requirements agreed at the beginning, agile projects deliver in a series of much more limited increments and involve a close collaboration between developers and end users. Requirements for additional changes and improvements are agreed between the developers and the end users as part of a series of rolling time-boxed cycles, often called 'sprints'. A set of incremental requirements are agreed at the start of each sprint. Work is then done to design, develop, test and implement what is needed to meet these requirements. At the end of the sprint, the team reviews what has been done and then moves on to begin the next sprint and so on.

The advantages of agile include flexibility and designing what the users really need now, rather than what was known at the beginning of a waterfall project. However, there's also uncertainty, because often we won't know what an agile project is going to deliver in future sprints, because the requirements aren't yet known or agreed. This makes planning and contracting others to do some of the work much more difficult!

So, what has all this got to do with Design Thinking? We think you'll recognise the links between agile and Design Thinking. Both approaches involve working closely with end users to understand their needs and both deliver changes in an iterative way. In fact, many agile projects use Design Thinking techniques – for example to better understand their end users and to develop ideas which will turn into requirements for each sprint to deliver.

Equally, an agile project might not formally use Design Thinking techniques, or a project team applying Design Thinking may never use the word 'agile'. There are also different agile frameworks and approaches; some of the more fashionable ones are Scrum and Kanban. We include some materials on these in the further resources section at the end of the chapter. But let's not get hung up on words here, the important bit is understanding how agile differs from traditional approaches, and that agile management aligns well with Design Thinking. By now, it should also be easy to see how the Design Thinking activity 'Hills' can help agile teams to re-evaluate and articulate what is needed for a given 'sprint'.

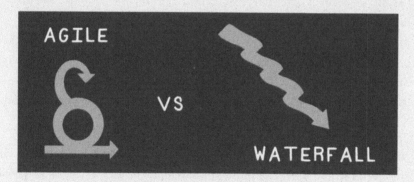

FIGURE 7.5: Agile versus waterfall

DESIGN THINKING STORYBOARDS

You will have noticed that a Design Thinking Hill already has some of the features of a story, which we discussed in the previous chapter. And indeed, once we have developed one or more Hills, it is usually helpful to pursue this a bit further and develop a story that communicates our idea in a more engaging way.

Design Thinking Storyboards provide a simple but easy to use structure and technique for creating such stories. The story is typically developed using six (or sometimes eight) sections. Each section is a step in the story. Each step is usually described by a simple sketch, supported by one or two sentences of text.

Although a storyboard can be used to tell a story once it is populated, often it's simply used to help us to develop the story's key structure and messages, which we can then build into our presentations and demonstrations of the prototype, which we'll discuss later in the chapter.

Your storyboard might tell a more detailed story about one of the Design Thinking 'Hills', really bringing out the wow factor. A good Design Thinking storyboard includes:

1. **Characters** – Who the audience will care about.
   - Usually, the characters include one or more of our end users – who we mention by name.
   - Often, we create a story focused on the end user(s) we created in our End User Personas and Empathy Maps.
2. A **setting** – Where the events happen.
   - This will be somewhere relevant for our end users in the context of the challenge and our idea – at home, in a hospital, in a shop, travelling on a train, etc.
3. A **plot** – With a beginning, middle and end – and usually conflict and resolution.
   - Usually, we begin by describing the problems our end user has today and the negative impact this has on them – this is the conflict.
   - In the middle of the story, we show how our idea and solution addresses these problems – this is also where we often include a demonstration of our prototype.
   - At the end, we highlight the positive impact our idea and solution have on the end user – and often highlight the value for the sponsor and wider organisation – this is the resolution.

Stories that really bring out the value and impact of our idea and solutions in a human-centric way are incredibly useful for prototype development. As we'll see shortly, when we create a prototype, we don't want it to be a fully-fledged solution. It may even just mimic one or two functions. Demonstrating these functions by using the prototype as we tell our stories is a great way to engage end users and sponsors alike.

Sometimes we have students who feel uncomfortable about the drawing process or consider the whole exercise as somewhat 'childish'. Rest assured; it is not! Many of the most innovative firms use storyboarding on a daily basis. Moreover, remember that this is not just about the output (though we are always thrilled to see the storyboards in the end) but also about the *process*. By coming to some agreement about the key elements of the story, dividing it into six (or eight) steps, considering what is most important to highlight (both visually and in the text), you are reflecting on your solution at a deeper yet practical level. By contemplating the pattern of the story, and learning how to develop an engaging plot, you're also strengthening your communication skills. And if you are not one for drawing, someone else in your team may be – and/or there are also many online tools that you can use (see further resources section).

The guided activity below should be carried out to create a storyboard for each selected story the team wants to tell. Before you start, read through the instructions and make sure you have all the materials you need.

TEAM ACTIVITY: STORYBOARD – ESTIMATED TIME 30–40 MINUTES

Carry out this step to create a storyboard for your idea.

1. PREPARE TO RUN THE ACTIVITY

- Place a flip chart onto a wall or use a virtual whiteboard.
- Create a storyboard template, using the format shown in the template in Figure 7.6.
- There's no need to write out the words 'Sketches' and 'Scene descriptions' and include the numbers. These are included purely to indicate where sketches and scene descriptions should be placed on the template, and the order of the scenes.
- Alternatively, if using MURAL, you can make use of our online template.

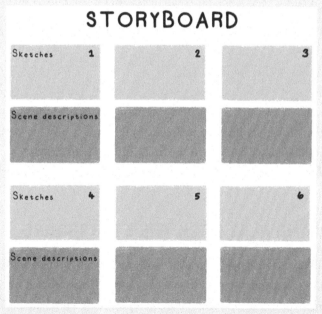

FIGURE 7.6: Storyboard template

2. THE TEAM CONVERGES TO DEVELOP THE STORYBOARD FOR YOUR IDEA

- The team converges to develop a story and the storyboard for your idea.
- Facilitation tip – We recommend you use sticky notes for initial sketches and the scene descriptions. If you need to change anything, you can then simply recycle the sticky note and replace it with an updated sketch or scene description.
- Start by reviewing the other outputs you have created in the other Design Thinking activities. In particular, the Empathy Map, Idea Description and Hills will be very useful.
- When developing your story, consider:
  o Who are your characters? Make them real and give them names so we care about them. Usually, the protagonist or main character will be one you developed an End User Persona and Empathy Map for.
  o Where is your setting or settings?
  o What is your plot?
  o For example, you could begin by showing the issues the character (one of your end users) is facing today and the pain this causes them. Make us care about them!
  o What is in the middle? Show how your idea and solution will change and improve the character's life and experience. Make us feel the improvement.
  o How will you end? Demonstrate the value and impact of your idea and solution. Make us think or say wow!
- Once the story begins to take shape, starting at the beginning, create a sketch and add a scene description for each step.
- Facilition tip – Remember, this isn't a drawing contest so don't worry if your sketches won't win an art competition. Equally, if your diverse team includes a good artist, ask them to lead the sketching activity. (You can, of course, also 'cheat' by finding some good free to use images online for the pictures.)
- Continue until you have completed the final scene of your story.
- Figure 7.7 shows an example of a completed storyboard from the charity organisation challenge.

3. REVIEW AND PLAY BACK THE STORYBOARD

- Once the storyboard is complete, the team converges to walk through the storyboard – have an honest discussion and discuss how you can improve the story and the way you tell it.
- If possible, find somebody else and tell the story to them – get their feedback and think how you can improve the story and the way you tell it.

- Note, you're not expected to use the storyboard in a presentation or pitch. Instead, the idea is you will use the storyboard as inspiration to tell human-centred stories and also to help shape your prototype.

4. MAINTAIN AND UPDATE THE STORYBOARD

- The storyboard should be kept accessible during the project and be referred to from time to time as needed.
- The storyboard can also be updated over time as the team gathers more knowledge.

The exercise can be repeated, if desired, to create additional storyboards for additional aspects of your idea, but don't create too many, as this will over-complicate things! The output of the activity is one or more completed storyboards.

Storyboard

Sara wants to make a difference but doesn't know which charity to support. She's also worried she won't know how her money will be used.

Sara sees a post about ChangeMakesChange on Instagram. An influencer explains how she has chosen a community to support and how she can see the impact of her donation.

Sara signs up to the ChangeMakesChange campaign - using the easy to use affordability recommendations to set up a monthly direct debit donation.

Sara installs the ChangeMakesChange app and elects to support island communities impacted by climate change. Sara can view examples of how her money is being used by real people in these communities 24/7.

Each month Sara gets a notification reminding her to check the difference her money is making.
Jonah and Fiafia tell Sara how their family home was damaged by flooding in a storm and how donations from people like Sara have enabled them to rebuild their house on higher ground.

Sara's happy to know she's helping the charity make a positive difference to real people's lives. She's had a promotion and is considering making a second monthly donation to support communities generate their own electricity using solar power.

FIGURE 7.7: Storyboard example

REFLECTION POINT: HILLS AND STORYBOARDING

Reflecting on the activities above to communicate your ideas using Hills and Storyboards, consider the following questions. Make a note of your answers in the space provided and/or in your journal.

1. WHAT WAS YOUR EXPERIENCE OF DECIDING ON YOUR 'HILL(S)'? WHAT WOULD YOU DO DIFFERENTLY NEXT TIME?

2. DO YOU THINK YOUR STORYBOARD TELLS AN ENGAGING AND MEMORABLE STORY WHICH BRINGS OUT THE VALUE OF YOUR IDEA?

3. HOW DO YOU THINK THE STORYBOARD COULD BE IMPROVED?

PROTOTYPING

You've come a long way so far during this chapter. You've already reviewed and validated (and potentially changed) your selected idea using the Six Thinking Hats. You've also created one or more Hills to articulate who'll benefit from the idea, what they'll be able to do and why it is different and/or exciting. Lastly, you've created a storyboard, so you can tell a story which communicates the value and impact your idea will bring.

Now, it's time to develop a prototype. Often when people hear this word, they start to worry. They might think they have to build a device, create a fully working digital app or some other solution. This isn't the case.

A minimum viable product or 'MVP' is the bare minimum required to deliver enough capability to accomplish an agreed goal. MVPs are intended for 'live' use, so they are 'the real thing', whereas prototypes are usually not. The key objective of creating a prototype in this very early stage of the innovation management process is not to demonstrate full functionality but to communicate your idea and potential solution.

A prototype is a tool which enables you to demonstrate an idea or solution **and** on which basis later forms **can be developed.**

Usually, there are two audiences we develop prototypes for:

- **End users** – So they can give feedback on if they like it, verify if it will fix their issues and suggest how it can be further improved.
- **Sponsors and other key stakeholders** – So they can verify (in conjunction with the commercial value covered in the next chapter) whether it is worth investing in to create a fully working solution which can be delivered and/or commercialised for live use in the real world.

As you're only demonstrating and communicating, you don't need a fully functioning solution, just something which is 'good enough' to demonstrate the key features by telling a good story (using the output of your storyboard) which brings out the wow factor (from your Hills). You see, this stuff does all link together, after all!

It doesn't even need to be a functioning prototype, as long as you can mock it up to make it looks like it works. And there are different types of prototype. You might want to create a 'paper' prototype – this can be very powerful. Or perhaps you would prefer to create a digital prototype. Alternatively, not all innovations are digital – you might want to create a physical prototype. Again, there are many materials that can be used to mock up a device, including play-doh or 3D printers, which are increasingly popular.

These days, there is a lot of talk about *rapid prototyping.*

What is meant by this term is not just that you create a prototype of an idea or solution in a speedy manner but also that you start prototyping early in the innovation process (i.e., now). Rapid prototyping is key to agile project management, and related 'sprints', as it allows you to obtain and implement feedback from an early stage, and in an iterative manner. You may come through an entire series of 'quick and dirty' prototypes that mock up certain aspects and functionalities. Rapid prototyping also makes it less likely you'll become emotionally attached to a certain prototype than if you had spent ages (or lots of money) creating it. Why is this important? Because we still want you to love the problem, and not the solution!

To give you some great guidance from industry experience – and a break from reading – we recommend you now watch these three short videos on YouTube, as in this space a few (moving) pictures can paint a thousand words.

1. **Sketching and paper prototyping** – This a great video from Google's rapid prototyping series. You're welcome to watch the full video, but if you are in a rush, the first five minutes are the most relevant.
2. **Digital prototyping** – This is another video in the same series from Google. The full video will be very useful, but the first one and a half minutes will give you a good overview.

3. Physical prototyping – This great short video from Quirky demonstrates hints and tips for creating simple physical prototypes.

When deciding what type of prototype you want to create, you first need to consider your idea for a solution and the context in which you want to apply it. For example, if you want to create an app, you won't need a 3D prototype. Other ideas may suggest that a physical prototype could be useful. Second, it is helpful to consider the skills you have got in your team. For example, if you have Computing students or others with coding or development skills in your team, you may want to consider creating a compelling digital prototype. Alternatively, you may have Engineering or Design students, similar skills or just enthusiasm and plan to create a simple animated prototype or a physical prototype of some sort.

Third, rapid prototyping is about creativity and making do with what you have got. Often it is much quicker, cheaper and easier to go for a simpler first prototype. For example, when working on an app, it can be really useful to create a paper prototype first that shows the user interface and enables you to demonstrate how future users can use and derive value from the app. Once you have developed, tested and improved the interface aspect, you will be much clearer about what underlying functionality you really need.

While we are happy for you to work on digital or physical prototypes, we generally assume that you may have limited resources and perhaps lack experience in IT and engineering. This is why in the guided activity below, we'll walk you through the steps needed to create a simple paper-based prototype, digitising and animating it to some degree to enable the team to deliver a compelling demonstration and story.

EXPERT

PROTOTYPING

Gary Wilson is the Technical Manager for the IBM Technology Garage in the UK. He leads a team which uses Design Thinking, rapid prototyping and other techniques to enable enterprises to accelerate their innovation activities and work more like start-ups.

(Continued)

1. WHY DO YOU THINK RAPID PROTOTYPING IS IMPORTANT?

Rapid prototyping allows us to quickly formulate a model of an idea or product, and bring it to life for our stakeholders, without either party having to make huge time or financial investments. In conjunction with the type of hypothesis-driven approach to building solutions we experience using Design Thinking techniques, rapid prototyping allows us to iteratively build and test an idea with our users and ensure that what we are building is usable, viable and desirable.

This co-creation is key to ensuring that we are improving the experience of – and delivering value to – our end-users, as well as providing a positive business impact for the stakeholders we are working with.

2. MANY PEOPLE STRUGGLE TO DECIDE HOW FAR TO TAKE THEIR PROTOTYPE. HOW DO YOU JUDGE THE KEY QUESTION OF 'HOW MUCH IS ENOUGH'?

Rapid prototyping is a great way to quickly demonstrate and validate your vision, test ideas, learn, and align with your users and stakeholders. The great thing about proto-typing is that it can provide huge value, regardless of whether you are creating lower fidelity, lower cost paper prototypes or wireframes, or higher fidelity design mockups or functional prototypes.

Ultimately, a prototype should communicate the new experience your users will have with your solution, and how far you need to go will be very much dependent on how much of that experience you need to communicate and demonstrate to your stakeholders before they are confident in committing to and investing further in the idea.

3. PLEASE CAN YOU SHARE A FEW EXAMPLES OF PROTOTYPES YOUR TEAM HAS CREATED, AND PERHAPS DESCRIBE THE IMPACT THEY'VE HAD, TO BRING THE TOPIC TO LIFE?

I've been privileged to lead a multidisciplinary team focused on delivering prototypes for IBM's clients over the last few years. In that time, we've delivered dozens of design and functional prototypes to clients across many industries.

For example, we built a design mockup to demonstrate how a retail bank could reimagine the onboarding experience for small business owners using only a conversational interface, and another to show how a city council could communicate the impact of different pollutants on its vulnerable citizens, and test policy simulations so they could model and visualise the difference those policy decisions could make.

We've also created functional prototypes that prove that our artificial intelligence capabilities can create real competitive advantage for clients. For a retailer, we used visual recognition to automatically tag their extensive catalogue of images, so that they could be immediately recalled and used in their fast fashion marketing and social media campaigns. For a healthcare provider, we created a prototype to demonstrate how they could use text analytics and speech services to provide critical information to visually impaired patients.

In pretty much all instances, the prototypes we have co-created with our clients have had a significant positive impact on that client relationship and on the end-user experience we were trying to improve.

TOP TIP

Remember, the goal when prototyping is to collaborate and subsequently align with your end users and other stakeholders on a key concept, build something that gives it 'form', and test it with them. It's not about building the whole solution!

HOW MUCH IS ENOUGH?

When it comes to prototyping, this is a key question. How much capability should we create?

The answer we give is *'the minimum you can realistically get away with'*. If you were working for a company here, they haven't yet decided to make a major investment into your innovation. You've made sure you really understand (and maybe by now even love!) the problem, you've focused on your end users, created and begun to develop your idea, and now you need to demonstrate the value of it.

The idea is to get someone in the organisation (the sponsor) so excited by the potential value of your idea they want to invest further to make it a reality. But if they decide not to, everything done to date will have been a valuable learning experience, but it won't go any further.

It's the same for your project now. You want the people you present to and/or write your assignment papers for to be excited by and see the value of what you've done and what you've learned, but you don't want to spend every living hour working on your prototype.

So, don't just slap something together which isn't compelling, but don't spend an eternity creating the ultimate level of perfection either.

As a team, discuss and agree between yourselves how much will be enough, in the context of your project and your course or module. You want to ensure you learn key employability skills and get a great grade, but how much work on your prototype is going to be enough to achieve this?

PAPER PROTOTYPING

The guided activity below can be used to create a paper prototype for an app, web-based or similar digital solution, as this is what many (but not all) of our student teams tend to focus on. As prototypes vary wildly, we haven't included time estimates and it will be virtually impossible to detail every step. Also remember that innovation is iterative, and capability development is usually carried out in parallel with commercial development, which we discuss in the next chapter.

We also appreciate that you may wish to create a more sophisticated prototype than the type of simple paper prototype described below. This is fine, but even if you do, it may be useful to create the paper-based version first and use this as a guide of what to create in your digital, etc. version.

TEAM ACTIVITY: PAPER PROTOTYPING

We recommend viewing the Google sketching and paper prototyping video introduced above whilst progressing through the activity.

- Agree how much is enough.
  - The team **converges** to agree how much functionality the prototype will need to have for the team to be able to deliver an effective demonstration by telling one or more stories.
- Design the look and feel.
  - The team **converges** to agree overall look and feel – logo, colour scheme and so on.
  - This can initially be created using coloured pens and card or using a tool like PowerPoint or Keynote.
- Create screen functions and transitions.
  - The team **converges** to create (screen) designs for each function.
  - The team creates designs of interfaces to show how data will be entered and options selected, etc. – for example by using drop-down menus.

- Create an animation.
  - The team **converges** to create an animation to demonstrate one or more transactions.
  - This can be created by taking still photographs and combining them into a short video.
  - Or a tool like PowerPoint or Keynote in presentation mode could also be used to create a video.
  - The key for this step will be to align the animation with the story about the end user, highlighting the value and benefits to them and to the sponsor.
  - Depending on the approach used, you may wish to have the ability to start, pause and restart the animation to maintain alignment with the story being told.
- Review and play back the prototype.
  - Once the paper prototype is ready, the team **converges** to walk through the prototype whilst telling the story – have an honest discussion and discuss how you can improve the prototype and the story and the way you communicate them.
  - If possible, find somebody else to demonstrate the prototype and tell the story to – get their feedback and think how you can improve the prototype and the story and the way you communicate them.
- Maintain and update the prototype.
  - The prototype should be kept accessible during the project and be referred to from time to time as needed.
  - Prototyping is an iterative process – the prototype should be updated as needed – particularly following constructive feedback from end users, sponsors and other stakeholders.

The output of this activity will be a completed paper prototype.

REFLECTION POINT: PROTOTYPING

Reflecting on the activities above to create a prototype, consider the following questions. Make a note of your answers in the space provided and/or in your journal.

(Continued)

1. HOW EFFECTIVE DO YOU THINK YOUR PROTOTYPE WILL BE?

2. HOW CAN THE PROTOTYPE BE IMPROVED?

3. WHAT CAN YOU DO DIFFERENTLY NEXT TIME TO CREATE A BETTER PROTOTYPE?

CONCLUSION

This chapter has taken you a long way, from a rough idea to a first prototype. To begin with, you learnt how to analyse and validate ideas (in this case using the Six Thinking Hats technique). You used Design Thinking Hills and Storyboarding techniques to communicate your idea in a way that is accessible and engaging and really brings out the value.

Of course, there are other Design Thinking techniques for this stage which we have not covered, such as an activity that is all about how we can define success for the different stakeholders involved. Don't feel short-changed, there is always more to explore! In our experience, the programme of activities we have included in this book can be used for a huge range of challenges and ideas. It is just good for you to know that there is more, and that if you want to become a Design Thinking wizard later in your life there is a lot more to explore and look forward to.

For now, it is about knowing what is *really* needed, a bit like in prototyping! In our experience, the ability to communicate what lies at the heart of an idea, and to judge what is the *minimum required to succeed* (and not just to avoid failing) is key to Design Thinking – and these are also important employability skills. At university, we sometimes do not practise them enough, as we learn to communicate facts (rather than stories), often using jargon, and usually we have just one attempt to create outputs (assignments) rather than engaging in a process of iterative and collaborative learning and improvement.

The activities included in this chapter have also encouraged you to use lateral thinking and creativity, again two very important skills for graduate jobs in the 21st century. Chances are you have also had a number of disagreements amongst members of your team – and had to find ways to deal with them! So, while this chapter was not about creativity and teaming, the activities it involved should have taught you a thing or two about communication, collaboration and other skills too.

Analysing, validating and prototyping ideas is all about *capability development*. You start out with an idea of what you want to do, but then it requires hard work to understand how this may work more specifically, and what the requirements and tasks are that have to be completed in order to get there.

You have learnt how Design Thinking, agile and rapid prototyping connect and form a more flexible approach to capability development that is currently deemed superior in many industries. No matter if you plan to work in a tech company, in the arts, in government or the civil sector, understanding the potential of agile and what it involves can be incredibly useful.

A number of our previous students have told us they have used the methods for capability development presented in this chapter for the development of the products and services in their own start-up companies. Others have said they've also found these very useful when working in organisations large and small. This said, in the development phase of the innovation management process, we typically develop our idea and capability in parallel with the commercial elements of the solution. These are covered in the next chapter. We hence recommend reading Chapters 7 and 8 in close succession.

KEY LEARNING POINTS

- After creating new ideas, it's useful to spend some time analysing them, verifying their value and feasibility, and perhaps improving them.
- Creating a Design Thinking Hill helps to identify which end users will benefit, what the idea will enable them to do, and what is different or exciting about it.
- You can have the best idea in the world, but if you can't communicate the idea and the value, the idea will go nowhere.
- Effective storytelling is a key business skill. Great stories make us care about and remember about what we've been told. They have engaging characters, a believable world or a setting where the action takes place and a plot – with a beginning, middle and end. Design Thinking Storyboards provide a simple but easy to use structure and technique for creating such stories.
- Prototypes are crucial for demonstrating ideas and new solutions, but they don't (always) have to be sophisticated. We should always ask 'how much is enough?'
- Rapid prototyping is an agile strategy used throughout the innovation and development process.
- When it comes to rapid prototyping, the aim is to develop a first prototype that shows or imitates the key capability needed, and to use it for obtaining feedback and capability development.

ACTION POINTS

- ☐ Run the team activities.
- ☐ Make sure that you document and keep copies of *all the outputs* you produce, and that you keep them in a place where all team members can access them (for example, save pictures and/or screenshots in a shared folder). If using online tools, you should also create backups of your work.
- ☐ Please complete the reflection points and exercises.

EXERCISE

Below we have included some examples of Design Thinking Hills. Some are a bit better than others. Can you tell why? (Answers can be obtained from our companion website.)

1. Young professional banking customers can access and make transactions on their account online and through a mobile app.
2. Citizens with a health emergency can choose which specific hospital emergency department to attend based upon current waiting times and how long it will take to travel to each hospital from their current location.
3. Delivery drivers are informed which location to deliver to next using a world class app-based solution.
4. Domestic solar panel owners can automatically turn on and off domestic appliances without having to do anything once the system is set up.
5. Students can read this book and automatically get an excellent grade.

Note: Sample answers for this exercise are available online but please do have a go at the exercise first.

FURTHER RESOURCES

Dr Edward de Bono (who devised the Six Thinking Hat activity) has a website with further resources on lateral thinking:

www.debono.com/

This short report from IBM shows how Design Thinking and agile can be used together:

IBM Institute for Business Value. 2018. *Integrating Design Thinking into an Agile Workflow.*

A useful website on agile in government services:

www.gov.uk/service-manual/agile-delivery/agile-government-services-introduction

There are many introductions to different agile frameworks and approaches. The following book is a very short introduction to Scrum, one of the most popular ones:

Sims, C., & Johnson, H.L. 2011. *Scrum: A Breathtakingly Brief and Agile Introduction*. Foster City, CA: Dymaxicon.

 Another popular approach is Kanban (pronounced 'kahn-bahn') and the following website provides a great introduction to this method:

www.planview.com/resources/guide/introduction-to-kanban/

Byrne's article about how and why Steve Jobs first failed and then succeeded at storytelling:

Byrne, D. 2020. *Steve Jobs' Lesson about Storytelling*.

 A short and useful video about the importance of storytelling in Design Thinking with an example:

www.youtube.com/watch?v=1lDt-cd-VIs

Kelley's bestselling book on his work with IDEO provides some useful insights in Design Thinking, features some great examples and includes a great chapter on prototyping:

Kelley, T., Littman, J., & Peters, T. 2017. *The Art of Innovation: Lessons in Creativity from IDEO, America's Leading Design Firm*. London: Profile Books.

 An insightful TED talk on physical prototyping (admittedly for engineers) about how it has changed over the past decade:

Standaert, L. 2015. *Prototypes, Not PowerPoints*. TEDxGhent.

A really useful book on Design Thinking in the context of healthcare with two short but very useful chapters on prototyping and storytelling:

Ku, B., & Lupton, E. 2020. *Health Design Thinking: Creating Products and Services for Better Health*. Cambridge, MA: MIT Press.

COMMERCIAL
AWARENESS
AND VALUE

Chapter contents

Goals

- To develop an understanding of commercial awareness in general, and what employers want from graduates in particular.

- To learn about elements of commercial awareness that are useful for applications and interviews.

- To identify potential funding sources for innovation projects.

- To develop an understanding of the business value (to the sponsor and organisation) of your idea(s) and solution(s).

- To develop an understanding and means of communicating the value of your idea(s) and solution(s) to end users.

INTRODUCTION

This chapter is all about understanding and developing value. Commercial awareness has been identified by many employers as one of the major skill areas graduate applicants and new hires are lacking in (QS, 2019). Are you wondering what commercial awareness is? You are not the only one. While commercial awareness is talked about a lot, many people don't quite 'get' or understand what it means. After all, there's a commercial element to most things. How much rent do you pay? Is it a good price? How do you know? Why do universities charge tuition fees? And what do they do with the money? Have you ever wondered why the same tin of beans costs more in one well-known supermarket than another? Don't worry, we don't expect you to provide answers to all of these questions at the end of the chapter… or discover a secret passion for all things finance! Rather, in the first half of this chapter, we look to explain what commercial awareness is, how you can develop it and how this knowledge can help you with your career.

In the second half, we will also take a closer look at the commercial elements of your innovation project. Specifically, we'll help you to develop an understanding of the structure (rather than the specific numbers) of the business case for the solution you might wish to develop from your idea. This will focus on the sponsor and organisation who would ultimately be paying for any further development and the delivery and/or commercialisation of the solution. To ensure we don't forget about the end users (would we ever?), we'll also guide you through the development of a powerful value proposition statement. This highlights key value and benefits from your idea and solution for the user, in ways which are designed to make them want to use and/or buy it!

Lastly, as we highlighted in a previous chapter, 'capability' development and commercial development go hand in hand, so at times you may wish to duck and dive between Chapters 7 and 8 and read these chapters in conjunction with each other.

In this chapter, we're still focusing on the second phase of the simple innovation management process – but this time we're looking at the commercial development aspects.

WHAT COMMERCIAL AWARENESS IS AND HOW TO GET IT...

The Cambridge Business English Dictionary defines commercial awareness as 'knowledge of how businesses make money, what customers want, and what problems there are in particular areas of business' (Cambridge Business English Dictionary, 2011).

We'd like to extend the definition further. **In our view, all organisations need to be commercially aware, even the ones that do not seek to make a profit.**

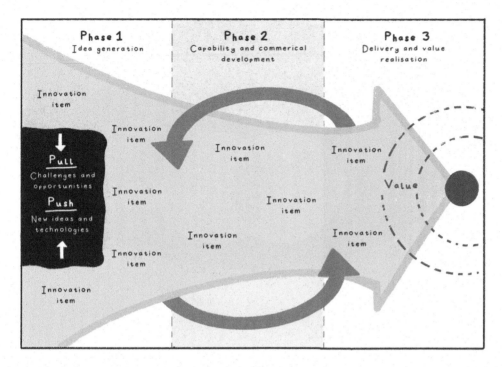

FIGURE 8.1: Phase 2 of the innovation management process

For example, the National Health Service (or NHS) in the UK provides free healthcare at the point of care for its patients, but commercial awareness is key to the organisation's success. All treatments and drugs are analysed to understand the value and benefits against the costs. The NHS needs to balance the money it spends with the income provided by the UK government. In turn, the government balances and prioritises what it spends on the NHS and everything else against revenue generated from taxpayers. It may decide to spend more and have to borrow to fund it, although it's likely it will have to pay the money back, including the interest one day (even if that might be in the far distant future!).

As the example shows, **commercial awareness can be examined at different levels.**

Figure 8.2 shows these different levels as concentric ovals. There is the ***organisational level*** (for example, a GP or hospital trust within the NHS) as well as the ***macro level*** of the wider healthcare system, and of government and society more broadly. But we can also zoom in more, so to speak, and focus on the ***project level***. So, for example, we could have a project that looks into improving patient data management in a hospital.

In the first half of the chapter, we examine commercial awareness on an organisation and macro level. In the second half of this chapter, we explore commercial awareness with a view to your innovation project.

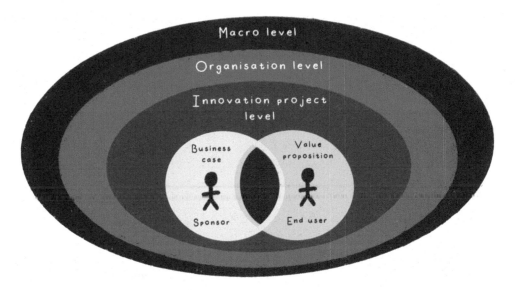

FIGURE 8.2: Levels of commercial awareness

ORGANISATION LEVEL

Let us now turn to the organisation level, which is sometimes also called the 'micro level'. Here, we focus our interest on specific organisations or sectors. We want to know how they work, what sustains them, what makes them tick. For that we need to have a degree of interest and empathy – and often we need to do some research, too.

Let's take an organisation you might be interested in working for one day. What would be useful to know about them?

- **What sector or industry are they in?** The rules of the game can differ a lot for different sectors and industries.
- **What is at the core of their activity?** What do they do? What products or services do they sell?
- **Who are their customers or clients?** Sometimes it can also be useful to do some initial stakeholder mapping.
- **Where does their revenue come from? What is their 'business model'?** For example, if the organisation sells something, do they sell individual items or subscription services or both? If you're applying for a job in a bank, do you know how they make their money, for example? Or when you consider the governmental sector, you also have different sources at different levels. For example, in 2018/19, local authorities in England received less than 20% of their funding from retained business rates, about a third came from government grants and about half from council tax (IFG, 2021). In other countries this pattern may look very different.

- **When does the organisation make its money or revenue?** In typical years, for example, some airlines make profits for half of the year and a loss in the other half. Retailers and some charities make a lot of their money in the run up to Christmas. Some organisations yo yo, making a profit one year and a loss the next. When you apply to a government job you need to know about the budget process.

- **What are the organisation's main costs and who and where are their key suppliers?** Might there be a threat to their costs or their supply chain from tariffs in other countries, a rise in labour or energy prices, a typhoon in Asia, a ferry strike in Dover?

- Who are the organisation's **competitors**? How are they getting on?

- What are the main **strengths** and **weaknesses** of the organisation?

- **What are the opportunities and threats the organisation and the industry are facing?** Is the organisation innovative or are they likely to be left behind by a new wave of technology or changes and customer trends?

- **How ethical and sustainable are they**, or is it all just marketing and 'green wash'?

- And then there's more basic stuff. **What are the financial results, compared to their competition?** What is the outlook? Will the organisation exist in 12 or 18 months? What good and bad things are people saying about them? Does it sound like an organisation you want to work for?

If all this sounds like a lot, don't worry! We're confident you could answer most of the above questions in a couple of hours, simply by searching the internet. If you're really thinking of working for a company, surely it's worth a few hours investment to find out what they're all about! As we have said earlier in the book, it's about loving the problem and doing your research. We have put together a *list of questions for developing commercial awareness* for future use in job applications and the like. You can download this set of questions from our online resources.

When it comes to commercial awareness, loving your problem is about knowing (or at least researching) what an organisation does and evaluating where the challenges and opportunities may be. Applicants who can answer most (or at least) some of the questions above demonstrate that they have understood the 'game' their organisation is trying to play, the rules of the game as well as the strengths and weaknesses of the organisation playing it. Those of you who are into team sports will appreciate how valuable such knowledge is. You do not really want to have a player who does not know the rules or asks where the goal is! It is the same with commercial awareness. Those who have done their homework are simply more attractive to the recruiter. When they get asked questions, they'll easily be able to show they really know their stuff.

They may even come up with a few insightful questions of their own. (Of course, if you do this, be ready to answer them, as they'll likely be turned around and asked of you!)

One of the favourite pieces of feedback we've received was from a student telling us how they'd practically applied some of this knowledge during an interview for a job that they really (REALLY) wanted. The student landed the job and the recruiter said that the answers related to commercial awareness were the most impressive the company had ever received from a graduate. And that was from just a few hours of research. Remember, it is not rocket science – unless perhaps, you're applying to NASA or SpaceX.

MACRO LEVEL

Let us now shift gear and have a closer look at the macro level. The macro level is about the wider context beyond an organisation, the bigger picture so to speak. We are talking here about the world economy, a large industry and/or your home country. Is the economy in a period of growth, or recession? Are financial markets doing well or badly? Is the economic outlook positive or negative? These macro phenomena can have important implications for organisations and projects – even your own life. For example, you may decide to study abroad where fees are lower, but the cost of maintenance is higher. Or even simpler, if you're planning to go on a holiday or study overseas, is the dollar or the euro likely to be higher or lower when you go? This will determine if it's better to get some currency now or wait until you travel.

The main questions we ask ourselves here are what's the wider situation now, and how and why might it change? You can strengthen your commercial awareness at the macro level simply by taking an interest in business and current affairs. Watch the news, listen to podcasts, browse a few business websites, find the best sources of information for the specific industry you're interested in. We're only talking about a few minutes a day here, or even every few days, rather than spending every waking hour reading financial alerts. If you just do a few of these things, you'll soon find you have a very good grasp of commercial awareness at the macro level.

MORE IN-DEPTH: PESTEL ANALYSIS

There are many tools for assessing the macro environment of a project or organisation. One popular tool that was developed for strategic management is called PESTEL or PESTLE. It structures the analysis around six environmental factors, looking at both threats or challenges and opportunities. We include below a brief overview of the six factors that have given this framework its name: **p**olitics, **e**conomics, **s**ociety, **t**echnology, **e**cology and **l**aw.

- **Politics** refers to political issues in the broadest sense that may relate to government and state as well as civil society actors such as campaign groups – or political issues raised on social and traditional media.
- **Economics** is about macro-economic factors such as economic growth, currency exchange rates, interest rates, etc.
- **Society** encourages us to consider macro issues such as equality and wealth distribution, culture and education of the workforce but also geography and demographics. For example, many wealthy societies are aging societies with growing demand for products and services for the elderly.
- **Technology** refers to factors such as research and development funding, patents, and technological leadership and weaknesses, but also infrastructure such as internet access and mobile phone usage.
- **Ecological** factors are becoming increasingly important and relate to sustainable development and ecological impact, covering issues such as pollution control and greenhouse gas emissions but also recycling and waste management just to name a few.
- **Law** refers to legal factors of relevance to the project or organisation. These may include rules on ownership and taxation as well as regulations, such as the rights of workers, consumer and safety regulations, and data protection amongst many others.

You can find out more about PESTEL analysis in textbooks on strategic management (such as Whittington et al., 2019) but there are also useful resources online. While we do not believe that every project requires an in-depth PESTEL analysis, it can be helpful to consider the six factors and how they may impact on your project or organisation. It is this effort of 'thinking through' and understanding projects and organisations in their context that can really strengthen your commercial awareness. So next time you are preparing for a job interview, why not prepare by conducting an analysis using the PESTEL framework?

One last thing on this topic. We often get asked by students how can they gain practical commercial experience, to add to their commercial awareness.

The answer is by gaining a range of experiences – and then reflecting on them. This could include voluntary roles, part-time jobs, placements, internships, being an official for a club or society and so on. Each of these will give you an opportunity to understand how revenue is generated, what things cost, challenges and opportunities and so on.

Even some more mundane matters can be useful, if you take a little time to analyse and think about them. Perhaps you organise paying the rent and/or bills for a shared house. Develop and ask questions and work out the answers to some commercial questions about these things. How does your rent compare to other houses? Why did you have to pay a deposit? What costs might your landlord have? How are council and other taxes calculated? What do these pay for? Are you on the best energy tariff? What factors, other than cost, do some people use to select an energy provider? Or even just think about grocery shopping. How do shopping costs compare between a high-end and a budget supermarket? Why is there a difference? And why are some people prepared to pay a higher price by shopping in one rather than the other? These are commercial questions and knowing the answers will definitely make you more commercially aware!

EXPERT

COMMERCIAL AWARENESS

Mark Fearn is one of the founding partners of The Berkeley Partnership, an independent management consultancy based in London and New York. He has worked across a wide range of industry sectors including Insurance, Banking, Retail, FMCG and Pharmaceuticals, advising organisations on strategy and transformational change. He retired from Berkeley in 2021 and is now an independent business advisor and executive coach.

1. WHY DO YOU THINK COMMERCIAL AWARENESS IS SO IMPORTANT?

Well, you can't run a business without being commercially aware. By this I mean that commercial awareness is all about understanding the dynamics of your business, or in my case as a consultant or advisor, the dynamics of my clients' businesses.

My job is to look 'under the skin' of the business strategy and operating model of my clients. I need to understand what makes them tick, how they make money and what levers need to be pulled to help them to become more successful.

CAN YOU SHARE AN EXAMPLE OF WHAT YOU MEAN BY THIS?

Let's look at The Berkeley Partnership, the business that I set up. It's a management consultancy. Its main assets are its people, and so you have to ensure you keep those people busy. Every day a consultant isn't working on something chargeable for a client is a day lost, because we'll never get that revenue back. In that sense, consultancy is not that different from an airline or a hotel business – if they don't fill a seat or have someone stay in their hotel room overnight, they'll never get that money back.

Other businesses are different. Perhaps they hold stock. If they can't sell a widget today, they might be able to sell it tomorrow. And, of course, there are many types of business models! That's what I mean about looking at the operating model and being very clear about how an organisation works commercially so that you can truly understand where their revenues and costs come from.

HAVE YOU GOT ANY HINTS OR TIPS ABOUT HOW A STUDENT CAN GAIN COMMERCIAL AWARENESS?

Actually, this is not as difficult as it may seem. Every day, we interact with businesses and organisations, whether we're walking into a shop, using an app or website, phoning our bank or whatever it may be. One of the things we can do is take a step back and think for a moment about what makes that business or organisation successful – or not.

For example, if you walk into two supermarkets in the UK, let's say Aldi and Waitrose, they might be very different. This is deliberate. They both sell many similar things, so what do they do differently, and why? Who are their customers? Why are their prices different? Which business makes more profit?

The same is very true for other types of organisations such as hospitals or charities. What do they need to do to be able to operate effectively? How can they improve? What might cause them problems? What do they need to do to survive? What can they do to flourish?

(Continued)

DO YOU HAVE RECOMMENDATIONS FOR STUDENTS WHO MAY BE GOING TO JOB INTERVIEWS?

Absolutely. Before any student attends an interview with an organisation, I'd highly recommend they think quite hard about how that organisation operates. For example, if it's a commercial organisation, how does it make money? What are the major cost areas? What are likely to be the big risks that it needs to manage?

Before you go for an interview, do your research around these areas. These days, this is fairly easy to do. There is a lot of information online about almost every organisation – what they do, how they make their money, what their strategy is and so on. The next step is then to review the information available and really think through how the business operates, what makes it successful and what part you could play in that success.

TOP TIP

I'll go back to what I said before. When you interact with an organisation, take a moment to reflect on its strategy. What is its offer to the marketplace? Who are its target customers? How has it designed its operating model to deliver its products or services to the marketplace profitably and/or efficiently? Think about what makes it tick. The more you do this, the more commercially aware you'll become.

REFLECTION POINT: COMMERCIAL AWARENESS

Reflecting on the text above, consider the following questions. Make a note of your answers in the space provided and/or in your journal.

1. WHAT COMMERCIAL AWARENESS HAVE YOU GAINED FROM EXPERIENCE SO FAR IN YOUR LIFE?

2. WHAT ACTIVITIES CAN YOU UNDERTAKE TO GAIN FURTHER COMMERCIAL AWARENESS AND EXPERIENCE?

3. WHAT ACTIONS CAN YOU TAKE TO BETTER PREPARE YOUR OWN COMMERCIAL AWARENESS BEFORE YOUR NEXT JOB APPLICATIONS AND INTERVIEWS?

PROJECT LEVEL

Having considered commercial awareness at the organisation and macro level, it's time to return our focus to your innovation challenges and projects. While it is important to research the context of your project – and to be commercially aware of relevant factors at the organisation and macro level – when it comes to the project level, we need to very clear about *how this knowledge can be used to frame and develop our idea.*

This has a lot to do with understanding and articulating the value we think our solution will deliver – both to the user and to the sponsor. As Figure 8.2 shows, we need a **value proposition statement** that articulates the value for the user as well as a **business case** that explains how our solution will deliver value to the sponsor. We have a closer look at these later in this chapter. For now, we just want to ask the following question: how can we create a value proposition statement, business case and prototype (however basic) without resources? Usually this is not possible. And this insight takes us back to the six key enablers of successful innovation, which we highlighted in Chapter 2. One of them (and some may argue the most important of them) is **funding**, and this is of course very much focused in the commercial area.

Many graduates are surprised how difficult it can be in established organisations to obtain funding to develop innovation projects – even in organisations that are well known for their innovations! This has something to do with how budgets are allocated, responsibilities and the way decisions are made about budgets, which takes us back to commercial awareness at the other levels.

To summarise, when we think about commercial awareness at the project level, we need to consider:

- where **funding** for the development of the project could be obtained
- what **value** the project may have to users as well as the sponsor of the project
- the **costs** of our project (in relation to its potential benefits)
- how we can **'sell'** our project idea in the best possible way.

We'll take a closer look at each of these in turn.

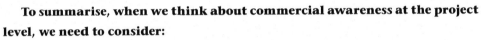

EXPERT

COMMERCIAL AWARENESS

John James has extensive experience in the retail banking industry. His roles have included being the Head of Mobile Banking for HSBC UK and more recently Head of Digital Product for First Direct.

1. WHAT DOES COMMERCIAL AWARENESS MEAN TO YOU?

For me, there are three aspects to commercial awareness. The first is about being curious and continually asking yourself 'Why?' For example, in a banking context, why do people use our products? What need is it we're addressing through the things we're selling. Some of the answers to these questions might be obvious but others aren't, and over time they can change.

The second aspect is about discovering and understanding how organisations make their money. What are the things which drive their revenue, cost and profit? Take retail banking. Many current accounts are loss making. It's the secured and unsecured lending part of the business which makes the most money. Commercial awareness includes developing a level of understanding of this type of thing.

Finally, it's about knowledge of what's happening in the wider industry and world. For example, what are the key trends you need to be aware of? In retail banking in recent years, there's been a huge focus on digital, but what are the other trends?

2. DO YOU HAVE AN EXAMPLE OF WHERE BEING COMMERCIALLY AWARE RESOLVED OR ADDRESSED AN UNFORESEEN PROBLEM?

A number spring to mind. One involves trying to appreciate the overall value of what you're trying to do. One cost driver for digital banks is the provision of support for myriad platforms and operating systems used by customers, some of which are quite old. Technology teams are often quite rightly keen to remove support from the oldest platforms.

Some of these will be used by relatively small percentages of a bank's customer base, often less than 1%. However, when you turn that percentage into customer numbers, they'd often fill multiple packed football stadiums. Yes, the change would reduce testing and maintenance time and costs, but each affected customer needs to be served elsewhere, potentially adding significant cost to other areas of the organisation. By taking the wider commercial view, we might conclude it's a great idea, but overall, not the best thing to do.

(Continued)

3. HOW WOULD YOU RECOMMEND STUDENTS GAIN COMMERCIAL AWARENESS DURING THEIR TIME AT UNIVERSITY?

By getting engaged with different things.

For example, volunteer to be part of a team which runs a club or a society and think of it as a mini business. Often, to get funding, you'll need to attract a certain number of members. To do this, you're going to need to do things to attract and retain them. You'll soon develop an understanding of what needs to be done to bring people into the club, which isn't really that different from attracting and keeping customers and making sales. The experience will help you to develop a good commercial awareness of what makes the club succeed (or otherwise) and you'll be ready to apply the learning elsewhere.

Second, be interested in what's happening around you! Ask yourself why do you and other people make the decisions you do?

4. WHAT DO YOU RECOMMEND STUDENTS CAN DO TO GAIN MORE COMMERCIAL AWARENESS ABOUT A POTENTIAL EMPLOYER BEFORE APPLYING FOR A JOB OR GRADUATE RECRUITMENT SCHEME?

I have two recommendations here. The first one won't always be possible but, if you can, investigate whether you can actually try out the products or services the organisation delivers. If you can, assess them as a customer and compare the experience to what the competition offers. For example, if you're applying to a high-end food retailer, how do they compare to a discount brand? Go into a store and have a look around, try their shopping apps and so on. How does the retailer pitch their offering compared to their competitors? Develop an understanding of the market they're in.

Second, remember, Google (other browsers are available!) is your friend. Research the company and their industry. Visit the company's website. Have a look at how they present themselves, what do they highlight as being important, access the latest annual reports and so on. Find out as much as you reasonably can about the organisation in general and use this information during the recruitment process.

TOP TIP

Stay curious and up to date. There have been lots of interesting commercial models over the years, but they've all had a lifespan. At one time, Kodak and Blockbuster were market leaders but things changed, and they went over a cliff. If you've identified a trend, is it a flash in the pan or will it last? Things evolve. Don't stay still, be curious.

FUNDING SOURCES FOR INNOVATION PROJECTS

Finding funding for the early stages of an innovation project is often challenging, because we haven't yet determined if there's sufficient value to justify paying to develop and deliver the innovation. Progressing our idea and developing it into a working solution is going to need resources – and resources typically cost money!

There are, however, a range of potential funding sources for the early stages of an innovation project, which we may be able to tap into, as shown in Figure 8.3.

- **Business unit budgets** – This is the most likely source of funding for most innovation projects within an established organisation. The head or another leader in a business unit may have an element of their budget allocated either to address this specific challenge we're looking at, or budget available to focus on other things – if we can convince them that it's worth doing by highlighting there is a positive business case. The person with the budget will usually be the sponsor for the innovation.

- **Internal innovation funds** – Some organisations have funding set aside to develop promising ideas, up to the point where the organisation can verify if they have sufficient value, i.e., a positive business case. Depending on how the fund is organised, the sponsor may be a committee or a dedicated person overlooking the fund. Sometimes, there are also internal competitions for such funding. Once the organisation identifies a positive business case, it's likely a business unit budget will be used to fund further development and delivery. If it appears there's not a positive business case, it's likely the project will be stopped.

- **Clients or partners** – Sometimes organisations co-develop and co-fund innovations with clients, suppliers or partner organisations. Occasionally (although not that often), there may be a special budget for joint innovation.

- **Investors and venture capital** – These are usually more relevant for start-ups rather than established organisations. Investors and venture capitalists may invest in a start-up or a specific innovation activity, in return for a commitment to be paid back with interest or for a share in the company (like, for example, in the popular TV show 'Dragon's Den').

- **Wider external sources** – In some industries and sectors, there may be specialist funding available from government or other bodies to develop certain types of innovation – for example, innovations which reduce carbon emissions or improve healthcare. Many of these are run like competitions.

The process of identifying sources of funding and applying to them is often a great exercise in commercial awareness. Applicants who have done their research, understand the context

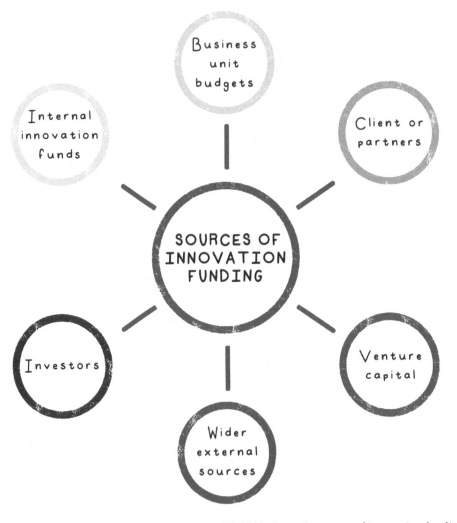

FIGURE 8.3: Example sources of innovation funding

and have empathy with potential sponsors are more likely to succeed. A cross-cultural study by Knight (1994) showed that venture capitalists in European, American and Asian contexts sought financial return as well as looked to work with entrepreneurs who are able to evaluate and respond to risk and who are familiar with the market. This points yet again to the importance of commercial awareness for obtaining funding from sponsors.

STRUCTURING A BUSINESS CASE

When applying for funding at any stage of the project, the business case is really important.

A business case makes the case to the sponsor(s), organisation and wider stakeholders that they should progress and fund an innovation, or other type of change project.

The idea of a business case takes us all the way back to Chapter 2, where we defined innovation as the application of new ideas (or existing ideas in a new context), which results in change that delivers value. A business case is all about that value and how it can be delivered.

The content of the business case includes an evaluation of the benefits, costs and risks of developing and delivering the innovation, to ensure the value and benefits are bigger than the costs.

Although the business case is primarily targeted at the sponsor(s), we also need to consider other key stakeholders, who may influence the sponsor(s) or have a key input into decision making. When considering a business case, it's hence often useful to look back at and potentially update the Stakeholder Map we created in Chapter 4.

Often, it can also be useful to think about competitors and markets more widely. Is our innovation a new solution for an existing market (i.e., are we trying to beat an existing offer) or are we attempting to create and capture a *new* demand? In management, we call this a *red ocean* versus a *blue ocean* strategy (Kim & Mauborgne, 2015). You can envisage this in the following way. When a lot of sharks try to compete in the same spot (i.e., biting each other) the ocean turns red. This does not happen when there is just one shark exploring a new part of the ocean – the *blue ocean* stands for a new market where there is little or no competition. Thinking about markets and competition in this way, and about novelty and types and levels of innovation (see Chapter 2), strengthens our commercial awareness and helps us to better understand the value we are seeking.

ELEMENTS OF A BUSINESS CASE

Typical elements of a business case for an innovation project include:

- The **challenge or opportunity** being addressed.
- The **rationale** to progress this change; this includes information on the proposed innovation.

- **Expected benefits**, often linked to an assessment of the size of the opportunity.
- **Costs**, investment and funding required.
- **Risks** – potential impacts on the business case and mitigation.
- **Timescales** – for delivery, incurring costs and benefit realisation which may include estimates of break-even points.

FIGURE 8.4: Elements of a business case

UNDERSTANDING BUSINESS CASES

The research and Design Thinking activities you and your team have already conducted allowed you to gain a deeper understanding of the more specific challenge or opportunity you want to address and the rationale for doing so. When drafting a business case, it is important that you now re-examine your idea for a solution from the perspective of the sponsor. How can you help the sponsor to appreciate the value of your solution? Remember the story we shared in Chapter 6 about Tony's first engagement with his new boss, where Tony re-interpreted his proposition in terms of a threat to revenue and related business opportunity.

Make sure that you too have empathy with your sponsor and frame the challenge and your proposed contribution in relevant if not lucrative terms.

Value and benefits can be measured in monetary terms and they often are, but this is not always the case. For example, benefits may be documented as additional sales revenues or reduced cost and spending. Non-monetary benefits can include measures such as increased customer satisfaction, addressing legal and regulatory compliance requirements, enhanced patient outcomes and so on.

In contrast, costs are usually measured in monetary terms. However, even a good business case can only include an estimated prediction of what the costs and benefits might be, rather than the actual numbers.

And it's not just about costs and benefits. Risks and timescales are equally important. The risks indicate what may go wrong, how likely it is this might happen and what will be the likely impact to the costs and benefits if it does. Some risks will be easier to manage and mitigate against than others. Risk can be assessed in probabilistic terms. For example, a firm will have statistics as to how many innovation projects of a certain type have failed. We can also look at risk in terms of managers' perceptions. Freeman and Soete (2004) show that R&D managers tend to doubt forecasts relating to revenue and product lifecycle more than those relating to technical success and development costs, with development time somewhere in the middle.

Often, budgets for innovation and other change projects will include a 'contingency' fund. This is an amount of money set aside to deal with unexpected problems. It can be tempting to increase the size of the fund but each extra pound (or euro or dollar, etc.) spent will eat away at the business case.

Finally, you need to consider timescales. How long will it take you to develop and implement your innovation? How long will it take to break even, and make a positive benefit? Clear and credible estimates are critical to the people who manage budgets and fund innovation and change. Once again, though, we can only create estimated predictions for these timescales. If something goes wrong, and we have to spend some time to fix a problem, this will likely delay our implementation and means the project will cost more, impacting the business case.

Remember, prediction is difficult, particularly about the future!

Here are three simple example scenarios.

- We may estimate we can create a new app in the next three months, but it will cost $20,000 to develop and roll-out. Once we do this, we estimate we'll gain an additional $75,000 in sales revenue over the next year. Therefore, as $75,000 is bigger than $20,000, the business case is positive. Of course, this is a simple example, and although we have included timescales, we haven't considered any potential risks.

- We now create a business case for an insurance company to implement a new automated process for reviewing and processing insurance claims, using artificial intelligence. In our business case, we estimate this will cost £750,000 but save £1,000,000. The first question we'll get back from the insurance company Operations Director (as the sponsor) will likely be 'How long will it take to save the £1,000,000?' We may reply, 'That's easy. We'll save £100,000 a year by reducing manual labour costs, so it will take ten years'. Even though the business case may seem to be positive, the Operations Director is likely to reject it. Why? Because it's going to take ten years to break even, even if everything goes to plan and there are no other changes. This is too long a period for most organisations to make a 'return on their investment'. Sometimes, you might hear this abbreviated as 'ROI'. Many organisations have strict rules for ROI, such as that an estimated break-even point must be within 18 or 24 months.

- We now create a similar business case for a charity to implement a smaller solution for a new automated process to identify the best people to target fundraising campaigns to, again using artificial intelligence. In our business case, we estimate this will cost £75,000 but generate £100,000 extra in donations. We'll get a similar question back from the charity's Campaign Director (as the sponsor) 'How long will it take to generate the £100,000?' This time we reply, 'We estimate we'll generate the additional £100,000 in donations in year one alone by better matching campaigns with the people most likely to make donations'. This time, the business case seems much more positive, due to the much quicker ROI. The Campaign Director will likely review the solution's feasibility, risks and detailed timescales to verify whether the investment in the project will be worthwhile, compared to where else they might spend their budget.

Hopefully, these examples have given you a simple flavour of what's in a business case and why it's important. It is of critical importance that the sponsor and other key stakeholders believe your business case is credible. Part of this will come down to how well you construct the business case. Doing your research, understanding the end users, verifying the costs, benefits, timescales and risks will all be important.

Equally, the team's prototype (as discussed in the previous chapter) will help to convince the sponsor and others your idea and solution is actually going to work. This is why we often develop the prototype and business case in parallel. Lastly, anyone you're pitching to will be looking at yourself and your teammates and judging how credible you are too, so the way you communicate all this is important. There's much more on this in Chapter 10.

Rather than including a detailed guided activity here, we've included a template for a structure for your business case with our online resources. We don't expect you to be including detailed numbers in this. You could, but at this stage these wouldn't really be credible. It is important for you to know though what elements should be in your business case, and when you come to present and pitch your innovation proposal that you can articulate the real value to the sponsor – and have more detail in your head ready to answer their questions.

TEAM ACTIVITY: DEVELOP YOUR BUSINESS CASE – ESTIMATED TIME 45+ MINUTES

1. Download the template from the companion page or using the QR code.
2. The team diverges, and each team member reads the templates and reflects on what should be included. Make sure to take notes on the template or using post-its.
3. The team diverges and discusses each element of the business case one by one.
4. The team discusses further steps: a) if/where the business case needs further work; b) if/what further research and development is required. Based on this discussion an action plan is created.

FIGURE 8.5: Business case failure

DEVELOPING A VALUE PROPOSITION STATEMENT

A value proposition statement makes the case to an end user of why they should use (and/or sometimes buy) the product, service or process created from our idea and innovation, by communicating the value and benefits in a clear and effective way.

Often, value propositions have a short tagline followed by one to four sentences with a greater level of detail. Good value propositions are meaningful, easy to understand and clearly communicate the value and the benefits the user will receive. They also differentiate the idea and solution from any existing solutions and/or the competition.

Here's an example. When Uber was launched, the value proposition statement was as follows:

> Uber: Tap the app – Get a ride
>
> Uber is the smartest way to get around. One tap and a car comes directly to you. Your driver knows exactly where to go. And payment is completely cashless.

Some students may struggle to remember a time before Uber but believe us, it did exist! Think then, if you'd never heard of Uber and generally used more 'traditional' taxi services. The statement above would be a good way of clearly communicating to most people what Uber was about – a smart way to get around.

And then there are the benefits and what makes it different. You don't need to call a number for a taxi company or find a taxi and wave it down in the street – you just tap the app and the car comes to you. More good news, you won't have the hassle of explaining to the driver where you're going, because they'll already know. Even better than that – you don't need to worry about having enough notes and coins, as the whole thing is cashless.

We're not looking to champion the benefits of Uber here. Other transport solutions are also available! However, we – and hopefully you – have to admit when it launched, Uber created a pretty good example of a value proposition statement for us to include in this book.

Here are a few others:

- Soundcloud (older version)
  - Find the music you love. Discover new tracks. Connect directly with your favourite artists.
- Spotify Free: Listening is everything
  - Millions of songs and podcasts. No credit card required.
- Soundcloud (newer version): Hear the world's sounds
  - Explore the largest community of artists, bands, podcasters and creators of music and audio.

- Evernote: Accomplish more with better notes
  - Evernote helps you capture ideas and find them fast.

Each of these has its own strengths. Like Uber, the first three focus on more general consumers, i.e., people like us. The older Soundcloud statement includes a differentiating item around connecting 'directly with your favourite artists'. In the meantime, Spotify has been successful, including bringing people in with the free version with the great benefit of 'no credit card required', before persuading them to get rid of the ads by upgrading to the premium paid version.

The newer Soundcloud statement draws out current differentiators around 'community' and 'creators'. The reason we've included two examples from Soundcloud is not because we love their solution, but because we want to highlight how value proposition statements can evolve and change over time.

Here's another example, focused on business users, rather than consumers:

- Freshbooks: Accounting software built for owners, and their clients
  - Balancing your books, client relationships, and business isn't easy. FreshBooks gives you the info and time you need to focus on your big picture – your business, team, and clients.

The tagline clearly shows the target audience, whilst the follow-on sentences highlight the pain points of small business owners, before succinctly describing the value and benefits they might get from using Freshbooks to address them.

In the guided activity below, you'll create a starter value proposition statement for your idea.

TEAM ACTIVITY: VALUE PROPOSITION STATEMENT DEVELOPMENT – ESTIMATED TIME 45 MINUTES

Use this step to create a value proposition statement to communicate the value of your idea to your end users.

1. PREPARE TO RUN THE ACTIVITY

- Place a flip chart onto a wall or use a virtual whiteboard.
- Write 'Value Proposition Statement' on the top.
- Alternatively, if using MURAL, you can make use of our online template.

(Continued)

2. THE TEAM DIVERGES TO PROVIDE INPUT – THIS STEP SHOULD BE CARRIED OUT IN SILENCE!

- Individual team members create one or more potential value proposition statements on paper or sticky notes – take input from the project's work to date and perhaps inspiration from some of the examples we've provided above.
- Remember a good value proposition statement:
  - is directly targeted at your selected end users
  - communicates the value and benefits to your end users – in a way they can easily understand: seek to avoid complex long sentences and jargon
  - includes an engaging tag line and one to four follow-up sentences
  - differentiates the idea and solution from any existing solutions and/or competition.
- When done, team members place their statements onto the chart so everyone can see them.

3. WHEN THE TEAM MEMBERS HAVE FINISHED, THE TEAM CONVERGES TO REVIEW AND DEVELOP A VALUE PROPOSITION STATEMENT THE WHOLE TEAM IS HAPPY WITH

- The team converges to play back and review each team member's potential value proposition statements.
- Facilitation tip: Sometimes we find items from multiple statements get combined to create something much more powerful than any of the individual inputs.
- Write down the team's agreed value proposition statement for your idea and solution.
- Check the statement(s) against the reminder in the previous step about what makes a good value proposition statement. If everything is covered, well done. If not, change, add or remove text until it is.
- Figure 8.6 shows an example of an agreed completed value proposition statement from the charity organisation challenge.

4. MAINTAIN AND UPDATE THE VALUE PROPOSITION STATEMENT

- The value proposition statement should be kept accessible during the project and be referred to from time to time as needed. For example, it should be used as a key input into playbacks with sponsors and end users and in important presentations and pitches.

- The value proposition statement can also be updated over time as the team gathers more knowledge and/or receives feedback from end users.

Value Proposition Statement

Change makes change - The easiest way to support a good cause. Donate what you can afford and select the type of communities you want to support.

Change makes change. Support a good cause of your choosing. Keep tabs 24/7 on how your money is making a difference with stories personalised for you, told by real people.

Change makes change! Verify how much you can afford. Donate to the type of community of your choice. Be informed by the people you're helping.

Change makes change. The affordable way to make a difference and keep in touch with how your money is being used.

Change makes change - Donate. Stay informed. Relax.

Change makes change!
The affordable way to make a difference. Donate to the communities and causes you most want to support. Be informed directly by the real people you're helping.

FIGURE 8.6: Value proposition statement example

REFLECTION POINT: BUSINESS CASE AND VALUE PROPOSITION

Reflecting on the text and activities, consider the following questions. Make a note of your answers in the space provided and/or in your journal.

1. WHAT DO YOU CONSIDER WILL BE THE MOST COMPELLING ASPECTS OF YOUR PROJECT'S BUSINESS CASE? WHY DO YOU THINK THIS?

(Continued)

2. DO YOU THINK YOUR SPONSOR WOULD BE LIKELY TO INVEST IN FURTHER DEVELOPING YOUR SOLUTION? IF NOT OR IF YOU'RE NOT SURE, WHAT CHANGES COULD BE MADE TO PERSUADE THEM?

3. DO YOU THINK YOUR VALUE PROPOSITION WILL APPEAL TO YOUR END USERS? IF NOT OR IF YOU'RE NOT SURE, WHAT CHANGES COULD BE MADE TO IMPROVE IT?

CONCLUSION

Commercial awareness is a critical requirement for employers, and also a critical employability skill for new graduates. Developing a level of commercial awareness and using this to carry out some commercial research about potential employers, as described at the beginning of the chapter, will put you in a much stronger position to identify which organisations you'd actually like to work for, and where you can add value.

When applying for jobs, being able to demonstrate commercial awareness will set you apart from many of the other candidates during your applications and interviews. It will also give you a fast start in your careers and often help you in your wider life. We hope some of the simple recommendations and tips we've shared with you will put you in a good place.

Commercial development during the early stages of innovation projects takes place in parallel with the development of our ideas, solutions and capabilities such as prototypes. We need both elements to be able to convince our project sponsors the project is worth investing in.

Although we haven't tasked you with doing this, structuring and populating a business case is critically important for an innovation project, well, for any change project really. As we've seen, a business case weighs up the costs versus the benefits and considers elements such as timing and risks. When developing business cases we are drawing on forecasts about the future, and this is a tricky business. There are different methods for such forecasting. While we have not included them in this chapter, we have included some pointers in the further resources section at the end of the chapter. The more certain we can be in the accuracy of our assessments and the more credibility we can demonstrate the better.

For most projects, not everyone in the team will be responsible for creating and managing the business case, but everyone in the team needs to be commercially aware. For example, we have to understand the commercial implications of our decisions. If the developers decide they want to take another couple of weeks to hone the development of our prototype from being good to being perfect, this will usually cost more money, as well as setting us back two weeks. Whether this is a good or a bad decision will depend on the project and the wider context, but we each have to consider and understand the commercial implications of our actions.

We also have to understand what value we're generating for our end users. The value proposition statement you've developed during this chapter is a great way of documenting and communicating this – using a structure we can share with the end users to gain their buy-in.

If you're thinking, 'Pah – this is just marketing stuff', then in a way you're correct. This is about 'marketing'. We have to convince the end users that what we're creating for them is of value to them and they should use it. If they don't, what's the point? If the end users won't adopt our solution because they don't see the value, we may have invented something new, but we certainly haven't delivered any innovation. Moreover, like a Hill, a good value proposition statement also helps us as a team to remain focused on what we have decided to be the key value we want to deliver. As you continue with the development of your project, you will see how useful this is.

KEY LEARNING POINTS

- Employers highly value commercial awareness in job applicants and new hires.
- Commercial awareness can be considered at the macro, organisational and project level.
- By taking a bit of time and carrying out some focused actions we can all develop, enhance and maintain our commercial awareness.
- Having good commercial awareness helps with job applications, at the start and right through our careers. By taking on some tasks and responsibilities that train your skills in this area, you can strengthen both your commercial awareness and practice.
- Creating a positive and credible business case, which shows how the benefits outweigh the costs, will be a key requirement to gain funding to develop and deliver innovation and any other change projects. The business case is targeted at the sponsor(s) and other key stakeholders, who may influence the sponsor or have an input into decision making.
- A value proposition statement is used to clearly communicate the value of an idea and solution to the end users, often showing how and why it is different and/or exciting and why they should use it.

ACTION POINTS

- ☐ Run the team activities.
- ☐ Make sure that you document and keep copies of *all the outputs* you produce, and that you keep them in a place where all team members can access them (for example, save pictures and/or screenshots in a shared folder).
- ☐ Please complete the reflection points and exercises.

EXERCISES

1. Look up some frameworks for the development of business models and value propositions. Start by searching online for different images illustrating a) Lean Canvas; b) Business Model Canvas; and c) Value Proposition Canvas. Compare and contrast these different approaches and consider what you can learn from them.

2. Search online for websites showcasing examples of powerful value proposition statements. Select a few that you really like and discuss these with your team. What do you think goes into creating a powerful value proposition statement?

FURTHER RESOURCES

When it comes to commercial awareness, one of the first follow-up tasks is to ensure that one engages with relevant political and business reviews on a regular basis. Making it a habit to read *The Economist*, the *Financial Times* or similar outlets is a great starting point.

A brief and useful book on how to strengthen your commercial awareness:

Stoakes, C. 2019. *All You Need to Know about Commercial Awareness*. Wendover: Christopher Stoakes Ltd.

It can also be useful to read an introductory strategy textbook as these usually introduce their readers to a number of common tools for assessing and developing businesses, including PESTEL (as introduced above), SWOT (a framework for evaluating strengths, weaknesses, opportunities and threats to a business) and Porter's Five Forces (competitors, buyers, suppliers, new entrants and substitutes). We suggest the following book, but there are others:

Whittington, R., Regnér, P., Angwin, D., Johnson, G., & Scholes, K. 2019. *Exploring Strategy*. 12th edn. Harlow: Pearson.

An overview of innovation competitions, funding and awards:

https://apply-for-innovation-funding.service.gov.uk/competition/ search

The following website lists some questions used in job interviews to test the applicant's commercial awareness:

WikiJob. 2021. *Commercial Awareness: Interview Advice*.

Another area of commercial awareness is the interpretation of forecasts such as the expected size of a market in years to come or the rise or fall of a certain technology. The following article summarises six rules for effective forecasting that are useful to know:

Saffo, P. 2007. Six rules for effective forecasting. *Harvard Business Review*, 85(7–8), 122–193.

For an excellent section on the development of business cases and value propositions in Design Thinking that includes some great complementary team activities have a look at the following excellent book, pages 212–264:

Lewrick, M., Link, P., & Leifer, L. 2018. *The Design Thinking Playbook*. Hoboken, NJ: Wiley.

There are many useful approaches and frameworks that can be used for the development of a business case, with the Business Model Canvas being one of the most prominent examples. The following article describes a Business Model Canvas for sustainability-oriented business model innovation:

Joyce, A., & Paquin, R. 2016. The triple layered business model canvas: A tool to design more sustainable business models. *Journal of Cleaner Production*, 135, 1474–1486.

As you progress towards your pitch you may want to have a look at this short video on how to communicate value:

Withers, J. 2017. *4 Steps to Create a Killer Value Proposition*. DiscoverOrg.

MANAGING CHANGE AND OVERCOMING SETBACKS

Chapter contents

Goals

- To learn about the iterative nature of Design Thinking, innovation management and change projects.

- To develop an understanding of the benefits of personal resilience, particularly when encountering change, setbacks and disappointments.

- To identify employability benefits of positively reacting to change and the development of 'bouncebackability'.

- To develop approaches for reviewing and reflecting on unforeseen changes and setbacks to turn issues into opportunities.

- To find out about approaches to managing change and iteration in team projects.

INTRODUCTION

In the world we live in, change is a certainty. Change may be driven by new discoveries and ideas, incremental or transformational innovation, changes in the climate, economy, society and so on. Things change – and we have to adapt. Sometimes we have a degree of control over what is changing and how – but often not.

We all have had experiences of serendipity, when things came together under a lucky star, as well as those of unexpected problems, when fate seemed to conspire against us. Innovation invariably involves both – eureka moments and moments of frustration. Innovation also usually requires us to go through several loops and iterations (as discussed in Chapters 2 and 3). These iterations usually happen for a reason, and often that reason is related to changes or setbacks, disappointments or failures. Sometimes, we make a mistake or fall love with our solution rather than the problem. Sometimes, change happens for reasons beyond our control. Perhaps a customer or an executive simply does not like our idea for all the wrong (or right) reasons.

Dealing with developments beyond our control isn't easy, whether they occur in our professional or our personal lives. When you think back to some of the bigger setbacks in your life, you will be reminded how important it is to develop the ability to bounce back.

 In the end, what matters most is not that we've had a problem or that we've made a mistake, but how we approached it and learnt from it! We all need to develop a level of resilience and the skills needed to address changes and setbacks with adaptability, foresight and professionalism. We can also *learn* how to turn problems into opportunities (well, perhaps not all of them – but more than you might think).

This is what this chapter is all about. It's about understanding the role of change and failure in innovation projects and strengthening your ability to bounce back. Change, setbacks and failure are challenging to process. So, we advise to have some chocolate at hand (or an alternative pick-me-up treat if preferred).

ITERATION IS PART OF THE PLAN

When we introduced the innovation management and Design Thinking processes in the initial chapters of this book, you may have made two observations.

Firstly, the flow of activities generally progresses *from left to right*. We begin with a challenge, a problem or an opportunity. We undertake research to better understand the challenge, and we carry out Design Thinking and other activities to develop empathy for our end users and key stakeholders. We generate ideas, select one or more of them, develop prototypes and create a view of their commercial value. If all goes well, we hope we'll gain funding to move into delivery and commercialisation. Ultimately, we're seeking to create value and generate benefits.

But then there is also the notion of *iteration*. In real life, things rarely develop in a truly linear way. In virtually every project, we encounter issues and stumble a few times along the way. Sometimes, we're able to quickly overcome such problems and move on. At other times, we may have no choice but to take a step backwards. For example, when we begin to develop an idea, we may realise such a solution isn't feasible. On these occasions, we may have to move backwards in the innovation management process and repeat certain activities such as idea generation and selection.

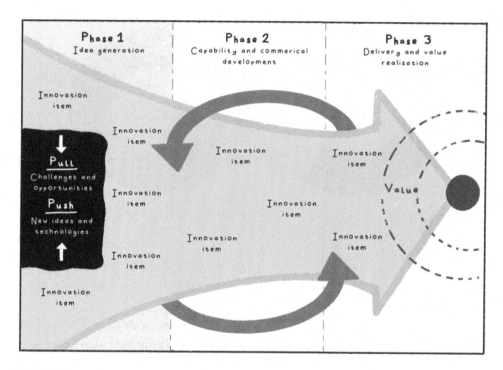

FIGURE 9.1: Innovation management process

In our illustration of the innovation process, this iterative nature of the innovation process is indicated by the two orange arrows. They show that stepping back and moving forward is not just a response to some accident – it is part of the plan!

When you consider some of the Design Thinking techniques we introduced in previous chapters, it will become even clearer how iteration is built into the innovation process. Sometimes, during Design Thinking activities you may find yourself having to repeat a series of similar activities a number of times until the users and sponsors are happy with the solution you've developed for them. For example, we often create prototypes and play them back to our end users. They may well tell us something like, 'We like this but not that – please can you change it?' Of course, this is the sort of feedback we want and need from our users. It ensures that we will create something which works for them. So, we'll go back and do some more development, before re-demonstrating the revised prototype again and... maybe again, until we get it right. This is why Design Thinking processes are often illustrated as two connected loops (see Figure 9.2).

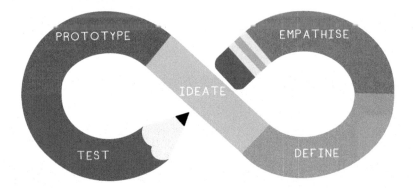

FIGURE 9.2: Design Thinking process

There are many different Design Thinking techniques for prototyping, testing, evaluation and development. In this book we introduce a number of them to you – but if you want to find out even more just have a look at the further resources section at the end of the chapter.

For now, the key learning points are that **it is helpful to have a clear understanding of the different stages of an innovation project; and that it is also helpful to have a plan – but when it comes to innovation processes more generally, and Design Thinking more specifically, iteration needs to be built into such a plan**. We need to be agile (as discussed in Chapter 7). It is a fundamental design principle.

MORE IN-DEPTH: MANAGING CHANGE

In order to survive and flourish, organisations need to deal with changes all the time. Changes can be emergent or planned. They can be forced or chosen. Sometimes the environment of an organisation changes very quickly – and an organisation needs to respond. For example, at the beginning of the Covid-19 pandemic, many universities had to switch to online teaching almost overnight. They *had to manage a change* that was beyond their control. This demanded a great deal of flexibility and effort from academics, professional staff and, of course, students.

While in most places face-to-face teaching has resumed, the long-term impact of this rapid shift to online delivery is still unfolding. New tools for online learning are being adopted. Researchers have gained more experience with online collaboration and conferencing. The prolonged period of remote working has encouraged more flexible working arrangements. While initially, everyone just responded to the abrupt change in a more ad hoc way, some universities developed new digital transformation strategies – as well as a larger number of online programmes. Universities anticipate and plan for transformational change in strategic ways. Such *drive for change* is something you will often see described as 'change management'. It involves a 'process of continually renewing an organisation's direction, structure, and capabilities to serve the ever-changing needs of external and internal customers' (Moran & Brightman, 2001, p. 111).

There are many frameworks and tools for the management of change that are beyond the scope of this book. For now, let us have a look at this very brief blog with five tips for managing change: **https://online.hbs.edu/blog/post/managing-change-in-the-workplace**

The author argues that when we manage change we need to pay attention to the *process* of change, the *forces* driving change, the *plan* for change, how change is *communicated* and the *roadblocks* we are likely to encounter.

When we work on innovation projects the same applies. We need to develop some understanding of the *innovation process* and the preparation, capability development, implementation and follow-through required for our innovation to be successful. We also need to understand what *forces* or pressures may aid implementation and adoption, both on the micro-level of a given project team or organisation as well as with a view to the macro environment (as discussed in the previous chapter). Like in change management, we need to have a *plan*. We need to be able to *communicate* how our innovation will deliver value, and we need to anticipate potential *obstacles* so that we can avoid or at least address them. So, when we develop an innovation project, we can learn a lot about change management and vice versa.

EMBRACING FAILURE

As we have already noted, innovation processes are fraught with uncertainty, challenges, and mistakes and this is normal, even expected, and therefore needs to be accommodated. This said, sometimes (in projects and in wider life in general), we may encounter a *major* problem. Something big, alarming and/or unexpected may happen, which we can't iterate our way out of.

Perhaps our project is considered to be a failure. Innovation, after all, is about doing something new. When we start, we don't know how things will turn out. We may be too late – or ahead of our time. We don't know if we're developing the next Tesla or Sinclair C5. (You've probably never heard of a C5 but this article will tell you why it is worth knowing about: **www.bbc.com/future/article/20141209-sinclair-c5-30-years-too-soon**)

Innovation, of course, is inherently risky, and therefore we have to be prepared to fail sometimes. The important thing is how we react, respond and bounce back from such failures. Sometimes, the project sponsor may change their mind, or have it changed for them. Perhaps their budget has been cut, and they have to halt the project, even though it's been a great success so far.

Of course, in our wider life we may encounter a more serious problem. We don't wish to be glib. There are some things that are extremely difficult to bounce back from. But here is the good news... when we're working on a change or innovation project, we can most certainly bounce back from the vast majority of setbacks and situations, no matter how bad things may appear to be at the time. The question is just *how* to achieve that.

ANALYSING AND REFLECTING ON FAILURE

A few details and names have been changed here to anonymise and protect those involved, but the following example is based upon real-life experience. Once upon a time, two organisations worked very closely together. One organisation was a bank. The other was an IT services company which had been contracted by the bank to support many of its IT systems and services.

The IT systems in the bank's branches were very old. The bank asked the IT supplier to create a proposal to modernise the branch IT systems. The two organisations spent a few weeks agreeing and documenting the requirements for the new systems. The IT company's team went away and spent several months (and a lot of money) creating a priced proposal for a new technology solution for the bank, which it believed would meet all of the requirements.

When the IT company was happy it had developed a compelling proposal, the two organisations met again. The IT company presented the new systems, change project and the price to the bank – but was very surprised and disappointed to find that the bank wasn't happy at all with the proposal. The bank said it would cost far too much and the technology solution wasn't what it had in mind. The IT company said the proposal was the most cost-effective way of meeting the bank's documented requirements and would deliver an industry-leading IT system. Unfortunately, it appeared the bank had been expecting a good and reliable solution but with a much lower price tag. Each organisation was upset with the other. For a time, it seemed like the bank might ask another IT company to do the work.

Some members of the IT company's team took a step back and reflected on what had caused this expensive mistake. Although they were angry and upset, as they'd done what they had thought the bank had asked for, they admitted that the proposal was a failure. They asked themselves what they had done wrong, and what they would do differently if they could go back in time and start the process again. One of their key reflections was that they had 'designed a Rolls Royce but the bank only wanted to pay for a Volkswagen'. While they had designed the best possible technology solution, this had led to a high price. A second reflection was that the two organisations had not communicated well enough during the development of the proposal. If they had worked more closely at that stage, these issues would have come out much earlier, and they could have been addressed along the way.

The IT company approached the bank and admitted its mistakes. It offered to work more collaboratively if the bank would give it a second chance to create a revised proposal. The bank agreed. The two teams collaborated for several months on both the technology and the commercial aspects of the proposal. There were disagreements and negotiations along the way, but in the end a proposal was developed, which was accepted by the bank's executives. The two organisations then created a joint team to deliver the more detailed design work and the testing and implementation programme. The project was a great success, as it was delivered on time and to budget, which can be quite a rare thing in industry! The bank's business benefited from the modernised IT systems and the IT supplier increased its revenue. The two organisations received a joint industry award for the project.

This is a great example of analysing and reflecting on a failure and doing something differently next time. The IT company was fortunate to get a second chance and made the most of it. Even if they hadn't, they applied the learning when they created proposals for their other customers.

One of the most important lessons was that **the team had admitted their failure, they analysed what had gone wrong and then they learned from their mistakes. By doing this, they turned a failure into a great success.**

EXPERT

WHAT IF PEOPLE DON'T LIKE OUR IDEA?

We introduced Tim Kastelle of the University of Queensland in Chapter 2. Here, Tim shares his thoughts on pitching.

(Continued)

1. WHAT HAPPENS IF WE PITCH OUR IDEA AND OUR STAKEHOLDERS DON'T LIKE IT?

 Getting negative feedback at the idea stage is the best possible outcome! If you are still in the early stages with your idea, it is still relatively easy to respond to feedback. It's much worse to find out that the idea isn't so great after you've built it and launched it.

Here's an example. My last job before I became an academic was in a small software start-up. I was the third person in the firm, and when I joined, the founder and investors had already sunk two years and a substantial amount of money into building the software. My job was to sell it. When I started talking to customers, it became clear that our software mostly duplicated open-source software that was available for free. This was not good for our business model. I learned this after two weeks of engaging with potential customers. What if these two weeks had been invested at the start of the process rather than at the end? The founders would have saved two years and a lot of their investors' money. It's never great to learn that your idea won't work, but it's much better to learn this early – before you have spent time and money executing your idea.

2. BUT DIDN'T HENRY FORD SAY, 'IF I HAD ASKED PEOPLE WHAT THEY WANTED, THEY WOULD HAVE SAID FASTER HORSES'?

There's no evidence that Ford actually said this, but it's still a very popular quote. It's true that people often have a hard time imagining how they might use an idea that they've never encountered before. So, yes, you might get a negative response to your idea pitch simply because of this challenge.

This is why we need to focus not on what people want right now, or think they want, but rather on what is giving them problems right now, or what their aspirations are. It's still our job to make the creative leap from this feedback to building something that people will love. Talking to stakeholders early is essential to any kind of innovation.

3. WHY DO PEOPLE AVOID HAVING THESE CONVERSATIONS?

I really don't know. My start-up experience is not uncommon – the founders seemed to prefer going out of business to actually engaging with customers and stakeholders to improve their chances of success. Part of this seems to relate to having a strong need to be right. Many people become much more attached to the solution they're building than they are to the problems of their stakeholders that they're trying to solve. If your focus is on your idea/solution, then negative feedback can be very damaging, and can even be misunderstood as an attack on your identity. I think this is what people are trying to avoid when they dodge feedback.

TOP TIP

Love your problem, not your solution. This is really important. If you hold the problems of your stakeholders tightly, and your solution lightly, your chances of successfully building something people will use go way up. When you do this, negative feedback about your idea might be a bit deflating at first, but after some time to reflect, you'll realise that you've been given a gift – a chance to make your idea even better. But if you get the same feedback after you've built and launched your idea, it's no longer a gift – it's a sign that you've gone down the wrong path. Which would you prefer?

REFLECTION POINT: ANALYSING FAILURE

Recall a situation where you experienced failure – at work, during your studies, at school or in another social setting. Consider the following questions. Make a note of your answers in the space provided and/or in your journal.

1. WHAT HAPPENED? WHY DID YOU CONSIDER THE SITUATION WAS A FAILURE?

(Continued)

2. HOW DID YOU DISCOVER THE PROBLEM, AND HOW DID YOU FEEL INITIALLY?

3. WHAT DID YOU DO NEXT?

4. DID YOU ANALYSE THE FAILURE? WHAT LESSONS DID YOU ULTIMATELY TAKE AWAY FROM THE EXPERIENCE?

5. IF YOU EXPERIENCED SUCH A SITUATION AGAIN, WHAT WOULD YOU DO DIFFERENTLY?

TURNING A PROBLEM INTO AN OPPORTUNITY

The previous examples were from industry. This one is from academia and closely related to the development of this book.

Much, though not all, of the contents of the book have been inspired by a module we run at the University of Leeds in the UK. For the first three years of its existence, the module was delivered in a collaborative teaching space. Design Thinking and other team-based activities were introduced and facilitated in the classroom and worked on by student teams, collaborating in their own allocated workspace. The students also met up on campus between the classroom sessions to undertake additional collaborative activities.

In 2020, the UK, like many other countries, was badly affected by the Covid-19 pandemic. A series of lockdowns and other social distancing rules were introduced. Universities, schools and many other establishments and industries were badly affected. Unfortunately, as many of you know, student learning was severely disrupted. As you may imagine, a module with students working closely together, huddled around a table in a shared working space isn't ideal during a lockdown, or when social distancing rules apply. So we faced a significant problem. Questions were asked. Should the module be cancelled or postponed?

One of the key reflections many prior students of this module had commented upon was 'bouncebackability' – encountering a problem, reacting positively and turning it from being an issue into an opportunity. As module leaders, we sat down and analysed if and how this could be done for the module during the pandemic-induced crisis. We had no wish to dilute the strengths of the module by focusing more heavily on theory and less on practice and teamworking. Tony had experience of running workshops online during his career in industry and investigated online collaboration tools for Design Thinking workshops. This is how we found out about the tool called MURAL.

We took a decision to re-design and deliver the module workshops to run online, using Zoom with breakout rooms and MURAL as the technology platform. Although this presented challenges, we worked through them. In this process, we realised the problem created a great opportunity. Even when the pandemic receded, online collaboration would be more important than ever before. In many industries and many multinational organisations, it already was. Enabling students to gain enhanced online collaboration skills would be a great addition to the employability skills already covered by the module.

There was also a parallel challenge with industry. Before the pandemic, we had run a major multi-day Design Thinking workshop on sustainable mobility with a team from the United Nations. The workshop ran face to face in Leeds, with a room, flip charts, sticky notes and so on. During the pandemic, we then delivered another online using Zoom (with

FIGURE 9.3: Bouncebackability

breakout rooms) and MURAL. If anything, this was an even greater success, with even more diverse participants from many more countries attending and nobody needing to travel, reducing costs and environmental impacts. As in the previous example, a problem was transformed into an opportunity.

You may think now that one cannot turn *every* problem into an opportunity – and in a way you are right. Sometimes things fail and we are not given a second opportunity.

More often than not, however, **we can learn from our experiences. And in this sense, we can indeed turn almost every problem into an opportunity to improve our 'bouncebackability'.**

DEVELOPING 'BOUNCEBACKABILITY'

So what is bouncebackability? Fundamentally, it is about being able to do three things:

1. *Accepting* change and *admitting* to problems or failures – both individually and in teams.
2. *Analysing* and *reflecting* on problems or failures – and *learning* from them.
3. Where it's possible to do so, *transforming* setbacks into opportunities.

Bouncebackability starts with the acceptance of problems or change. **It involves the** analysis of problems **with the aim of** learning and transforming setbacks **into opportunities.**

We prefer this somewhat unusual concept of 'bouncebackability' over that of resilience because bouncebackability is about agency and positivity. It is about *doing* some specific things – accepting, admitting, analysing, reflecting, learning – all with the aim of *transforming* a problem into an opportunity.

In contrast, resilience is often seen as an ability or capacity that one either has or has not. This is of course not entirely true – we know that like bouncebackability, resilience is something that can be developed. (See the further resources section at the end of the chapter for more information.) However, in this chapter we focus on bouncing back because it is part of what we do when we iterate in innovation projects. As Tim argues above, we really need to love the problem, embrace failure and plan for iterations if we want to be successful. After all, Design Thinking is all about turning a problem into an opportunity.

With change being a certainty, the ability to be resilient and demonstrate 'bouncebackability' is also a key employability skill. Careers today are more dynamic than they have ever been before (WEF, 2020). You simply won't be able to stand still even if you love your job. Some of the changes which happen you may wish for and embrace. Others may be forced upon you. A new competitor may enter your industry and disrupt your organisation. Your department may be merged with another. Your budget may be cut. Artificial intelligence may take over some or all of your role. To survive and thrive in such a changing world and changing jobs market, we need to be adaptable. This doesn't mean changes won't upset us. Some certainly will, but we need to be able to take the knocks and move forward.

With this in mind, let's have a closer look at the first and sometimes most difficult stage of bouncing back – the moment when we face the setback and need to accept or at least admit to our problems or failures. Nobody likes to be disappointed, and it is all too human to be upset or to look for guilt elsewhere. However, usually this is neither helpful nor empowering. The first step is to acknowledge our problem and to give ourselves agency in doing so.

EXPERT

DEALING WITH SETBACKS

Carly Gilbert-Patrick leads the Active Mobility, Digitalization & Mode Integration Team at the Sustainable Mobility Unit of the United Nations Environment Programme (UNEP), which supports countries around the world to de-couple increasing mobility and transport from increased emissions. Prior to this, Carly led sustainable transport programmes for UN-Habitat and UNEP and worked for Transport for London where she supported implementation of the London Cycle Hire Scheme and the London Low Emission Zone.

1. AT SOME POINT OR ANOTHER, WE ALL EXPERIENCE FRUSTRATIONS, SETBACKS OR REJECTIONS. THIS CHAPTER IS ABOUT HOW BEST TO DEAL WITH THEM. WHAT IS YOUR EXPERIENCE?

Working for a global programme for sustainable mobility, dealing with frustrations and setbacks is an everyday occurrence! Particularly in the areas of transport I focus on – walking and cycling – that are often overlooked and underinvested in even though they serve the majority of citizens. So, whilst I continue to advocate for better policies and investment, I hear a lot of 'nos' or things just don't move fast enough for my liking.

2. CAN YOU GIVE US AN EXAMPLE?

I would love to give the example of Nairobi, Kenya, the city I live and work in. I have been working with stakeholders in Nairobi for about ten years to introduce policies and investment for pedestrians and cyclists. However, the institutional setup and decision making processes are very complex, with lots of different organisations having a say. For the first six years, I was met by a lot of bureaucracy and little progress. I would sit in meeting after meeting. This experience left me despondent at the lack of momentum and change. However, I also built up a lot of networks and relationships over that time, and eventually I could see progress. In 2015, Nairobi launched a walking and cycling policy for the city and ringfenced 20% of their transport budget to investing in the needs of pedestrians and cyclists! So sometimes, it is useful to adopt a more long-term perspective.

3. WE ALL KNOW THAT THE ABILITY TO LEARN FROM OUR MISTAKES, BE RESILIENT AND MANAGE CHANGE IS IMPORTANT. AND YET, WHEN WE ENCOUNTER SETBACKS, IT CAN BE HARD TO SEE IT IN THIS WAY... DO YOU AGREE?

I totally agree. It's hard to be positive when coming face to face with a setback. Sometimes, in the face of adversity, we can be despondent. It's human nature.

4. IN YOUR EXPERIENCE, WHAT CAN WE DO TO TURN A SETBACK INTO AN OPPORTUNITY?

People always say 'treat others like you want to be treated'. But I also like to try and treat myself like I want to be treated. So, I try and give myself time and grace – a few hours or

(Continued)

days to sit with the setback and unpick it. I remind myself that we all make mistakes or suffer setbacks, and how I would treat my colleagues when they experience something like this. I try not to rush into solution seeking.

After sitting with the setback for a while, we can then start identifying the next steps. Setbacks often force us to slow down, re-examine and come up with new ways of thinking or doing. In most cases, this turns into an improvement and ultimately into something good.

TOP TIP

Sit with it and give yourself time to absorb the setback or change. Don't rush into seeking solutions. Also, consult and communicate with your team! A problem shared really is a problem halved. Don't be afraid to make mistakes and share your mistakes with others.

Carly gives us some great advice here on how to deal with setbacks. While we agree that a problem shared is a problem halved – not everyone wants to have a share of a problem. Sometimes, when we work in teams we may not (or at least not initially) agree on what the problem is – or even whether there is a problem. When the problem 'hits the fan', it can then be tempting to just assign blame. This is not a nice thing to do – and it is also rather unproductive. There is no need to assign blame in order to understand what has gone wrong. When team relationships turn sour, the chances of a successful recovery decrease rather than increase.

The first step of bouncebackability (*accepting* change and *admitting* to problems/failures) is hence first and foremost about coming to terms and dealing with emotions. Listening and empathy can go a long way in such situations. As Carly advises, treat yourself and others like you want to be treated.

The next step is then about *analysing* and *reflecting* on problems or failures – and *learning* from them. For that we have already introduced you to a great tool – Gibbs' Cycle we described in Chapter 1.

Gibbs' Cycle is indeed a brilliant tool for bouncing back both individually and as a team. When you hit a barrier or suffer a setback, it helps you to structure your response and invites you to a) describe what happened, b) make room and address

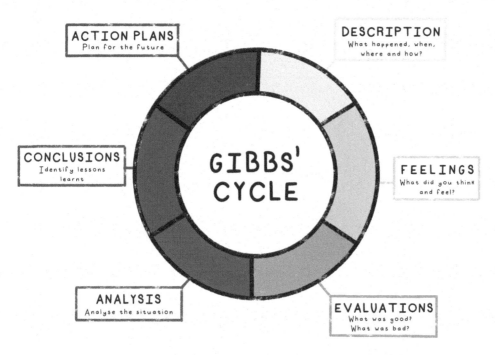

FIGURE 9.4: Gibbs' Cycle

your (often negative) feelings; it c) guides evaluation and d) analysis, so that you as a team can e) identify conclusions and f) make a plan to transform your setback into an opportunity. Our advice is therefore that when your team suffers a setback, try to be kind to each other and yourself and use Gibbs' Cycle to process what has happened in one or several team meetings.

Gibbs' Cycle and the Six Thinking Hats are great tools for analysing a change, problem or setback. There are also some additional frameworks available that you can use for the last step of bouncing back: *transforming setbacks into opportunities.*

It is true that whenever we have learnt something useful from a setback, we have turned it into an opportunity. This said, we often wish to go beyond that and recover a project and develop it further. For this, it can be useful to work with a tool that helps to reassess the more specific situation and what can be done about it. We propose the set of what and where questions in Figure 9.5 to start out.

We have now discussed how important changes, setbacks and even failures are for successful innovation projects. While nobody enjoys setbacks, we have shown that being able to deal with them professionally is a great employability skill to have. Bouncebackability

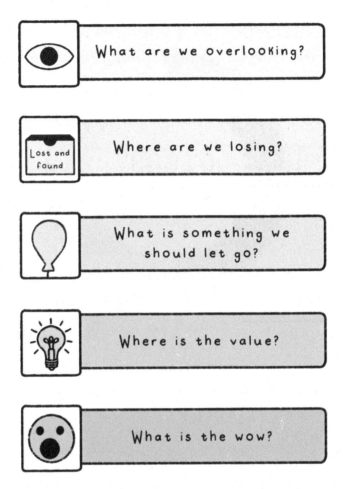

FIGURE 9.5: What and where questions for transforming setbacks

is something we can learn and practise, individually and as a team. The last question we have now is one for you: *Are you ready to bounce back?*

TEAM ACTIVITY: DEVELOPING 'BOUNCEBACKABILITY' SKILLS – ESTIMATED TIME 90–180 MINUTES

Warning! This activity can be challenging, but if you really immerse yourself in it, you will find it very useful.

Your innovation sponsor has been briefed about your project and they've just sent the email in Figure 9.6 to the team.

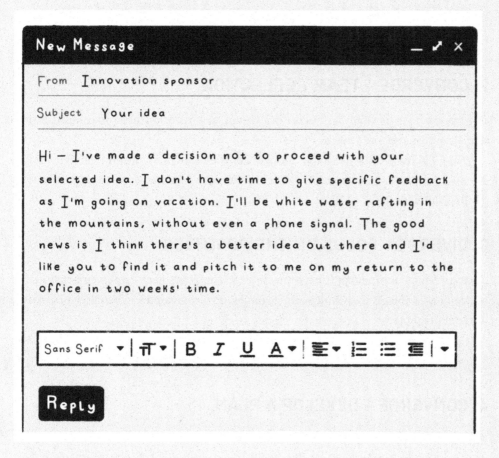

New Message — ↗ ✕

From Innovation sponsor

Subject Your idea

Hi — I've made a decision not to proceed with your selected idea. I don't have time to give specific feedback as I'm going on vacation. I'll be white water rafting in the mountains, without even a phone signal. The good news is I think there's a better idea out there and I'd like you to find it and pitch it to me on my return to the office in two weeks' time.

Sans Serif ▾ | T ▾ | B I U A ▾ | ☰ ▾ • ☲ ☲ ☲ | ▾

Reply

FIGURE 9.6: Email from innovation sponsor

Yes, we know this is frustrating! You've worked so hard.

Understandably, you want more feedback to understand the rationale for this decision, but unfortunately you can't get it.

This is an enforced and unexpected change beyond your control. Can you work with your team to bounce back and turn this problem into an opportunity?

1. DIVERGE – PERSONAL REFLECTION

Each team member should take five minutes to reflect and honestly write down on sticky notes what they feel about this news. Imagine this has just happened to you. How would you feel?

(Continued)

(Hint – if your feelings are primarily negative, that's fine, but ask yourself why this is. Have you fallen in love with the solution, rather than the problem?)

2. CONVERGE – TEAM REFLECTION

The team holds a ten-minute discussion, giving each team member an opportunity to share their feelings and reflections.

(Hint – What are the collective thoughts of the team? Many team members may be disappointed and/or frustrated. Others may consider the change as an opportunity to develop a better idea.)

3. DIVERGE – FOCUS ON THE POSITIVES

Place any disappointment or frustration aside for a moment. Each team member writes on sticky notes, stating the advantages the team has now compared to when they first started work on the project.

(Hint – you've learned so much through the course of the project, but how can this knowledge help you identify a different and potentially better idea?)

4. CONVERGE – DEVELOP A PLAN

The team reviews the advantages identified.

As a team, work through the **where/what** questions identified above (Figure 9.5).

Sketch out an action plan to identify and develop your new idea – stating which activities from the earlier chapters you should undertake in which order.

(Hint – Which previous activities (e.g., research?) should you simply review? Should you focus on a new category of end users or continue with the current ones? Which activities should you run through again (e.g., Big Ideas, Prioritisation Grid, Storyboarding and so on?))

5. IMPLEMENT THE PLAN TO IDENTIFY AND DEVELOP AN UPDATED IDEA

We appreciate within the confines of this book, your project, your module and the time you have available, this may not be possible, but in an ideal world, we would advise you to implement the plan and develop your second idea, create a new prototype, identify the value and so on.

To help with this, our MURAL template includes space to repeat many of the activities included so far in the book to enable you to develop a second iteration for your project.

WHY DO WE ASK YOU TO DO THIS?

1. Innovation management and Design Thinking are iterative. Repeating activities and working through multiple iterations happens all the time in industry, so it's a great idea to gain experience of doing this. It will also give you more experience of applying Design Thinking and other techniques.

2. In our experience of working with many student teams, companies and projects, the second idea is often much stronger than the first. This is because it has been developed with a lot more knowledge of the subject area than the team started with.

3. Finally, in the real world, stuff happens! Encountering and overcoming problems like this is a great way to develop bouncebackability and personal resilience. It also provides great experience and a story you can use in future job interviews.

CONCLUSION

This chapter has been all about facing issues and setbacks. Change happens! It is how we deal with it is that is important.

Both innovation management and Design Thinking are designed to expect and manage change and are very iterative in nature. This is because in real life, projects don't proceed forward in a straight line. Almost always, we will encounter changes and issues along the way. The more innovation and Design Thinking projects and activities you work on, the more experience you will gain in this area.

Sometimes, during an innovation project, you'll need to take a step back, as in the example situation in the guided activity above. Equally, during Design Thinking activities you may find yourself often having to repeat a series of similar activities, such as prototype development and user feedback, a number of times until the user and sponsors are happy with the solution you've developed for them.

We've provided you with a definition of 'bouncebackability' as involving three key steps – but whatever anyone calls it, learning from our mistakes, being resilient, managing change and sometimes turning an issue into an opportunity are key employability skills, and ones which we all need to develop to a degree.

A simple approach, like Gibbs' Reflective Cycle, can really help with your innovation and Design Thinking activities and your wider life too. We can all learn from our experiences but for this to work we often need to take a step back, reflect and think about what has happened, so we can work out what to do better next time, whether it is in an innovation project, getting a job or anything else.

Some people use this approach every time they have a job interview. If they don't get the job, they analyse what has happened and see what they can do differently next time, until they get the job they're looking for. Equally, we have used the same approach on the modules, projects and research activities we work on. We have, of course, failed several times, and faced difficult people, situations and changes beyond our control. This has taught us a lot about the importance of 'bouncebackability', supported by a healthy dose of empathy for those around us.

It is now time to take the project you've worked so hard on and move forward. Good luck with the closing chapters!

KEY LEARNING POINTS

- Innovation management and Design Thinking processes are iterative in nature – they are designed to expect and manage change.
- Coping with changes and setbacks isn't easy but we can learn to deal with them more effectively.
- Give yourself time to absorb setbacks or changes. Don't rush into seeking solutions. Consult and communicate with your team. Don't be afraid to make mistakes and share your mistakes with others.
- 'Bouncebackability' – the ability to learn from our mistakes, be resilient, manage change and sometimes turn an issue into an opportunity – is a key employability skills area.
- Use of a simple approach, like Gibbs' Reflective Cycle, can help us to reflect, think about what has happened and work out what to do better next time, whether in an innovation project or our wider life.

ACTION POINTS

- ☐ Carry out the team activities.
- ☐ Make sure that you document and keep copies of *all the outputs* you produce, and that you keep them in a place where all team members can access them (for example, save pictures and/or screenshots in a shared folder). If working online, don't forget to create backups of your work.
- ☐ Please complete the reflection points and exercises.

EXERCISE

DEVELOPING BOUNCEBACKABILITY SKILLS

Identify another situation in your life where you faced an unexpected challenge and related setback. Use Gibbs' Reflective Cycle to review and analyse the situation. You can do this in writing or as a discussion with your team.

- Step 0 – Take a few moments first to immerse yourself in the situation.
  - Think back to how you experienced the situation.
- Step 1 – Describe what happened.
  - Write down a short factual description of what happened on a piece of paper.
- Step 2 – Consider your emotional response.
  - How did you feel emotionally about the situation?
  - Were you angry, frustrated, worried, sad, apathetic, happy, excited, etc.? (This is a bit like wearing the Red Hat in the Six Thinking Hats approach.)
- Step 3 – Evaluate what was good and bad about the situation.
  - Describe what was bad about the situation and what went wrong. (This is a bit like wearing the Black Hat in the Six Thinking Hats approach.)
  - Describe what was good about the situation, usually there is always something. (This is a bit like wearing the Yellow Hat in the Six Thinking Hats approach.)
- Step 4 – Analyse the situation.
  - Looking at it now, can you see a way to turn this issue into an opportunity to do something different and better?
- Step 5 – Conclude what could have been improved/what you should have done.
  - Given your experience to date and your analysis in the previous steps, summarise what you think you should have done differently.
- Step 6 – Consider what you have taken away from this exercise and make a plan for what you would do if you were to face this (or a similar) situation again.

FURTHER RESOURCES

An insightful blog article with some practical tips on dealing with disappointment:

Kets de Vries, M. 2018. Dealing with disappointment: Research blog.

This very personal talk about resilience highlights three strategies that can help to build resilience when we deal with the larger challenges and tragedies in life:

Hone, L. 2019. *The Three Secrets of Resilient People*. TEDxChristchurch.

This brief blog identifies some additional (evidence-based) strategies to build resilience:

Newman, K.M. 2016. Five science-backed strategies to build resilience. *Greater Good Magazine*.

In any innovation process you may go through planned and unplanned iterations. The following article presents a tool that can help with planning and management of iteration:

Eppinger, S.D. 2001. Innovation at the speed of information. *Harvard Business Review*, 79(1), 149–158.

Not just projects and organisations go through iterations when innovating. The following research article provides some interesting insights into how policy feedback loops enabled China to successfully develop and implement early market reforms in the state-owned economy:

Leutert, W. 2021. Innovation through iteration: Policy feedback loops in China's economic reform. *World Development*, 138, 105–173.

For those of you who are interested in following up on change management, the following review could be a good starting point:

By, R.T. 2005. Organisational change management: A critical review. *Journal of Change Management*, 5(4), 369–380.

The following blog post adopts a more practical perspective and offers some useful tips for managing organisational change:

Stobierski, T. 2020. 5 tips for managing change in the workplace. *Harvard Business School Online*.

PITCHING INNOVATION AND WOW FACTOR

Chapter contents

Goals

- To learn about key elements of a successful innovation pitch.
- To draw on all the outputs your team has created in the development of a compelling innovation pitch.
- To develop additional communication skills for presenting and pitching.
- To build upon and combine the skills developed over the course of your project and deliver a compelling innovation pitch.

INTRODUCTION

We're now coming to a critical time in the book and your project. You've worked with your team to understand and research your assigned challenge. You and your team have generated empathy and an understanding of the needs of your end users. The team has generated and prioritised diverse ideas, and you've selected and developed an idea, created a prototype and articulated the value for both the sponsor and end users. The final step in your project is to 'pitch' your idea in order to get support to move it forward. You're almost there!

At this stage, you mustn't forget all the things you've learned along the way. In addition to applying innovation and Design Thinking skills, you've collaborated with different stakeholders and worked in a diverse team. You've applied critical thinking skills and solved complex (and sometimes 'wicked') problems. Your commercial awareness has increased greatly, and you've applied a wide range of communications skills. You've managed and navigated difficult changes and developed personal resilience. Lastly, you've used your initiative and actively reflected upon and learned from your experiences.

In this chapter, you're now going to bring all of these skills together and apply them to develop and deliver a compelling innovation pitch. The pitch might be targeted at project sponsors or your module tutors. If you're working through this book independently, you might end up pitching to us. As a reminder, you can join our LinkedIn community and get involved in our competition (if it's currently active).

Alternatively, if you're creating your own start-up business, either now or in the future (some of our students have done this), your pitch might be aimed at investors. No matter who your audience is, you need to have an objective and generate empathy for them, communicate your idea and the value, and convince the audience it's worth giving you a good grade or investing in your idea, your solution or start-up. Good luck!

In terms of the innovation management process, we're now at a crucial stage, one of the major review points or 'stage gates' in the process. Before the project can continue, you need to convince your sponsor(s) or investor(s) to agree your idea and project is worth investing in, so the idea can be fully developed and delivered, so the value can be realised.

COMBINING AND BUILDING UPON WHAT YOU'VE ALREADY LEARNED

Here's a reminder of the seven key skill areas you've focused on in this book due to their particular importance to graduate employers.

To create your innovation pitch, you'll need to apply all seven sets of skills focused on in the book:

1. **Innovation and Design Thinking** – You'll need to review the output of the techniques you've used to date and verify which elements and Design Thinking artefacts should be included in your pitch.

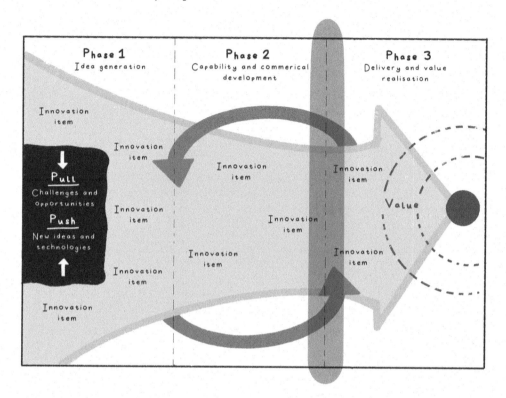

FIGURE 10.1: 'Stage gate' between Phase 2 and Phase 3 of the innovation management process

2. **Collaboration and teaming** – You'll need to work closely with your teammates to develop a compelling pitch, which makes use of the diverse skills of individual team members and the collective power of the team.

3. **Initiative and active learning** – Using your initiative will be key for developing and delivering the team's pitch. Practice makes better, and the more you practise, the more issues you'll find and need to overcome. You'll also need to reflect on what you've learned and apply the results to improve your final pitch.

4. **Critical thinking and problem solving** – Think of the pitch as a problem in itself. You need to design, develop and deliver a compelling pitch in order to achieve your objectives of addressing the problem or achieving a good grade and/or approval and funding to progress your idea further.

5. **Empathy and communication** – You'll need to generate empathy for your audience, by considering what's most important to them – rather than you – when developing the

pitch. During the pitch itself, you'll need to engage with your audience and positively communicate the value and wow factor of your idea.

6. **Resilience and managing change** – When delivering a pitch, no matter how well you prepare and practise, something unexpected may well happen or go wrong on the day. For example, a team member becomes ill, or the technology doesn't work, or an audience member asks an unexpectedly awkward question, and so on. You'll need to be resilient when such problems happen and manage and overcome such changes when they occur.

7. **Commercial awareness** – We bet you know what we're going to say next! You can have the best idea in the world but if you can't communicate it – and communicate the value of it – it's likely to go nowhere. Being able to articulate the commercial value of your innovation to your sponsor or module leaders, and the value to end users, will be key enablers for the success of your pitch.

PRESENTING AND PITCHING

Presenting is about one or more people communicating with an audience. The objective generally is to share information to increase levels of knowledge and understanding, although sometimes it may also be about providing entertainment. There are many different forms and formats for presentations. These include lectures, briefings, speeches and so on. If you think about it, even stand-up comedy is a form of presentation – and we can actually learn a lot from having a look at what stand-up comedians do when they engage with their audience.

An innovation pitch is simply one specific type of presentation. As with all presentations, there are presenters, an audience and objectives. Typically, the objectives of a specific pitch will go well beyond increasing levels of knowledge and entertaining the audience. The primary objective is usually to persuade or convince someone to support and perhaps invest in your idea or solution, so that it can be further developed and ultimately delivered to generate value.

In order to get someone to agree to invest in your idea, you'll need to convince them of (at least) two things:

1. **The idea will work** – And really will address the problem(s) you're looking to solve.
2. **There's sufficient value** – The value generated is likely to be significantly large enough to outweigh any costs and investment, taking into account risks along the way. That's not to say a positive outcome will be guaranteed. Most sponsors and investors understand this, but they do need to be convinced that the potential benefits are large enough to justify taking the risk that the project may fail.

Effectively, in an innovation pitch you're 'selling' the feasibility and value of your idea to your audience, whether they're module leaders, project sponsors or external investors.

Before you can effectively do this, you first need to know who your audience will be, generate empathy and understand what is most important to them. Once you've done that, you can develop your pitch.

Innovation is a competitive field. You want your pitch to stand out. Think about some of the 'presentations' you've attended in the past.

What adjectives would you use to describe each one? Boring, dull, interesting, informative, useful, very useful, entertaining, funny, laugh out loud funny, inspiring, motivating?

Why were some of them memorable and impactful and others instantly forgettable? Think about this as you develop your own pitch. To persuade or convince your audience, you're going to need to show them that your idea will work, has sufficient value and that your pitch stands out from the crowd. To make it stand out, it's going to need a wow factor. We'll come back to this shortly.

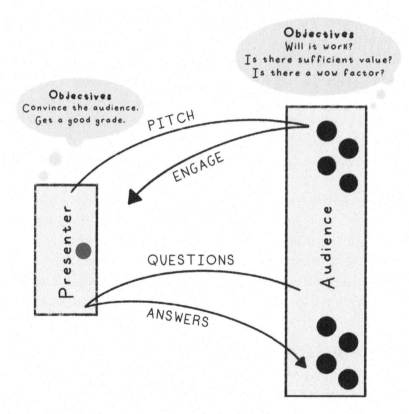

FIGURE 10.2: Elements of a pitch: Presenter(s), audience and objectives

KNOWING YOUR AUDIENCE

Knowing and having empathy with your audience is critically important.
This is good news really, because you can tap into many of the things you learned earlier
in this book and so far in your project. When we tasked you with understanding the
problem, you spent time undertaking research. Now we recommend that you do the same
with your audience. What do you know about them? What's important to them? What do
they like and dislike? Depending on the specific audience, you might be able to speak to
them directly beforehand or speak to people around them and/or carry out some research
online to find out more about them.

For example, when one of the book's authors, Tony, worked for IBM, each year he
presented IBM's latest view of technology futures to IBM clients. When he was asked to
speak to a specific client organisation, he would ask the IBM team who knew the client
well a set of questions. 'Who will be there? What is most important to the individuals
and their organisation? What do they like? What do they not like? What else do I need
to be aware of?'

One year, Tony was asked to present to a senior executive and his team at a major
pharmaceutical company. As part of his preparation, Tony discovered that the executive
hated presentation tools like PowerPoint. Knowing this, Tony reworked his presentation,
so he could deliver it without PowerPoint, by drawing up six flip charts. The session went
really well. Afterwards, the executive informed Tony that it was one of the best presentations
he'd ever attended, saying, 'It was almost as if you knew how much I hate slides'. Of course,
Tony did know this – but only because he'd researched his audience.

Whenever we present, we should find out what we can about the audience and adapt
accordingly.

In addition to carrying out research, you can also tap into many of the Design Thinking
techniques you've already used to generate empathy and so on. If you don't know the
audience very well, or even if you do, why not create an End User Persona and an Empathy
Map for them? This will help to ensure you see things from their perspective, rather than
your own. Thinking through what an audience might do, say, think and feel about your
presentation or pitch is likely to give you some great tips on which areas to focus on and
which to avoid.

KNOWING YOURSELF AND YOUR TEAM

Knowing the audience is one thing, but you also need to understand your own and
your team's strengths, weaknesses and preferences. You have now worked together
for a while.

PRESENTATION IS A SKILL WHICH CAN BE LEARNED

At this stage, we want to reassure you. We understand and appreciate presenting and pitching can appear to be quite a daunting task for many people, including many students. Please don't worry unduly about this. To reassure you, most people are NOT naturally gifted presenters from birth. Even the best presenters and public speakers didn't start out that way. They use hints, tips, techniques and experience to get better and more confident over time.

The great news is that there are some extremely accessible and easy to use hints and tips which can help you to improve your presentation and pitching skills very quickly.

IT'S NATURAL TO BE NERVOUS

In fact, a level of nerves is a good thing – it means you care about what you are doing. Even when they've been performing for a number of years, many leading sportspeople and actors continue to feel nervous in the run up to a major match or event, or before they step onto the stage. For many, this nervous tension helps make them so good at what they do.

Presenting and pitching is similar. When you've watched a great TED talk, it's likely you were unaware how nervous the speaker might have been before the camera started rolling. Once again, there are hints and tips which you can use to make you feel more comfortable and confident when the pitch starts. We'll get to these shortly.

Before we do, we recommend you review your own and your team's strengths and preferences in two steps. Firstly, by diverging and carrying out a personal individual reflection, and secondly, by converging and reflecting on the overall power and preferences of the team.

REFLECTION POINT: PRESENTATION AND PITCHING – KNOWING YOURSELF

Consider the following questions. Make a note of your answers in the space provided and/or in your journal.

1. WHEN IT COMES TO PRESENTING, WHAT DO YOU CONSIDER ARE YOUR PERSONAL STRENGTHS AND PREFERENCES?

(For example, potential strengths may include experiences gained from previous presentations, confidence when speaking to an audience and so on. Preferences may include small

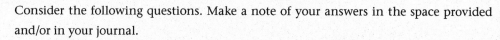

(Continued)

or large audiences, presenting on one's own and/or with a team, generating interactions with the audience, use of humour and so on.)

2. WHEN IT COMES TO PRESENTING, WHAT DO YOU CONSIDER ARE YOUR POTENTIAL AREAS FOR IMPROVEMENT AND/OR CONCERNS?

(For example, potential areas for improvement and concerns may include limited experience gained from previous presentations, concerns over confidence, answering questions and so on.)

3. WHAT AREA(S) WOULD YOU MOST LIKE TO BE INVOLVED IN WHEN DELIVERING YOUR TEAM'S PITCH? ANSWER IN ORDER OF PREFERENCE, WITH 1 BEING THE AREA YOU'D MOST LIKE TO BE INVOLVED IN AND 10 BEING THE ONE YOU'D LEAST LIKE TO BE INVOLVED IN. (YOUR ANSWERS WON'T MEAN YOU WILL, WON'T, SHOULD OR SHOULDN'T COVER SPECIFIC AREAS, BUT IT WILL BE USEFUL TO KNOW WHEN YOUR TEAM CONVERGES.)

Area	Preference (1 high to 10 low)
Opening the pitch	
Explaining the challenge	
Describing the idea	
Demonstrating prototypes	
Storytelling	
Role play	
Articulating the business case	
Closing the pitch	
Answering questions	
Other item – add a row for each	

Once all team members have completed the above reflection, it's time to converge and understand each team member's preferences for delivering the pitch.

TEAM ACTIVITY: KNOWING THE TEAM – ESTIMATED TIME 30 MINUTES

Arrange a meeting with all team members with one of you agreeing to act as organiser and facilitator. All team members are asked to prepare the reflection exercise above in preparation for the meeting.

1. AT THE BEGINNING OF THE MEETING, WALK THROUGH TEAM PREFERENCES TO UNDERSTAND TEAM MEMBER PREFERENCES.

a. Create a simple table (or spreadsheet) as shown below or use the table in the book.

b. Populate the table with each team member's preferences, as identified in the previous self-reflection activity.

(Continued)

Area	Person	Person	Person	Person	Person	Person
Opening the pitch						
Explaining the challenge						
Describing the idea						
Demonstrating prototypes						
Storytelling						
Role play						
Articulating the business case						
Closing the pitch						
Answering questions						
Other item – add a row for each						

2. HOLD A SHORT GROUP DISCUSSION, WALKING THROUGH EACH ROW OF THE TABLE TO BRING ALL TEAM MEMBERS UP TO SPEED REGARDING TEAM MEMBER PREFERENCES.

3. AGREE THE FOLLOWING POINTS

- Team member preferences in the table will be taken into account when allocating areas of the pitch to team members.
- Not every team member will get their ideal preference.
- The team will allocate sections of the pitch based upon the agreed structure of the pitch and what the team collectively decides will be best for the team as a whole.

ACTIVITY OUTPUT

- The output of this activity will be the completed table, which the team will return to later.

WOW FACTOR

An innovation pitch needs to stand out from the crowd. For this, you'll need a wow factor.

The concept of the wow factor is about incorporating a quality or a feature of something else in your pitch that will make your audience feel excited about it and make them remember what they've seen and heard for a long time afterwards.

You want to leave your audience thinking and/or saying 'Wow!' about the pitch.

FIGURE 10.3: Wow!

You'll remember in Design Thinking the wow factor is a key element of a Hill, with Hills being structured as follows:

- **Who** – A specific user or a group of users.
- **What** – What the user(s) will be able to do.
- **Wow** – Why this is different or exciting.

During commercial development, you created a value proposition statement for your idea. Many value proposition statements include a differentiating factor which shows how the solution is exciting or different. This is also a wow factor.

Hills and value proposition statements describe potential wow factors for end users.

The wow factor for sponsors may come from elsewhere. This could be in the business case. If your innovation generates or saves a huge amount of money, or addresses another key performance indicator – for example, significantly reducing patient waiting lists in a hospital – this would certainly make most sponsors say 'Wow!'

In terms of pitches, the wow factor can take many forms. Here are a few examples:

- The idea itself.
- Demonstration of the prototype.
- The value proposition statement.
- Elements of a business case – particularly the size of the benefits.
- Specific presentation content – e.g., use of stories, role play and/or videos which make the pitch stand out.
- A high impact opening and/or close of the pitch.

There may be different wow factors for the end user and the sponsor. You may want to bring out both in your pitch.

The key thing for you to consider and plan for when developing your pitch is to ensure your pitch does stand out and does have a real wow factor for your specific audience.

DEVELOPING THE INNOVATION PITCH

The term 'pitch' is usually used for very short presentations that pitch an idea, concept, service or product. Short 'elevator pitches' draw on the idea that one should be able to communicate a summary of one's idea or enterprise in the time span of an elevator ride. On the other end of the spectrum, some detailed project presentations can last up to an hour – or even longer!

When we work with students, we usually ask for team presentations of about seven minutes. This gives a team some time to elaborate but also forces the team to be very clear about what needs to be included. It is important to remember that whatever form a pitch takes, both content and delivery count. Even if delivered in a very engaging way, a bad idea remains a bad idea. Conversely, a great idea may not be recognised as such if it isn't communicated effectively.

Before we proceed, we recommend each team member, or the whole team collectively together if the team is physically co-located, watches one or more example pitches. There are many examples available on the internet, some from TV shows that involve pitching such as 'Dragons' Den' in the UK (or the US and Australian 'Shark Tank') but also recordings of pitches for start-up competitions such as the Canadian 'Startupfest' and others. Have a look and find some examples that you like. Perhaps you have a particular topic or setting you are interested in? Share some good examples with your team. Schedule a meeting and discuss the pitches each of you had selected.

- What did you like about it? What didn't you like?
- Was this about the content or the way it was delivered?
- Did anything stand out? Was there a wow factor that you'll remember in future?

UNDERSTANDING PITCHING

There is an entire literature on how to deliver the perfect pitch. Numerous frameworks, strategies and templates are promoted in books, articles, videos, podcasts and blogs. But how do we know what works? Powerful examples and anecdotes can inspire us – but they do not provide a solid evidence base.

Research has shown that in the initial assessment, investors often do not use a complex decision model with a large number of attributes; rather, they look for fatal flaws on which basis they could reject a proposition (Maxwell et al., 2011). Using stories and metaphors can be of great advantage not just because they engage the audience in a personal or emotional way, but also because they cannot be scrutinised like statistics (Anderson, 2005). 'The best narratives draw in the audience to create a familiar reality that otherwise does not exist' (Pollack et al., 2012, p. 919) – after all a pitch is about the *future* in which such reality may come into existence. Familiarity builds credibility.

While it helps to engage with the audience's emotions (remember our sections on personas and storytelling), there are limits. A research study on 'entrepreneurial passion' showed that preparedness rather than passion had a positive impact on the decisions of venture capitalists to invest (Chen et al., 2009). An analysis of pitches aired on television also showed that for successful pitches, it is key to enact behaviours that give the audience an impression of preparedness and legitimacy (Pollack et al., 2012).

Research – as well as the diversity of different models and approaches – shows that there isn't one right way to deliver a compelling innovation pitch. Your successful pitch should therefore engage and entertain, it should deliver a great idea and make the audience feel wowed – yet at the same time, you need to be well-prepared and credible. When we are asked if we can provide a template with the best steps and suggested structure for a good pitch we always (very politely) answer, 'Sorry, no we can't'. We're happy to provide recommendations and hints and tips, but each pitch should be different. After all, we want you to wow an audience with *your* idea! In some modules (and competitions!), there may be ten, twelve or even more teams pitching one after another. If we provided a standard format for this, the presentations would soon become very boring indeed.

IMPORTANCE OF BEING UNIQUE

You can take lessons learned and positive approaches from other pitches and presentations you've seen. You can also learn a lot from professionals sharing tips online and from our industry experts Paul and Eva (see their interviews later in this chapter).

Ultimately, however, you should aim to make your own pitch unique.

Instead of providing a template, we're therefore highlighting a series of 'considerations' of what we think you might wish to include in your team's innovation pitch. Please read and review these but feel free to diverge from them, where you feel it makes more sense to do so. Feel free to innovate and do your own thing – based upon your knowledge of your challenge, idea, the value, your audience, your own and team's strengths, weaknesses and preferences, and what you've been tasked to do.

We've listed the considerations below. We recommend you review these, become familiar with them and reference them again during the team-based 'Develop your innovation pitch' activity below, as they should be very useful.

CONTENT AND MEDIA

Here is a list of the potential content elements we think will generally be most useful to consider when developing your team's own innovation pitch:

- The **challenge and/or the problem** your team is looking to solve.
- The **idea and solution**.
- A **demonstration of the prototype** – typically built around an end user story (see below).
- The **value** of the idea to the **end user**.
- The **business case, value and benefits** for the **sponsor(s)**/investor(s).
- A **wow factor** (see below).
- **Anything else you consider will be valuable and meet the objectives** and expectations of your audience – for example, for a financial audience detailed numbers may be most important.

The figure below summarises the elements which can be included in an effective pitch.

Some people prefer to have these things organised in a canvas with different boxes – a little bit like the prominent Business Model or Value Proposition Canvas. In our experience, it can be difficult to fit everything into such a document, so we suggest that you work with a flip chart and post-its, a shared document or use a blank space on you team MURAL.

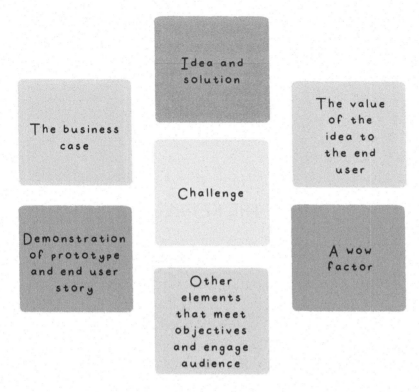

FIGURE 10.4: Considerations for your pitch

EXPERT

PITCHING

Paul Hallett is the Co-Founder of Vet-AI, an innovative start-up organisation which is using ground-breaking technologies, such as artificial intelligence, to revolutionise the pet care industry.

1. BEFORE YOU PITCH, DO YOUR RESEARCH YOUR AUDIENCE?

Yes, definitely. In particular, we verify whether an investor will be a good fit for our business or not. At Vet-AI, we get enquiries from potential investors every week, so there's a lot of filtering to be done before we can even think about a pitch.

(Continued)

This is important. We need to know if an investor will be a good fit for us, and whether it's likely we'll be a good fit for them. If not, we'll both end up wasting time and effort.

The questions asked might be different for each organisation. For us, it's about asking whether they have B2C [business-to-consumer] experience, what sort of projects they normally invest in and what's in their existing portfolio? Additionally, we consider commercial and operational aspects. For example, what sort of shareholding in our business, or other commercial approach, might they want to consider? How actively might they want to be involved in decision making?

It's only once we've done this homework and agreed a good fit, we'll begin to plan the pitch.

2. WHAT ARE SOME OF THE KEY ELEMENTS YOU INCLUDE IN A PITCH?

Obviously, we've got our ideas and value proposition. It's then about communicating the opportunity and size of the business case, articulating the final vision and commercialisation plan. We need to show how we're going to convert all this into real revenue. For example, by highlighting what we've got is something customers want and will be willing to pay for.

But there's something else too. For us, it's really important to amplify the 'why' behind what we do. Our focus centres on mental health and animal welfare. These are the core motivations for everything we do. And we track these things beyond profit. Of course, this is an interesting message to take to an investor, but we can also show how profit comes as a consequence from delivering things which have a real meaning for people.

Our pitches are also very visual. A great picture paints a thousand words.

Lastly, it's important to have a great structure and close. It's like a book. You've got to generate interest in the first chapter. Then you've got the body of the book and it needs to end well. You need to ensure your audience leaves that meeting with something they're going to remember.

3. OFTEN OUR STUDENTS PITCH AS A TEAM. DO YOU HAVE ANY RECOMMENDATIONS FOR TEAM-BASED PITCHES?

We always do team pitches. We have a great team. Each member has their own key strengths and areas of expertise.

We prepare for each pitch as a team. Each slide and key message is given an owner, the expert in that area. And we rehearse together.

For the pitch itself, we walk into the room as a team. We pitch as a team and, at the end of the session, we leave as a team.

My recommendation for students is to take the same approach. Make use of your individual strengths and expertise but work collectively for the good of everyone in the team.

Working in this way with multiple personalities and voices is also much more engaging, so much better than listening to one person speak for the whole time.

4. WE KNOW PITCHES SOMETIMES FAIL. PERHAPS THEY DON'T QUITE HIT THE SPOT. WHAT MIGHT YOU DO AFTER A LESS SUCCESSFUL PITCH?

Get feedback. There will always be failures, the important thing is what we learn from them. Ask the audience, 'What can we improve? What did we miss that you were looking for?' and so on.

5. CONVERSELY, WHAT DO YOU DO AFTERWARDS WHEN A PITCH GOES WELL?

Build momentum. We'll follow up quickly with agreed actions and more information. Often, we'll send details of a strong and relevant case study to demonstrate an example of the work we do and where we can take this together. Once we've got interest, momentum is key. We need to find out if we're going to partner and, if so, move forward.

TOP TIP

Most importantly for me, it's about putting the problem front and centre. Generate a clear understanding of why you're doing what you're doing. Once you've done that, you can go on and show how you're going to solve this problem.

Having decided on the content, it is now time to consider the media you want to use in your presentation.

Contrary to some beliefs, presentations and pitches do NOT have to use a presentation tool such as PowerPoint, Prezzi or Keynote! Of course, slides (particularly visual ones) can be a great aid and provide structure for your pitch, but it's the message, and the way you convey your message for your specific audience, which are more important.

You may decide to just speak, use a presentation tool, show a video, use role play, demonstrate a functional prototype, draw up flipcharts, provide handouts, use props and so on. Most teams will use a combination of a number of these and other approaches.

If using slides, in general we'd suggest you make them visual, rather than wordy. Ensure they align with, enhance and reinforce what the team are saying when they're on screen.

Equally, ensure they don't distract attention away from the team's main messages. You don't want the audience to be busy reading words from the screen, rather than listening to, hearing and reacting to what you're saying.

If you plan to use multiple technologies and/or screens, ensure you have smooth transitions between them. As recommended below, practise the changeovers.

One additional point to consider is what media works best depending on whether your pitch will be delivered in a physical room or online. We'll return to this point below. Let us first have a closer look at the structure of an innovation pitch.

STRUCTURE OF AN INNOVATION PITCH

In Chapter 6, we highlighted the power of storytelling. If you remember, most stories have a common structure, as shown in Figure 10.5.

It is often helpful to structure your team's pitch just like in a story:

1. Beginning – with a strong opening – to capture attention.
- For example, saying something like, 'Today, we're going to show you how you can save 20 million pounds' will likely get people listening to you. Of course, if you make a claim like this, you'll need to back it up during the rest of your pitch.
- The important thing with the opening is to grab the attention of your audience. How you do this is down to you and your team to decide.

2. Middle – the majority of the content – explained in an engaging way to maintain attention.
- This is where you may highlight the problem, the idea, solution and value.
- We recommend you centre the demonstration of your prototype around a powerful end user story. In the context of your pitch, this will be telling a 'story within a story'.
- The **characters** are likely to include one or more end users. Give them names and make the audience care about what happens to them. Characters can be developed using End User Personas, etc. Sometimes, you can also use your own experiences or that of the persons you pitch to.
- The **setting** will be a home, a workplace or other location, which is relevant for the challenges and end users.
- Develop the **plot** using a storyboard. Begin with the end user's problems (the conflict), in the middle show how your idea and solution will address these, for example by demonstrating the prototype (the resolution) and end with the value (the happy ending) for the end user and sponsor.
- Of course, there will be other things which you may wish to include in the middle of your pitch.

3. **End** – with a strong closing – so you'll be remembered.
   - Avoid ending on an anti-climax by saying something like, 'Well, um, ah well, that's the end of our presentation'.
   - We recommend you end instead with something which will be important and memorable for your audience. How you do this is down to you and your team to decide!
   - If you use visuals, also make sure that you end on a high – and certainly not just a 'thank you' slide. You want to end with something you want them to remember!

4. Questions and answers.
   - Pitches usually end with Q&A sessions.
   - You need to be prepared. This is where your research and thinking throughout the project will pay dividends. As part of your development and preparation, think about what questions are likely to be asked by the audience – and practise answering them. You may have some materials prepared, a slide with a diagram or some stats, but don't overdo that. Think about the practicalities (you don't want to sift through lots of papers or scroll through additional slides).

Now, at last, it is time to develop your pitch!

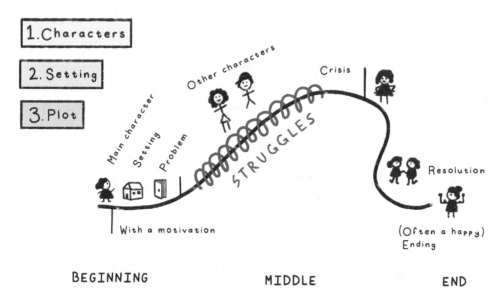

FIGURE 10.5: Structure and elements of a story

TEAM ACTIVITY: DEVELOP YOUR INNOVATION PITCH – ESTIMATED TIME 60 MINUTES PLUS

Arrange a team meeting – either face to face or online. Make sure that one of you has agreed to prepare and facilitate.

1. UNDERSTAND THE OBJECTIVES AND RULES OF THE GAME

- Before you start, ensure every team member understands and agrees of the objective(s) of the pitch. That way, you'll be moving forward together towards achieving a common goal.
- Ensure you have reviewed what you've been tasked to do. For example, most modules will provide some structure, guidance and/or constraints for your pitch. This might include scoring criteria, marking criteria, guidance on the audience, objectives, content, structure, timing and so on.
- Create a checklist of what you're being tasked to do.
- Research and discuss your audience – who will you be pitching to? What is their motivation? What are they interested in? Consider creating an empathy map for your target audience.

2. DEVELOP A STRUCTURE FOR YOUR PITCH

- Create a structure for your pitch – with a strong opening, engaging main section and a strong close, as described above.
- Some teams may decide to create a storyboard for this – often with more than six blocks.
- In the middle section, e.g., where you demonstrate your prototype by telling a story, you may decide to create a storyboard within a storyboard.

3. INCORPORATE THE WOW FACTOR

- Identify the wow factor element(s) in your pitch.
- Agree how this will be included and communicated.

4. ALLOCATE SECTIONS OF THE PITCH TO INDIVIDUAL TEAM MEMBERS

- Using the output of the 'Knowing the team' activity above, where possible take into account each team member's strengths and preferences.
- Agree which parts of the pitch will be allocated to each team member.

- Assign role(s) for use of technology – e.g., who will present slides, share screen, drive prototype demonstrations, etc.
- Create a backup plan for the use of technology – e.g., if a team member's device or connectivity fails, who will present, e.g., if a prototype demonstration fails, what will the team do and so on.

5. DEVELOP THE DETAILED CONTENT

- Depending on the pitch and team, some of the detailed content may be developed by individual team members, pairs or small groups or the whole team.
- Once the individual sections have been completed, bring the content together to create the whole. Ensure slides are formatted in a consistent way to give the pitch material a distinctive and coherent look and feel.

6. CHECK YOU'RE ADDRESSING THE RULES OF THE GAME

- Walk through the checklist you created in the first step above.
- Ensure you have addressed everything you need to.
- If there are gaps, iterate and address them by updating the structure and detailed content as required.

ACTIVITY OUTPUT

- The output of this activity will be a completed storyboard or other documented description of the pitch structure, and the developed content of the pitch.

EXPERT

COMMUNICATING VALUE

Dr Eva-Marie Muller-Stuler is Chief Data Scientist and leader of the Advanced Analytics and AI practice of IBM Middle East and Africa. Eva has developed and implemented large-scale AI projects for over 15 years. She is also a successful investor, consultant and mentor for innovative start-ups, both fin-tech and other.

(Continued)

1. YOU HAVE DELIVERED SO MANY PITCHES BOTH INTERNALLY AND FOR CLIENTS. CAN YOU PERHAPS SHARE WITH US ONE EXPERIENCE WHERE YOU LEARNT A LOT ABOUT PITCHING?

 A good pitch is about preparation – but you also need to have your wits about you. I was once at a client with the wrong brief as to what they needed. My team had thought that the client wanted new spreadsheets but early into the conversation it turned out that such an approach would not solve their problems. What they actually needed was a complete setup of their data governance. Of course, this was more expensive at first, but it resolved their underlying problem. Everything else would have been just another short-term workaround. When I raised this, my pivot was welcomed by the client, and I won the pitch and the project.

Two lessons I took away from this experience were to always ensure that you and the client are on the same page, and to adopt an agile approach to every meeting. Even when pitching, you have to be able to take on board new information. Also, have the courage to be open and honest. It can help to build trust and rapport when you say: 'I have to think about this and will get back to you'.

2. WHAT ARE THE KEY INGREDIENTS NEEDED FOR A GREAT PITCH?

There is a great saying: 'the bait has to be appetising for the fish not for the fisherman'. To further this point, there are three key 'ingredients' to consider.

First, you need to know your subject. If you know your subject matter better than anyone you know, you have the confidence to be more than just a pitch giver, you are a subject matter expert. This makes the client feel comfortable with your level of knowledge. You want to move from a Client–Salesperson relationship to a Patient–Specialist one.

Second, you need to understand the real problem. We are often brought in to sell or deliver our solution to a problem that was posed by another group, department or organisation. This scenario often leads to confusion and the wrong problem being solved. By focusing on the actual problem, identifying the true stakeholders and finding out what the pain points are, you are able to address the heart of the problem, which makes your expertise even more trustworthy.

Third, you need to empathise with the client. We can find ourselves in situations where we face criticism from the very people we seek assistance from, and this creates a negative spiral of self doubt and harmful justification. An example of this could be in the dentist chair or our first meeting with a personal trainer. This is the last feeling we want our clients to experience. The right way to avoid these situations is to use our true empathy and focus on our client's pain as our own.

3. HOW BEST TO COMMUNICATE VALUE?

Don't ever let your customer confuse price with value. We too often see the conversation focus around if the competition can offer something cheaper, but it should be to build something of quality that adds value, ensuring the client achieves their ambition. It always pays off to be as customer-centric as possible. In order to deliver value, we need to understand it from the client's business perspective. If we do not understand their ambitions, the 'value' we create won't be that valuable. So, it is imperative to focus on what will make the most valuable impact for the client and explore it together with them. Once this exercise is complete, it is time to consider your communication strategy.

This is where being as clear as possible about this value and how it can be achieved has served me well. Don't leave the client guessing; it's not a good idea to play games with ambiguous messages. Rather be specific about what has been discovered, what is being suggested and how it will be achieved.

4. IN YOUR EXPERIENCE, WHAT DELIVERS THE BEST WOW FACTOR?

Presenters often focus on the media rather than the message. A glossy PowerPoint presentation doesn't necessarily come across that well. My advice when delivering a pitch?

Understand the problem better than your customer. Tell the story and communicate the solution. Be brief; our client's time is valuable so treat it with respect. Be direct; tell the client what they need to know to be able to move forward to the next stage and from there to contract. Build the relationship and interact.

5. WHAT THINGS ARE BEST AVOIDED? ANY EXAMPLES?

Often, I see people being overconfident when pitching their first offer to the client, and not really caring about or understanding the underlying issues. In software development we say: if the client comes to you because he wants a bridge, before you go ahead and build the first

(Continued)

bridge you have some material for, ask yourself if the problem is actually about the best way to cross the water – and there might be better and cheaper solutions than building a bridge.

TOP TIP

The experience of the Covid pandemic showed us how important it is to stay agile and adapt to new circumstances. Within days, we had to move from face-to-face workshops to doing it all remotely. Too many calls involved one person presenting slides for an hour and more, completely losing the audience in the process. When you are presenting virtually, it's even more important that you stay focused on your clients. There are many useful tools out there that enable you to have more interactive sessions. Virtual whiteboards, project management applications, virtual backgrounds and coffee places (just to name a few), they all allow us to stay connected and engage with others in more creative and often more personal ways.

PRACTICE MAKES BETTER (MUCH, MUCH BETTER)

Once the team has allocated sections to team members and the structure and content has been developed, it's time to practise – on your own and with your team.

We considered calling this section 'Practice makes perfect' but decided this was unrealistic. After all, unexpected issues and mistakes will likely still occur, no matter how much you rehearse. However, practice will make your personal contribution and the team's overall pitch better – usually much, much better.

We love this quote, often attributed to a famous golfer, who was quite upset because people in the media claimed he'd only won so many tournaments because he was a 'lucky' golfer. This is what he said: 'The funny thing is the more I practise, the luckier I get'.

It's exactly the same for your presentations and pitches.

The more you practise, the luckier (and better) you'll get!

Here are our recommendations for preparing and practising your pitch. Most are relevant for any type of presentation.

PERSONAL CONSIDERATIONS

- Think of the audience as your friends.
  - Most audiences will want you to succeed.
  - Think of it as like giving a speech at a wedding. You may be nervous – but the happy couple and all the guests want you to do well.

FIGURE 10.6: Perfect pitching

- Play to your strengths.
    - Do or say things which will make you feel comfortable.
    - If you like interaction rather than just a one-way communication, ask the audience some questions. If you have a big audience, you can ask for a show of hands. If you're using an online tool such as Zoom, you can ask people to put 'Yes' or 'No' into a chat or use polling tools.
    - Some people find humour makes them feel comfortable, so say something relatively funny (while still being professional) to raise a smile and calm your nerves.
    - The above are just two examples. Think about what might make you comfortable and will play to your strengths and try it out to see what works best for you – and your audience.

- Take your time.
  - If you talk too quickly, the audience will struggle to take in and react to what you say.
  - Say out loud what you plan to say and practise slowing yourself down. Take a breath now and then. It will really help.
- Keep your wording and messages simple.
  - Simple language and simple words will be easier for you to deliver and for your audience to understand.
- Pause at key points.
  - Pauses allow your audience to take in what you've said.
  - When you make a key point, or if you ask a rhetorical question, take a breath and pause.
  - Use the time to gauge the reaction of the audience.
  - This way, you'll gain maximum impact.
- Try out the 'The Rule of Three'.
  - This is a great public speaking tip which lots of professional presenters and politicians use.
  - For some reason, our brains seem to like processing information in lists of three. Short lists of three stick much better than lists of four or five, etc.
  - Here are a few examples:
    - 'Veni, vidi, vici' (I came, I saw, I conquered) – Julius Caesar.
    - 'Blood, sweat and tears' – General Patton.
    - 'There are three kinds of lies: lies, damned lies and statistics' (popularised by Mark Twain).
    - 'The good, the bad and the ugly' (the famous spaghetti western film).
    - 'There are three main stages of the innovation management process: ideation, development, delivery' (the authors of this book!).
    - We ask you which sounds better: 'Bacon, lettuce and tomato' or 'Bacon, lettuce, mayo and tomato'? (Yes, the rule of three is in part to blame for the success of the BLT across the British Isles and beyond…)
  - Consider how you can use the 'Rule of Three' in your own presentations and pitches.

PRACTICE

Usually, we recommend having some individual as well as team practice ahead of the big day. Let's start with the **personal practice**:

- Practise what you plan to say – first on your own and later on with your team.

- You can create a script to start with, but don't try to remember it verbatim or repeat every word. Improvise around the main points. Use a cue card with a few words as a summary for each key point if useful.
- Practise speaking the words out loud – this will make a big difference.
- If you're comfortable, use a mirror or record yourself. Don't worry if it freaks you out initially, just focus on the positives – what was good and what can be further improved?
- Identify words or phrases you find yourself stumbling over – if you keep stumbling over them, change them and say something else.
- Identify phrases which have impact or wow factor – and practise pausing for effect as described above when you've said them.
- The more you practise, the more comfortable and confident you'll become.

It is also important to practise together as a team:

- Each team member delivers their own section.
- Practise the hand overs between team members, cues for next slides, etc.
- Practise how you'll manage the timing (many pitches run under time constraints).
- Agree how you'll handle questions and think of any difficult questions which are likely to come up – have an allocated team member ready to answer them.
- Practise in the same room or using the same online technology which will be used for the pitch. This is really important. If you do this, things are much more likely to go right on the day because you'll have already encountered and addressed what might go wrong.
- Think through what might go wrong and be prepared... The more you think about and prepare for what might go wrong, the fewer problems you're likely to have.

When it comes to the actual speaking bit, we usually suggest learning from the best. Just think back to a talk or pitch you really liked and consider what the speaker did. There are also some great resources such as a TED talk playlist about presentation skills.

We appreciate that some of you will find public speaking more difficult than others. Not everyone feels comfortable speaking in front of a large audience! Some of you will be asked to present in a language that you still do not feel entirely confident to use. Lena (one of the authors) still remembers very well how terrified she was when she was asked for the first time to deliver a presentation in English! She practised and practised and practised. In the end rushed it a little (maybe because she could just reel it off...) – but she came through it and learnt from the experience. Now she can present with confidence in both German and English. So, the investment was definitely worth it. And we all keep on learning! At a seminar with a professional from an Opera House, Lena discovered that she used different voices when speaking English and German (yes, such things exist) – and that she could improve her breathing. Again, this discovery made a huge difference when she then started to deliver longer lectures.

There are many challenges when it comes to public speaking – but also many ways to rise to these challenges. It makes sense to invest in these skills. After all, good communication skills and the ability to deliver a good talk or pitch can make a huge difference to your future career. So, if you start on a lower level, this is not a big deal. It just means that you can benefit even more from studying some good examples and engaging in some practice. Sometimes, we need to push ourselves a little and go beyond our comfort zone. You will find that doing so regularly shifts the boundary of your comfort zone, making it bigger and opening up new opportunities.

IF/WHEN THINGS GO WRONG

Practising and preparing will really aid your team. However, unexpected issues, difficult questions and even mistakes will sometimes happen. Once again, our advice here is don't worry about it. It happens (and has happened many times) to the best presenters. The good news is that to a degree you can prepare for this, too!

Think back to the previous chapter and the content and recommendations we made about managing change and becoming resilient. This is the sort of approach you need to take. In addition, we've provided some additional hints and tips below about if or when things go wrong during your presentations and pitches.

When things go wrong...

- Correct the problem, or find a way around it, and continue.
- Stuff happens and most of us have been there. Most experienced audience members will feel empathy for you.
- In general, if something goes wrong (let's say a demo fails or connectivity drops), you can offer a polite apology but don't dwell on the negative side of things or apologise too much. This may detract from your overall positive message, which is much more important. So, better to move on ASAP!
- In general, the audience wants you to do well, so they'll forgive the odd glitch or mistake. Sometimes, you can even make a joke about it.
- If you get your words wrong – simply correct the mistake and move on.
- If you forget something – don't worry.
    - This is something we (the authors) personally used to fret too much over – if we forgot to say this or that when delivering a lecture, pitch or a webinar. The truth is the audience didn't know what you were going to say, and so probably didn't even notice you left something out.

- o If you remember in time, perhaps you can cover it later. If not, try not to worry. Anything you've forgotten to say will usually be far outweighed by the much greater amount of good stuff you and your team remembered.
- o Remember, you can help each other out! Sometimes a team member can pick up what you have forgotten to say, and sometimes this is not possible.
- o We've learned to forgive ourselves for occasionally making mistakes. You can, too!
- If you have one of those blank moments…
  - o We've all been there. Things are flowing along nicely and then wham! Your mind goes blank, and you can't remember what you were going to say next.
  - o When/if this happens to you, take a breath. Take a moment. It may come back to you. If it does, no one has probably even noticed. You can just continue.
  - o If it doesn't, perhaps a team member can help.
  - o If not, relax. Move on to what you were going to say next. Unless it's an absolutely key point, you can probably simply miss it out.

FINAL PREPARATIONS

Finally, we've reached the stage where you and your team can deliver your innovation pitch. We provide below a final checklist for preparing to deliver your pitch, for a physical room and for online.

Let us start with **face-to-face presentations**. Here we suggest paying special attention to:

- Personal appearance.
  - o Consider your personal appearance and ensure your choice of clothing is appropriate.
- Team member positioning.
  - o Agree the positioning of team members in the room – in relation to each other, the projector, screen and audience, etc.
- Minimise disruptions.
  - o Close down unnecessary apps and programs on the presenters' laptops or other devices, switch off sounds and alerts on everyone's laptop and smartphones, etc. Check if you have any overdue updates that could disrupt your presentation.
- Have slides, demos and props ready.
  - o Ensure slides are pre-loaded and set to screen show mode, ensure demos and props are where they should be.
  - o Ensure alternative team members have alternative devices ready in case of issues. Make sure that you have all login details ready if you use presentation tools from an online platform. (Lena once had a speaker who struggled to access his colleague's presentation…)

- Engage the audience when you're speaking.
  - Engage members of the audience when speaking using eye contact and positive facial expressions and body language.
- Be engaged and supportive when you're not speaking.
  - Use supportive facial expressions and body language when other team members are presenting. Nod your head if someone says something important, smile if they say something funny, etc.

Let us now consider **online presentations**. As you will see there is some overlap – but also a number of additional things to consider:

- Personal appearance.
  - As with presenting in person, consider your personal appearance and ensure your choice of on-screen clothing is appropriate.
  - Ensure your head and shoulders are in the centre of the screen when the camera is on.
- Check room lighting and background.
  - Don't go overboard, but check the lighting is okay and look at what can be seen in your room. You don't need to redecorate, but nobody wants to see your socks drying on a radiator behind you!
  - Optionally, you can use a background filter. If you do, get someone to check this looks okay on screen. Bear in mind your audience and objectives. A photo of a beautiful beach in the background can be part of the pitch – or a major distraction from it!
- Video sharing platform settings.
  - Set your first and second name in your profile. This way, everyone knows who you are when you're speaking (and when you're not).
  - Include a good 'head and shoulders' profile picture. This way, everyone can recognise you, even when your video is off.
- Minimise disruptions.
  - Close down unnecessary apps and programs on laptops or other devices used for presenting and/or connecting to the meeting, switch off sounds and alerts on everyone's laptops and smartphones, etc.
  - If you live in a busy house, put a 'Do not disturb – important online meeting in progress' sign on your door.
- Have slides, demos and props ready.
  - Before sharing screen, ensure slides are pre-loaded and set to screen show mode. Ensure options such as 'Share computer audio', 'Optimise for video clips', etc. are selected.

- o Ensure demos and props are ready to share and use, etc.
- o Ensure alternative team members have alternative devices ready in case of issues.
- o Consider having a second, alternative channel where team members can communicate if the need arises (hopefully not…).
- Audio settings.
  - o Ensure mute and unmute are selected at the right times.
- Video settings.
  - o Switch video on during the pitch if possible, unless you have connectivity or other issues.
  - o If you don't want to see yourself on screen, change the settings so you don't have to.
- Engage the audience when you're speaking.
  - o Engage members of the audience when speaking using positive facial expressions and body language. Even when we're online we can smile and use our hands, etc.

DELIVERING THE INNOVATION PITCH

Yes! It's time to deliver your innovation pitch!

If you've reviewed all the recommendations and hints and tips above and practised on your own and as a team, things are likely to go very well. Issues and mistakes may happen, but we're sure you can handle them.

We haven't included a team activity for this, as it would simply say something like – Prepare/Deliver the pitch/Take questions/Relax!

The specific format of your pitch will depend on your course, module, project and scenario, etc.

If you're working through this book independently and have formed a team through our LinkedIn network, you may have an opportunity to deliver your pitch online to us as part of our competition (if the competition is currently active).

You've done all the hard work, so now enjoy your pitch. It's a valuable experience and we (and your audience) wish you well. One last piece of advice: make sure that you have some time together after the pitch – to debrief and to celebrate! It is such a special moment to share.

Good luck!

REFLECTING ON THE INNOVATION PITCH

Congratulations! You have done it. Delivering the pitch is the culmination of much of your team's collaboration and hard work together. We are sure you have done great and hope that you have also found some time to celebrate together.

Before or after the celebration, we also strongly recommend you take a step back to reflect upon the experience of developing and delivering your pitch and what you've learned.

REFLECTION POINT: REFLECTING ON YOUR PITCH

Consider the following questions. Make a note of your answers in the space provided and/or in your journal.

1. WHAT DID YOU PERSONALLY ENJOY ABOUT THE PITCH, AND WHAT WAS THE MOST REWARDING ELEMENT?

2. REFLECTING UPON THE EXPERIENCE, WHAT WOULD YOU DO DIFFERENTLY NEXT TIME?

3. REFLECTING UPON THE EXPERIENCE, WHAT WENT WELL AND WHAT WOULD YOU DO THE SAME (OR MORE OF) IN FUTURE?

CONCLUSION

For most courses, modules and programmes, you're now at the end of your team's project journey, although we appreciate you may still have assignment papers to complete.

We hope this chapter and the experience of delivering a pitch have shown to you that we can all learn how to present and pitch better – despite the fact that most of us weren't born as naturally gifted presenters. Of course, issues and mistakes will happen. It's how we overcome them that's important! Being nervous isn't a bad thing. It shows that you care. Practice doesn't make perfect, but it will make your presentations and pitches much, much better.

You've come a huge way from the start of the book, in terms of the skills you've developed and your team's project. You've done it once. You can do it again. During your future career, it's likely you'll work on many more change and innovation projects, often addressing diverse issues and working with diverse teams. Communicating and sometimes pitching your ideas and solutions may be an important part of this.

No matter who your audience is, you'll need to have an objective and generate empathy for them, communicate your idea and the value, and convince the audience your ideas are worth progressing and/or investing in. When developing an innovation pitch, we need to think about what will make it stand out and be memorable. When we deliver it, we need to be unique and include a wow factor.

KEY LEARNING POINTS

- **You can have the best idea in the world, but if you can't communicate the idea and the value, the idea will go nowhere. This is repeated from a previous chapter, but as it's such an important message, we're happy to include it twice.**

- When developing a compelling pitch, we draw on skills and outputs we have developed throughout the course of the innovation project.
- Innovation pitches are a form of presentation. The primary objective is usually to persuade or convince someone to support and invest in an idea or a solution, so that it can be further developed, delivered and/or commercialised to generate value.
- As with any communication, we need to understand and generate empathy for the audience we're pitching to.
- When developing an innovation pitch, we need to think about what will make it stand out and be memorable. When we deliver it, we need to be unique and include a wow factor.
- Most people are not born with presentation skills, but we can all learn to present and pitch more effectively.
- Practice makes much, much better. The more you practise your sections, and the team practises the overall pitch, the better it will be.

ACTION POINTS

☐ Run the team activities.
☐ Please complete the reflection points and exercises.

EXERCISE

EVALUATION AND SCORING

In this chapter, we talk a lot about the main elements of a successful pitch and things you might wish to consider when pitching. While research has shown that, at least initially, investors are often focused on major flaws that should lead them to reject the proposition, in pitching competitions and academic settings your presentation or pitch will also be evaluated according to certain criteria.

Based upon what you have learnt from engaging with this chapter, we ask you to design a score sheet that could be used to evaluate an innovation pitch.

What criteria are important? How would you evaluate and score them? What would be a good design? We encourage you to share your score sheet in our LinkedIn Community.

FURTHER RESOURCES

There are lots of books on communicating ideas and pitching. This one focuses on why we remember some ideas better than others, and explains the role of key characteristics of sticky ideas such as unexpected, concrete, credible, emotional, stories. Sounds familiar? Great – but from this entertaining book you can learn a lot more about how you should present ideas so they are of interest to others.

Heath, C., & Heath, D. 2007. *Made to Stick: Why Some Ideas Survive and Others Die*. New York: Random House.

For those of you who are interested in research into successful pitching, here are two of the articles that we have refered to in the 'more in-depth' section above:

Chen, X.P., Yao, X., & Kotha, S. 2009. Entrepreneur passion and preparedness in business plan presentations: A persuasion analysis of venture capitalists' funding decisions. *Academy of Management Journal*, 52(1), 199–214.Pollack, J.M., Rutherford, M.W., & Nagy, B.G. 2012. Preparedness and cognitive legitimacy as antecedents of new venture funding in televised business pitches. *Entrepreneurship Theory and Practice*, 36(5), 915–939.

A useful video of TedX speech coach David Beckett on how to deliver a perfect pitch:

Beckett, L. 2016. *How to Give the Perfect Pitch*. Young Creators Summit 2016.

This comprehensive article on pitching for start-ups was published in *Nature*. It considers not just the pitch but also the choice of the right type of investor and partner:

Dance, A. 2019. Develop the perfect pitch to launch a start-up. *Nature*. Career Feature.

A useful talk on five of the most common pitch mistakes – and how to use story arcs to fix them. This builds on and expands on some of the content of this chapter:

Baker, B. 2015. *5 Pitch Mistakes Entrepreneurs Make, and How to Fix Them*.

This website on pitching innovations provides links to a series of useful articles published in McKinsey Quarterly:

McKinsey. 2021. *Getting Your Story Straight*.

There is also the TED playlist on giving great presentations which we mentioned earlier:

TED. 2021. *How to Make a Great Presentation*.

Finally, one more book – this one has some strong sections on understanding audiences and the connection between story and presentation:

Duarte, N. 2010. *Resonate: Present Visual Stories that Transform Audiences*. Hoboken, NJ: Wiley.

APPLYING THE LEARNING

Chapter contents

Goals

- To reflect upon what you have learned.
- To understand your strengths and development opportunities.
- To enable you to apply the seven skill areas when applying for jobs and in your future career.
- To consider how you can apply Design Thinking in a wider context.
- To encourage lifelong learning.

INTRODUCTION

Congratulations! You have reached the closing chapter of this book. You have developed a great project and delivered an excellent pitch. But more than that – you've learned so much!

It was only a matter of weeks or months ago when you probably knew very little about innovation, Design Thinking, your challenge and project area. Think about how much you know now about the specific issues your project has been addressing, about the end users, your project sponsors and the different types of benefits and values each stakeholder group may be looking for. You've probably learned a great deal about the specific industry, about innovation and the innovation management process. So much knowledge developed in such a short space of time!

Critically, you've also developed and enhanced a set of key employability skills which you can use for the rest of your life. This final chapter is all about **reviewing and applying your learning** and how this can have a positive impact on your future career and quality of life.

For this, we invite you to revisit the four-step learning model and the seven skill areas we introduced in the first chapter. We ask you to discover and chart how much you have taken away from the experience of engaging with this book, your project and/or module – and to consider how this learning can help you with what you want to do next.

We'll introduce you to some of our former students, who'll share how they've benefited from their first Design Thinking project, and how they've applied some of their learning when applying for jobs, in the workplace and even when starting their own businesses. We trust that these examples will be useful – and in some cases even inspiring. After this, we'll continue with a section on Design Thinking more specifically and examine how you can use it for your own career development.

The last section is about lifelong learning. This may sound a little daunting but don't worry! Your career may well be more diverse, dynamic and sometimes more demanding than those of previous generations. At times it's also likely to be exciting and impactful. Lifelong learning can help you rise to your future challenges, do great things and also enjoy yourself while you are at it.

We learn best from our own experiences, as well as those of others. This is what lifelong learning is about – and why we hope you'll stay in touch with us and the others who have worked with this book via our LinkedIn community.

But first things first!

THE FOUR-STEP LEARNING MODEL AND SEVEN SKILL AREAS

Back in the very first chapter, we introduced a simple four-step learning model: Research – Doing – Reflecting – Further Research.

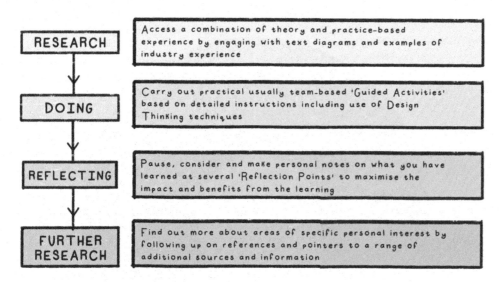

FIGURE 11.1: Four-step approach to learning

Your innovation project and learning journey through this book was designed to help you apply this model to the skill areas highlighted in the book. In each chapter, we invited you to do the research or learn about a topic or skill, to engage in a series of individual and team activities, to reflect on what you have done and learnt, and to build on that – or go deeper – with the 'more in-depth' and 'further resources' sections.

Here's a quick reminder of the seven skill areas:

1. **Innovation and Design Thinking** – The ability to identify problems and opportunities, and to develop and implement new solutions in a strategic way.

2. **Collaboration and teaming** – The ability to work constructively with others on a task, in particular working in diverse teams.

3. **Critical thinking and problem solving** – The ability to use information to develop, evaluate and implement solutions.

4. **Commercial awareness** – The ability to understand 'business' considerations and priorities and their practical implications.

5. **Empathy and communication** – The ability to communicate effectively in many different situations and with different audiences.

6. **Resilience and managing change** – The ability to cope with challenges, changes or setbacks.

7. **Initiative and active learning** – The ability to understand and analyse what we've done, identify whether we've succeeded or failed, and adapt, so we'll do better next time.

FIGURE 11.2: The seven skill areas

Do these skill areas sound familiar? Good! Over the past few weeks and months, you have learnt a lot about all of them. But what have you learnt exactly, and where do you want (or think you need) to do a bit more? This is where skills assessment comes in.

REFLECTIVE LEARNING

When we work with students, we usually assess their performance in the course or module through a reflective report of their learning around key skill areas. For this, we encourage them to go through their project notes and 'reflection points' and pull out all their own personal key learning points on each of the skill areas.

Often, we don't grade the final pitches at all because we think that you can learn just as much from a 'failed project' as you can learn from a 'successful project'. Moreover, at university, a grade should reflect individual learning rather than team performance (whether we approve of such an approach or not).

The main point here is that you worked through this book not just to deliver an amazing project but to learn something.

This learning will only have a lasting impact if you give yourself the opportunity to reflect and follow up on it. In this book, we invite you to do just that by engaging with a final learning review and team debrief.

Your final learning review is perhaps the most important exercise for enhancing your employability skills in the long term. It involves three steps. First, a review of what you have learnt since you started working with this book. Second, a self-assessment of what skills you have developed, and what skills may need further work. You will develop your own personal skills profile – something very useful to have for future job applications! The third and final step is to identify action points that will help you to further improve your employability skills.

We appreciate that this all sounds like a lot – but because of all the previous reflection points, it is actually not that hard to do. For most, the final learning review is a rewarding and empowering experience. After all, you will see how far you have come, and how you can build on what you have now got! (Plus, this exercise is also key for writing a great report or essay, if such an assessment is part of your module or course.)

As this final reflection point is so important, we've included a special section for it in the template for your personal reflective journal. Of course, you can also use the blank spaces below for your notes, but you may find that this time this is not enough space.

REFLECTION POINT: LEARNING REVIEW AND PERSONAL SKILLS PROFILE

1. LEARNING REVIEW

Reflect on how your employability skills now compare with where you think you were when you began reading this book. Have a look through all your notes and reflection points. Note down your key learning points in each of the seven skill areas in your personal reflective journal and/or the blank space provided below. Ask yourself:

(Continued)

a. What are the key things I have learned in each skill area?

Innovation and Design Thinking:

Collaboration and teaming:

Critical thinking and problem solving:

Commercial awareness:

Empathy and communication:

(Continued)

Resilience and managing change:

Initiative and active learning:

b. How have I learnt these things (by reading, by doing and reflecting, by watching others…)?

Innovation and Design Thinking:

Collaboration and teaming:

Critical thinking and problem solving:

(Continued)

Commercial awareness:

Empathy and communication:

Resilience and managing change:

Initiative and active learning:

2. PERSONAL SKILLS PROFILE

Once you have completed this process, it is time to develop your own personal skills profile and to identify some action points. Start by considering each of the skill areas. Think about what skills they cover. You can also download a sample list of employability skills for each section from our online resources.

a. Now have a look at Figure 11.3 below. The figure shows a matrix with the seven skill areas against different levels of confidence, with the *crying face emoji* indicating a skill area you don't feel at all confident about, the *happy face* standing for a skill level where you are already quite confident but still see room for improvement and the *emoji with the heart eyes* standing for skills that you feel you are already really good at. We have added two more for the stages in between.

Your task is now to identify some specific skills for each box. For example, looking at the 'communication and empathy' skills area, you may consider that you are great at storytelling (heart eyes), and also quite strong at visual communication and perhaps active listening (happy face) – but that written correspondence is still more of a mixed bag (smiley face). Contributing to team meetings may still be a bit of a challenge (expressionless face) and

(Continued)

presenting without reading from a script may be outright scary (tearful face). This is just an example – your skills profile is likely to be very different. Everyone is different in terms of their own experience, skill sets and in the kind of skills they wish to develop!

We also appreciate that it is not always possible to write a specific skill in each and every one of the boxes. For example, you may be a genius at teaming and have little to improve. Or you simply don't feel very comfortable at all about your commercial awareness. That is all fine, the main point of this exercise is to reflect and obtain some deeper insight about your strengths and weaknesses when it comes to employability skills!

By looking at each skill area, thinking about what you're already happy with and what you may want to improve, and filling in the boxes, you visualise your own personal skills profile. Such a resource is very useful to have when preparing for job applications or reviewing career ambitions!

	😢	😐	🙂	😄	😍
Innovation and Design Thinking					
Collaboration and teaming					
Critical thinking and problem solving					
Commercial awareness					
Empathy and communication					
Resilience and managing change					
Initiative and active learning					

FIGURE 11.3: Individual skills profile

There is space for your notes below and also in your personal reflective journal, which also includes a larger version of the matrix.

b. Finally, identify *at least one action* which can help you to develop further each of the skills that you wish to strengthen or improve in (as identified in your personal skills profile).

For example, if you cannot present without reading from a script, you may decide that you will volunteer for more presentations in future. Or if you still struggle with team dynamics, think about if there are additional resources and training that can help you to address this aspect. List your action points below and/or enter them in your personal reflective journal. The list of potential personal improvement actions is virtually endless. If you can, identify SMART targets. These are targets that are **s**pecific, **m**easurable, **a**chievable, **r**elevant and **t**ime-bound (i.e. have a deadline). This makes it more likely for you to follow-up on the actions and achieve the improvements you are looking for.

Make sure to identify actions that you will follow through with and review your progress every couple of months, setting yourself some new goals and actions. Some people spend a lot of money on coaches when simple methods such as a personal skills profile and a regular progress review can help a lot to develop one's future career. Good luck!

FEEDBACK

Self-reflection is great but we also need input from others.

All projects should end with a team debrief to make sure that both happen. Some of you may see this as a nerdy thing to do – but we encourage you to do it anyway. You owe it to one another! (Also, who says such a meeting cannot be followed by a little celebration or party?)

Before we get into the team debrief activity, we want to highlight that **being good at giving and receiving feedback are important skills to have**.

Everyone who has been at the receiving end of bad feedback knows that. And yet, we often do not pay a lot of attention to how we provide feedback and what actually helps – or does not. There is a personal and cultural dimension to this. Some people are more polite than others, and in some settings people are more used to critical feedback than in others. However, providing constructive feedback in a polite and respectful manner is ultimately about professionalism. So, let's share some tips for how to provide feedback.

1. Think about why you give feedback. What do you want to achieve?
2. Prepare your feedback. **Always consider whether and how the person receiving the feedback can benefit from this.** Make sure it is about them – and not about you!
3. Empathy and active listening go a long way when giving and receiving feedback.
4. Always ask if the person wants your feedback.
5. Focus on a few issues, usually no more than three. When providing critical feedback, focus on specific instances and examples. Don't say 'you always do this or that'. Do say 'when we prepared for the talk on Wednesday...'.
6. Make sure that you provide feedback from your perspective. Focus on what you have thought or felt. For example, say 'I learnt a lot from you doing this' or 'I felt supported/disrespected when you did this or that'. Avoid being judgmental.
7. Start and end with something positive.

Want to try this out in practice? The following team activity will give you an opportunity to do just that.

FIGURE 11.4: Constructive feedback

TEAM ACTIVITY: FINAL REVIEW – ESTIMATED TIME 90 MINUTES

This workshop is all about sharing the learning. It can be run in a physical room or online. If the workshop is to be held face to face, you'll need a room with chairs and a table and a flip chart as well as some post-its and marker pens. If the workshop is to be run online, you'll need a video conferencing tool and a virtual whiteboard or a blank space on your team MURAL.

(Continued)

1. DIVERGE

All team members go through their personal learning review and identity some key learning points for each skill area. Give yourselves at least five to ten minutes to complete this task. Try to be specific and feel free to add as many points as you want, both large and small.

2. CONVERGE

Review the learning points. Start with one skill area. Go through all the comments and arrange them around themes. Discuss where you have added similar or different points. Who feels that they have learnt more (or even the most) in each of the areas? When you are done, move on to the next skill area until you have completed all seven of them.

3. LOOK AT THE LAST SECTION OF YOUR PERSONAL LEARNING REVIEWS

What can you do to improve your skills further? Share some of your ideas and plans for action. Take notes where you feel you could benefit from a similar action.

4. CLOSE WITH A ROUND OF FEEDBACK

Tell your teammates where they did great and what you learnt from them. Make sure that everyone has at least one positive comment for each team member. Remember, the ability to give feedback is a great collaboration and communication skill in its own right!

If you want, you can also agree on having one positive and one negative (but constructive!) comment for each team member. But in our experience, the positives are more important.

EXPERT

REFLECTIVE LEARNING – WITH DESIGN THINKING

We introduced Professor Jeanne Liedtka of the University of Virginia in Chapter 6. Here, Jeanne shares her thoughts on the power of reflective learning.

1. WHEN YOU THINK BACK TO YOUR EARLY CAREER, CAN YOU RECALL A PROBLEM YOU LEARNT FROM A LOT?

Relatively early in my career, I was a junior member of a team creating a new education programme for a large group of businesspeople. Unfortunately, during the design process, the team weren't given access to the users we were going to be educating. By the end of day two, we had a full-scale mutiny on our hands, because the attendees weren't interested in our content. They felt it was a waste of their valuable time.

So, I found myself in a room with 60 angry and frustrated executives and a number of upset educators! At that moment, I learned a valuable design lesson. You have to engage the people you're designing for. As I was young and had doubts about the course design anyway, I wasn't afraid to say, 'Why do you feel this way? How can we improve this training, so it meets your needs and the needs of your business?' We spent the next two days productively creating and delivering a much more effective training course.

Effectively, I fell in love with the problem, not the solution.

2. AND YOU MADE A GREAT CAREER OF IT! AS A LEADING EXPERT IN TEACHING DESIGN THINKING TO STUDENTS, WHAT DO YOU ENJOY MOST?

The rush of watching someone discover their creative capacity. The positive impact this has on them can be incredible.

Also, I often ask students to write reflective journals each week. When I read them, it's brilliant. It sometimes makes me cry because I can really see the impact the Design Thinking process and activities have had, what the students have learned and, in many cases, how this has changed their view of themselves and their creative confidence. I don't have to wait five or ten years to be told by the alumni how the classes changed their life. I can see it in the moment! For an educator, it doesn't get much better than that.

3. HAVE YOU GOT RECOMMENDATIONS FOR STUDENTS WISHING TO LEARN MORE ABOUT WORKING WITH DESIGN THINKING?

Yes. The value of peer coaching is often underestimated. When we ask students to critique each other's work against their design brief, they spot flaws in that work which

(Continued)

they couldn't see before in their own. This experience is a great opportunity for learning and has helped many of my students to learn how to better evaluate their own work – as well as that of others.

TOP TIP

Inviting feedback, even though we might not like some of it, is extremely helpful. It ensures that we understand the people we're working with, and that we continue to learn and refine what we do.

APPLYING THE LEARNING

This book, your project, course or module and the learning review – these are not things we and your instructors have asked you to engage with for the sake of it. We don't ask you to strengthen your employability skills simply to achieve a good grade (although of course we do want you to do this) – but to help you to have a successful and rewarding career! So now you have identified some great learning points, what are they good for? How can you apply the learning?

We thought long and hard about how best to demonstrate this. We can of course explain how, for example, active listening and empathy can allow you to write a much better job application and engage the person or panel interviewing you for your first job, a future job or promotion. Or how enhanced commercial awareness can help you stand out from the crowd in interviews or to obtain funding for a new innovation or project... or how better collaboration skills can improve relationships of all kinds. This is all very nice – but is it worthwhile and, more importantly, how useful is it for you and your own career and life?

We decided instead to ask some of our former students to share what they have taken away from their learning with us, including undertaking their first Design Thinking project and practically applying a range of employability skills.

We feel that this is not just more authentic but also more engaging than any words we could have come up with. So let us introduce you to Dilan, Poonam, Taras, Lorenzo and Charlotte!

EXPERT: APPLYING THE LEARNING

Dilan Uludag works for Global Investment and Innovation Incentives, which is a professional services network. Inspired by topics revolving around innovation, she is about to embark on a Strategic Innovation Management Masters degree.

After graduating, Poonam Parmar joined a two-year graduate scheme with Arm. She has sinced moved into a role as a Project Manager within their Technology Operations Services Group.

Taras Lanchev created his own start-up business while he was still studying. His company, called Calbot, provides meeting scheduling and meeting planning software for law and accountancy practices.

After completing a student exchange programme to the UK, Lorenzo Zanutto continued with his Master of Science in Management at Bocconi University in Milan. He got involved in some consultancy projects for Italian start-ups and a research project on digital technologies for healthcare delivery. He now works for a software company that implements some of the findings of this research.

Drawing on Design Thinking methods, Charlotte Gray founded a start-up and developed a grade tracking app for university students called UniMate.

1. WHAT DID YOU ENJOY MOST ABOUT WORKING ON AN INNOVATION PROJECT WITH STUDENTS FROM VARIOUS BACKGROUNDS?

Dilan: I appreciated being put into a team that included students from various backgrounds. I truly enjoyed how we were all looking at our project from different perspectives. We all got inspired by the diversity of skills and knowledge offered within our team and complemented each other. Given the choice, one usually tends to work with those one is already friends with, so I learnt a lot from this experience.

Charlotte: What I enjoyed most was that everyone had their different strengths. Coming together as a team allowed us to produce great results that we would not have managed to achieve alone or with a more homogenous team. Personally, I learnt a lot from working with computer science students, as they made me appreciate the technical side of the project that was new to me.

Taras: Yes, thanks to our computer science students, we discovered quite quickly what ideas would be very hard to accomplish within the given timeframe. We had to adjust and take everyone's viewpoint into account. This was challenging, but a very worthwhile task. The idea we settled on in the end capitalised on the strengths of each team member and took their experience, knowledge and learnings into account, which resulted in a much better pitch.

Lorenzo: I found the double-step process of 'diverging and converging' very useful to leverage the full potential of the team. I also enjoyed learning more about teamwork. The ups and downs of an innovation processs are inevitably mirrored by corresponding group dynamics. If we want to innovate successfully, we need to be able to manage tensions and conflicts – and we need to know how to motivate and engage with different team members.

2. DURING THE PROJECT YOU APPLIED DESIGN THINKING AND OTHER INNOVATION TECHNIQUES. HAVE YOU USED THEM SINCE?

Charlotte: I did a lot of Design Thinking when I developed my app, in particular user personas and rapid prototyping. Before starting the designs for my app,

I made sure I had written out my key user personas to try and empathise with my future users. After creating the initial designs, I used rapid prototyping rather than coding the app right away to test out the designs and basic functionality. Even now, a few months after launching my app, I still use Design Thinking techniques on a regular basis.

Taras: When I started working on Calbot full-time after graduating from university I knew I needed to test my key assumptions about the problems professionals in law and accounting sectors were facing when it came to meeting scheduling. I ran several Design Thinking workshops and user interviews. This showed me very clearly that some of the assumptions I had made were wrong. People didn't struggle with meeting scheduling as such. They struggled with managing their time and running effective meetings for their clients. The fundamental problem they faced was not about scheduling – it was that if those professionals ran bad meetings, they would lose their clients. This completely changed the direction of our product and has probably saved us a lot of time and money. Always remember, love the problem, not the solution!

Lorenzo: I used Design Thinking tools in a consultancy project with a student association. We worked with an Italian start-up in the field of immersive videos and virtual reality technologies. Their value proposition was vague, and we suggested using Design Thinking tools to enhance clarity and alignment. We developed different personas in different contexts, looking for problems that could be solved using immersive technologies. Once we had identified some promising personas and problems, and considered the underlying emotional processes, we used Design Thinking Hills and a Prioritisation Grid to identify the solutions with the best wow-factor. This narrowed down the start-up's value proposition to three industries, and realised one minimum viable product for each. Our clients were impressed by the Design Thinking approach, which helped them to strengthen their commercial awareness as well as enhance their value proposition and business case.

3. HAVE YOU BEEN ABLE TO MAKE USE OF SOME OF THE EMPLOYABILITY SKILLS YOU DEVELOPED DURING THE COURSE?

Dilan: Commercial awareness is, I now know for a fact, one key ability employers look for – and they want to see applicants are wholeheartedly interested in

(Continued)

working for them. I made quite an effort to better understand how organisations operate, perform and prioritise. I engaged in work experience, read the news and used the university library's business research tools when preparing for job interviews… and it has paid off!

Poonam: The three vital C's (communication, collaboration and change) are hugely important for whatever career path you choose. Communication is probably one of the most used skills I try to embed into my working life on a daily basis. I converse with a wide range of people, from team members, senior programme managers to project stakeholders on a daily basis. I now always consider my target audience when I communicate – something I learnt when preparing for our final project pitch.

Charlotte: I constantly have to pitch my idea to various people. One technique that has proven to be particularly useful is storytelling. It helped me win a university start-up pitch competition!

Taras: I think communication skills involve not just knowing how to talk and what to say, but also knowing when to be quiet and when to let others do the talking. When I worked with users, I wanted potential customers to do the talking, so that I can learn from them. When it came to communication skills during user interviews, it was also very important to know how to ask the right question. There are 1,000 different ways of asking for something, but you need to be careful not to ask a closed or a leading question.

Lorenzo: I learnt a lot about giving and receiving feedback. It is true that negative feedback (if fair and well delivered) can be a great source for personal development. However, when working on this project, I also witnessed the power of positive feedback. Creating a sense of belonging and support is really important for a team. Positive communication such as encouragement and praise are key to good teamwork. It is now something I pay attention to and try to apply myself.

4. WHAT IS YOUR TOP TIP FOR STUDENTS READING THIS BOOK?

Charlotte: Actually, I have got two. My first top tip would be to make sure that all team members have a voice during the entire process. It's sometimes easy for someone to dominate and take the lead in a group project, but Design Thinking works best when everyone contributes. It's all about collaboration and building on each other's ideas, so make sure you create an environment that promotes that. My second tip is to always reflect on what went well and on things you wish you could have done better, both personally and as a team. That's why after each app launch or update, I get my whole team to reflect on how it went. It helps us improve as we progress and learn from each step but also allows us to appreciate the wins, which is equally as important.

Poonam: I agree. Self-reflection is still one of the key concepts I use in industry today. I also think that we need to accept that we can't be brilliant at everything, I'm certainly not – but that's what each day is about; finding your feet, growing and focusing on what you excel in.

Taras: I also think that reflection is a very important tool for perspective. J.C.R. Licklider wrote 'People tend to overestimate what can be done in one year and to underestimate what can be done in five or ten years'. Journaling offers a written log of where you were a week/month/year ago and so gives you that perspective of how much you have achieved since then.

Lorenzo: We can apply self-reflection in different ways: you can write in a journal, discuss with other people, or simply reflect on the 'bigger picture', asking yourself 'and so what?'

Dilan: We also need to remember that the innovation process is not a linear process. It involves iterations and cycles. Great ideas do take time to develop and require changes along the way. We need to keep a positive mindset and stay motivated because this will positively affect other team members, too. Our positive outlook and ability to adapt to changing requirements was our key to success.

Lorenzo: I agree. In the past, I associated innovation mainly with the application of new technologies. I now know that there is so much more – and always has been. Even when the solution was simply to rotate crops in order to preserve the fertility of a field. I now look at technology as a means, and not as the starting point. As innovators, we must first get our hands dirty when investigating the problem we want to solve. We need to understand better what is *actually needed* so that we can develop suitable solutions and communicate them effectively. Innovation always involves obstacles and setbacks. But when you look at it in this way, **when you really fall in love with the problem, you will find that it is likely to become both a more successful and also more enjoyable process**.

We hope that you have enjoyed meeting Dilan, Poonam, Taras, Lorenzo and Charlotte – and their reflections have inspired you in one way or another. Do you want to join this conversation? Please do! Join our LinkedIn group and let us know about what you have taken away from your first innovation project.

DESIGN THINKING YOUR LIFE?

Over the course of this book, you have applied Design Thinking as a process for solving complex problems. Figure 11.5 reminds you of the steps which took you from empathising, problem definition, ideation and capability development to prototyping, perhaps even testing. You experienced some setbacks along the way, so chances are you had to circle back a few times to ensure that you fully understood the problem.

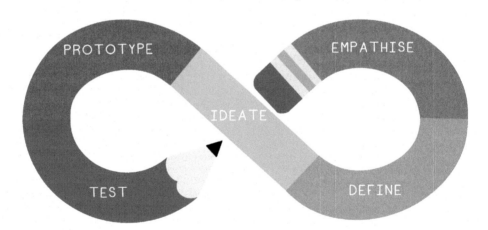

FIGURE 11.5: Design Thinking process

There are now several leading designers and innovation scholars who argue that we can also apply this process (at least in principle) to our own lives. We appreciate that at first, this may not sound very appealing. Who wants to think about their life as a problem to be solved? And yet, we feel there is much currency in this. Are not our lives the most complex projects we will ever undertake? In the 21st century, most of us do not walk into a job straight after completing a training or degree. Also, as we will discuss in the next section, few of us stay in the same job or even career path for our entire life. As we continue to explore and adjust, we face a lot of obstacles but also many choices. Often, we do not know what we really want to do with our lives. Not just what job to do, and where, but also whether or when to start a family, how to achieve a good work–life balance and so on. Sometimes, we must compromise – and sometimes, we just have to try a little harder or try something different altogether.

When we look at our lives like this, it may become more obvious how Design Thinking can help.

- **Design Thinking invites us to explore at a much deeper level what we and others want and need.** Applying this approach at different stages of our lives and careers is a great way of defining what we really wish to achieve (*Define and Empathise*).
- As with any good problem definition activity, Design Thinking helps us to differentiate between the facts we cannot change and solvable problems. Using a holistic approach, and taking into account value and feasibility, Design Thinking encourages us to explore diverse options and develop specific solutions for achieving our goals (*Ideate*).
- Our careers and lives are iterative, but we can only take so many steps at a time. Advocating a positive and forward-looking mindset, Design Thinking helps us to identify specific steps to try out at each stage of the journey (*Prototype*).
- Once we've taken a step, we need to reflect and gather feedback. Self-reflection and input from others will confirm what we're doing well and areas where we need to improve (*Test*).

Once we've done all this, we're ready to move on and go back through the loop. Of course, there will be problems and setbacks (it's an iterative process after all!) but at least we'll have a plan to use and adjust and improve as we go along. Most importantly of all, the plan is rooted in what's really important to us.

You may think now that this is self-help talk that you are not interested in, thank you – and that's fine! You may have *the* plan and that's great! But if you are one amongst many who are not so sure whether they have fallen in love with a solution (a job available) rather than the problem (i.e., what they really want and need to do with their lives), then this approach could be something for you. For you, the next question would be – how to do it? Do you create your Personas and Empathy Maps for yourself and colleagues? Isn't that a bit weird? Perhaps, it is, although for some people, it may be a valuable thing to do.

What we're suggesting here is not necessarily to apply every single Design Thinking activity and technique at every step – but to follow the general process and pick out techniques which work best for you. The good news is that there are Design Thinking leaders who have developed great frameworks, methods and templates for this process of designing one's life. The bad news is that we cannot really cover them in this book, as we're fast coming to the end. What we can do, however, is point you to some great resources. You may want to start with this video in which Dave Evans, co-author of the bestselling *Designing Your Life*, talks you through their approach in how to 'design your life': **www.youtube.com/watch?v=29V2xRitBGc**

We also list some additional resources in the further resources section at the end of the chapter.

DON'T STOP NOW!

This takes us to the last section of this chapter. We titled this 'Don't stop now!' because this is what many people do. They undertake a course, a module or a project – and then they stop. Job done. Grade obtained. Box ticked.

But of course, life goes on! We live in a world that keeps changing, and our role in the world keeps changing, too. In order to progress, we may decide to get better at some things we do reasonably well already. You may have already identified some opportunities like this when completing your review and debrief. This section is about the things we have yet to encounter, explore and learn from.

Nobody knows for sure what the future will hold – but some people earn their living from creating forecasts, trends and scenarios. When we look at such activities, the field of work in general and employability skills in particular, many people assume the lives of the next generation will be quite different from their own. Think how different your own lives may be from that of your parents and grandparents.

MORE IN-DEPTH: TOP SKILLS FOR NOW AND THE FUTURE

Digitalisation of work processes, automation, artificial intelligence and remote working all create a huge pressure for reskilling and upskilling. A recent survey by the World Economic Forum (WEF) found that 'on average, companies estimate that around 40% of workers will require reskilling of six months or less and 94% of business leaders report that they expect employees to pick up new skills on the job, a sharp uptake from 65% in 2018' (WEF, 2020, p. 5).

It is no secret that there are many uncertainties about what the future of work will look like. What will a graduate role look like in 2030, 2040 or beyond? What jobs will be in demand and sought after? One thing seems certain, **there will be more currency in the things people can do that machines and artificial intelligence can't do (or at least not as well).**

Creativity and empathy, for example. Lateral thinking and dynamic problem solving. As the world faces huge challenges, the ability to collaborate across disciplines and cultures will be in high demand. The report lists 15 top skills for 2025 (WEF, 2020). Have a look at them and you will see how many of these you have strengthened by working on your project and with this book!

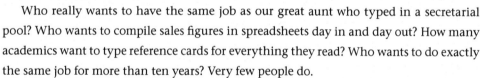

Fast-paced change is a challenge, and it can give us this restless feeling that whatever we learn, we are never done! This is true. **We are all in for lifelong learning! What we want to highlight here is that lifelong learning is not a lifelong sentence but a lifelong opportunity.**

Who really wants to have the same job as our great aunt who typed in a secretarial pool? Who wants to compile sales figures in spreadsheets day in and day out? How many academics want to type reference cards for everything they read? Who wants to do exactly the same job for more than ten years? Very few people do.

So how do we then navigate this brave new future of work? What skills will we need? If you now have a look at the list of the 15 top skills for 2025 you will notice something. You have strengthened most if not all of them to a degree by delivering your project and engaging with this book and/or your course or module. You already have a foot in the door to a dream job, so to speak. Don't stop now – but make something of it. Active and reflective learning can take you so much further. And remember, fall in love with the problem – not the solution!

CONCLUSION

So, this is it. In this final chapter, we have invited you to review and assess what you have taken away from your project and from working with this book and/or your course or module. We have revisited the huge opportunities that arise from adopting an active and reflective approach to lifelong learning. We have also provided examples of how others have applied some of the learning to inspire you to do the same. There are great opportunities ahead, and we have looked at how Design Thinking may help you to identify and realise some of them.

We hope that you have been able to engage in a project debrief, and that you have identified some very useful learning points and next steps as well as received constructive feedback. We love constructive feedback too – and if you have any for us, please do get in touch via LinkedIn or email. We'd love to hear from you. We wish you all the best with your future careers and as always we provide some further research resources below that hopefully will take you that bit further.

KEY LEARNING POINTS

- In order for our learning to have a lasting impact, we need to make time for self-reflection and team debriefs.
- We can apply self-reflection in different ways: you can just take time to think something through, write in a journal or discuss with others.
- Providing constructive feedback is an important communication skill that can be learnt and improved. Inviting feedback, even though we might not like some of it, is extremely helpful.
- Design Thinking can also be a useful approach for career development. The overall process as well as some of the methods and techniques can help us to design our lives with empathy and purpose.
- Lifelong learning can be challenging but is also a huge opportunity.
- Employability skills that are predicted to remain in high demand relate to activities that cannot be done by machines and artificial intelligence (or at least not as well) and include many of the skills that you have strengthened by working with this book.

ACTION POINTS

- ☐ Please complete the reflection points.
- ☐ Engage in the team activity, identify some useful learning points and provide constructive feedback to others in your team.
- ☐ Have a go at the final exercise below, which will help you to draw on your learning when applying for jobs.
- ☐ Join our LinkedIn group.

EXERCISES

SHOWCASING YOUR LEARNING

Your work with this book and the experience of developing an innovation project have advanced your employability skills. Now it's time to tell the world about this – and make sure that you can apply the learning!

1. Revisit your learning review and update your last curriculum vitae (CV) or resume with the knowledge and skills you have developed whilst working with this book, your project, module and/or course. You can download some useful tools and templates via the QR codes in the margin. Your university may also provide you with some additional support and resources.

   For graduates, we usually recommend a qualification or skill-based style. Such a format gives you a great opportunity to showcase your learning. (By placing work experience second, you also draw less attention to the fact that you may lack direct work experience in the role you apply for...) Make sure that your CV includes both a brief headline profile statement (which positively communicates who you really are) and qualification descriptions that are focused, engaging and about *you* (i.e., not copied and pasted).

   a. *Guardian CV* templates with a useful template for a qualification-style CV.
   b. *University of Leeds* – Skill-based CVs.
   c. *University of Manchester* – CVs for different purposes.

2. Many job interviews involve situational or behavioural questions where you are asked to share a story of how you have dealt with a certain situation or problem in the past. We include some sample questions of this kind below. Have a look at these questions and consider what experiences you have had while working on your project/with your team/with this book and your module or course, and how they could help you to land the job you are after. Your answers should contain: a problem/issue/challenge you faced; your solution; and a reflection on how such an approach could benefit your future employer.

   a. Tell me about a time you had to collaborate with a team.
   b. Describe a situation where you saw a problem and took steps to fix it.
   c. Tell me about a tough challenge you faced. How did you solve it?
   d. Tell me about a time when you needed to use communication skills.

FURTHER RESOURCES

Two really useful books about how to use Design Thinking for career development are listed below. The first one is a bestseller that has been around for a little while. It is really useful for thinking through the process and helps to reframe some of the questions we ask ourselves when we think about our future selves – after all, it is all about defining the problem, right? The second book draws on a wider range of exercises and techniques and is more visual. We like them both!

Burnett, B., & Evans, D. 2016. *Designing Your Life: Build a Life that Works for You*. London: Random House.

Lewrick, M., Thommen, J.P., & Leifer, L. 2020. *The Design Thinking Life Playbook: Empower Yourself, Embrace Change, and Visualize a Joyful Life*. Hoboken, NJ: Wiley.

There are also some related talks available online such as this one by Bill Burnett:

Burnett, B. 2017. *5 Steps to Designing the Life You Want*. TEDxStanford.

As well as one by his co-author which we also referred to in the section on Design Thinking your life:

Evans, D. 2018. *Design Your Life*. TEDxLiverpool.

When we look at the future of work, there are many resources to draw on. We cited some findings of a recent survey by the World Economic Forum:

WEF. 2020. *The Future of Jobs Report*. World Economic Forum.

But there is so much more to engage with – both in terms of academic research as well as industry reports. For example, McKinsey regularly produces new reports and analysis on the future of work. For example, they recently ran an international survey examining the skills citizens will need in the future world of work:

Dondi, M., Klier, L., Panier, F., & Schubert, J. 2021. *Defining the Skills Citizens will Need in the Future World of Work*. McKinsey & Company.

There are many good books and online resources about career development and how to find a job as well. You may also want to have a closer look at support provided by your university. With a view to graduate skills, these two websites can be really useful:

Office for Students (OfS). 2021. *Graduate Employment and Skills Guide.*

Higgenbotham, D. 2021. *How to find a job. Prospects.*

Finally, an insightful, useful book about how we learn:

Claxton, G. 1999. *Wise Up: The Challenge of Lifelong Learning.* New York: Bloomsbury Publishing.

And a bestselling guide on how to get going with your project ideas:

Knapp, J., Zeratsky, J., & Kowitz, B. 2016. *Sprint: How to Solve Big Problems and Test New Ideas in Just Five Days.* London: Bantam Press.

Finally, if you want to deepen your understanding of Design Thinking, Jean Liedtka and collegues have recently published a new book on the Design Thinking process that separates doing vs experiencing vs becoming, and makes for an insightful follow-up read:

Liedtka, J., Hold, K. & Eldridge, J. 2021. *Experiencing Design: The Innovator's Journey.* New York: Columbia University Press.

BIBLIOGRAPHY

Adams, K. 2007. *How to Improvise a Full-Length Play: The Art of Spontaneous Theater.* New York: Allworth Press.

Anderson, A.R. 2005. Enacted metaphor: The theatricality of the entrepreneurial process. *International Small Business Journal, 23*(6), 587–603.

Archer, W., & Davison, J. 2008. *Graduate Employability: What Do Employers Think and Want?* London: Council for Industry and Higher Education.

BCG – Boston Consulting Group. 2021. *The Most Innovative Companies Ranking over Time.* [Online]. [Accessed 4 August 2021]. Available from: www.bcg.com/publications/2021/most-innovative-companies-overview

Beckett, D. 2016. *How to Give the Perfect Pitch.* Young Creators Summit 2016. [Online]. [Accessed 22 November 2020]. Available from: www.youtube.com/watch?v=Njh3rKoGKBo

Bessant, J.R., & Tidd, J. 2015. *Innovation and Entrepreneurship.* 3rd edn. Hoboken: Wiley.

Bid, J. 2019. *Design Facilitation: The Secret Sauce of Great Designers.* [Online]. [Accessed 1 January 2021]. Available from: https://uxdesign.cc/design-facilitation-the-secret-sauce-of-great-designers-880de684d14f

Biesenbach, R. 2018. *Unleash the Power of Storytelling.* Evanston, IL: Eastlawn Media.

Brown, T. 2008. Design Thinking. *Harvard Business Review.* June, 84–92. [Online]. [Accessed 24 November 2020]. Available from: https://hbr.org/2008/06/design-thinking

Brown, T. 2009. *Change by Design: How Design Thinking Transforms Organizations and Inspires Innovation.* New York: HarperCollins.

Brown, T. 2021. *Design Thinking Defined.* [Online]. [Accessed 6 August 2021]. Available from: https://designthinking.ideo.com/

Buchanan, R. 1992. Wicked problems in Design Thinking. *Design Issues, 8*(2), 5–21.

Burnett, B. 2017. *Five Steps to Designing the Life You Want.* TEDxStanford. [Online]. [Accessed 2 January 2021]. Available from: www.youtube.com/watch?v=SemHh0n19LA

Burnett, B., & Evans, D. 2016. *Designing Your Life: Build a Life that Works for You.* London: Random House.

By, R.T. 2005. Organisational change management: A critical review. *Journal of Change Management, 5*(4), 369–380.

Byrne, D. 2020. *Steve Jobs' Lesson about Storytelling.* [Online]. [Accessed 2 January 2021]. Available from: www.linkedin.com/pulse/steve-jobs-lesson-storytelling-dave-byrne/?articleId=6694940202449956864

Cambridge Business English Dictionary. 2011. Commercial awareness. Cambridge University Press. [Online]. [Accessed 2 January 2021]. Available from: https://dictionary.cambridge.org/dictionary/english/commercial-awareness

Chen, X.P., Yao, X., & Kotha, S., 2009. Entrepreneur passion and preparedness in business plan presentations: A persuasion analysis of venture capitalists' funding decisions. *Academy of Management Journal, 52*(1), 199–214.

Chesbrough, H. 2016. *Open Innovation vs. Open Source.* UC Berkeley Executive Education. [Online]. [Accessed 24 November 2020]. Available from: www.youtube.com/watch?v=y-h0dq-XSJNY

Chesbrough, H., Vanhaverbeke, W., & West, J. 2006. *Open Innovation: Researching a New Paradigm.* Oxford: Oxford University Press.

Claxton, G. 1999. *Wise Up: The Challenge of Lifelong Learning.* New York: Bloomsbury Publishing.

Clegg, B. 1999. *Creativity and Innovation for Managers.* Oxford: Butterworth-Heinemann.

Dam, R.F., & Siang, T.Y. 2020. *Design Thinking: Select the Right Team Members and Start Facilitating.* Interaction Design Foundation. [Online]. [Accessed 22 November 2020]. Available from: www.interaction-design.org/literature/article/design-thinking-select-the-right-team-members-and-start-facilitating

Dance, A. 2019. Develop the perfect pitch to launch a start-up. *Nature.* Career Feature. [Online]. [Accessed 22 November 2020]. Available from: www.nature.com/articles/d41586-019-02252-w

De Almeida Kumlien, A.C., & Coughlan, P. 2018. Wicked problems and how to solve them. *The Conversation,* 18 October. [Online]. [Accessed 24 November 2020]. Available from: https://theconversation.com/wicked-problems-and-how-to-solve-them-100047

De Bono, E. 1992. *Serious Creativity: Using the Power of Lateral Thinking to Create New Ideas.* London: HarperCollins.

Detert, J., & Burris, E. 2016. Can your employees really speak freely? Despite their best intentions, managers tend to shut people down. *Harvard Business Review, 94*(1–2), 80–97.

Dietz, D. 2012. *Transforming Healthcare for Children and their Families.* TEDxSanJoseCA. [Online]. [Accessed 24 November 2020]. Available from: www.youtube.com/watch?v=-jajduxPD6H4

Dondi, M., Klier, L., Panier, F., & Schubert, J. 2021. *Defining the Skills Citizens will Need in the Future World of Work.* McKinsey & Company. [Online]. [Accessed 8 July 2021]. Available from: www.officeforstudents.org.uk/for-students/student-outcomes-and-employability/graduate-employment-and-skills-guide

Duarte, N. 2010. *Resonate: Present Visual Stories that Transform Audiences.* Hoboken, NJ: Wiley.

Dutta, S., Lanvion, B., & Wunsch-Vincent, S. 2020. *Global Innovation Index 2020: Who will Finance Innovation?* World Intellectual Property Organization. [Online]. [Accessed 1 August 2021]. Available from: www.wipo.int/global_innovation_index/en/2020

Edmondson, A. 2012. *The Importance of Teaming.* Harvard Business School: Working Knowledge. [Online]. [Accessed 22 November 2020]. Available from: https://hbswk.hbs.edu/item/the-importance-of-teaming

Edmondson, A. 2018. *What is Teaming?* Harvard University. [Online]. [Accessed 22 November 2020]. Available from: www.youtube.com/watch?v=sZZHkqIY0Fo

Eppinger, S.D. 2001. Innovation at the speed of information. *Harvard Business Review, 79*(1), 149–158.

Evans, D. 2018. *Design Your Life.* TEDxLiverpool. [Online]. [Accessed 24 November 2020]. Available from: www.youtube.com/watch?v=29V2xRitBGc

Ewalt, D. 2019. *The World's Most Innovative Universities 2019.* [Online]. [Accessed 22 November 2020]. Available from: www.reuters.com/innovative-universities-2019

Fleming, I.O., Garratt, C., Guha, R., Desai, J., Chaubey, S., Wang, Y., Leonard, S., & Kunst, G. 2020. Aggregation of marginal gains in cardiac surgery: Feasibility of a perioperative care bundle for enhanced recovery in cardiac surgical patients. *Journal of Cardiothoracic and Vascular Anesthesia*, 30(3), 665–670.

Freeman, C., & Soete, L. 2004. *The Economics of Industrial Innovation*. 3rd edn. London: Routledge.

Gibbs, G. 1988. *Learning by Doing*. London: FEU.

Golesworthy, T. 2011. *How I Repaired My Own Heart*. TEDxKrakov October. [Online]. [Accessed 1 January 2021]. Available from: www.ted.com/talks/tal_golesworthy_how_i_repaired_my_own_heart?language=en

Grams, C., & Lindegaard, S. 2010. *Open Innovation and Open Source Innovation: What Do They Share and Where Do They Differ?* [Online]. [Accessed 22 November 2020]. Available from: https://opensource.com/business/10/10/open-innovation-and-open-source-innovation-what-do-they-share-and-where-do-they-diffe

Gray, D., Brown, S., & Macanufo, J. 2010. *Gamestorming*. Sebastopol, CA: O'Reilly Media, Inc.

Griggs, J., Scandone, B., & Battherham, J. 2018. *How Employable Is the UK? Meeting the Future Skills Challenge*. [Online]. [Accessed 22 November 2020]. Available from: https://home.barclays/content/dam/home-barclays/documents/news/2018/Barclays%20Lifeskills%20report_v10.pdf

Guo, P., Saab, N., Post, L.S., & Admiraal, W. 2020. A review of project-based learning in higher education: Student outcomes and measures. *International Journal of Educational Research*, 102, 101586.

Hambur, S., Rowe, K., Tu Luc, L., & Australian Council for Educational Research. 2002. *Graduate Skills Assessment: Stage One Validity Study*. Canberra: DEST.

Heath, C., & Heath, D. 2007. *Made to Stick: Why Some Ideas Survive and Others Die*. New York: Random House.

Higbey, T. 2013. What are the best stories about people randomly (or non-randomly) meeting Steve Jobs? *Quora*. [Online]. [Accessed 22 November 2020]. Available from: www.quora.com/Steve-Jobs/What-are-the-best-stories-about-people-randomly-or-non-randomly-meeting-Steve-Jobs/answer/Tomas-Higbey

Higgenbotham, D. 2021. *How to Find a Job*. Prospects. [Online]. [Accessed 8 July 2021]. Available from: www.prospects.ac.uk/careers-advice/getting-a-job/how-to-find-a-job

Hone, L. 2019. *The Three Secrets of Resilient People*. TEDxChristchurch. [Online]. [22 June 2021]. Available from: www.ted.com/talks/lucy_hone_the_three_secrets_of_resilient_people

IBM. 2020. *Enterprise Design Thinking*. [Online]. [Accessed 22 November 2020]. Available from: www.ibm.com/design/thinking/

IBM Institute for Business Value. 2018. *Agile, Meet Design Thinking: Get Better Experiences to Market Faster*. [Online]. [Accessed 22 November 2020]. Available from: www.ibm.com/thought-leadership/institute-business-value/report/designthinking

IFG – Institute for Government. 2021. Explainer: Local government funding in England. *Institute for Government*. [Online]. [Accessed 16 May 2021]. Available from: www.instituteforgovernment.org.uk/explainers/local-government-funding-england

Ignatius, A. 2014. Innovation on the fly. *Harvard Business Review*. [Online]. [Accessed 16 May 2021]. Available from: https://hbr.org/2014/12/innovation-on-the-fly

Ikeda, K., Majumdar, A., & Marshall, A. 2013. More than magic: How the most successful organizations innovate. *IBM Institute for Business Value*. [Online]. [Accessed 22 November 2020]. Available from: www.ibm.com/thought-leadership/institute-business-value/report/morethanmagic#

Jackson, D. 2010. An international profile of industry-relevant competencies and skill gaps in modern graduates. *International Journal of Management Education, 8*(3), 29–58.

Johansson-Sköldberg, U., Woodilla, J., & Çetinkaya, M. 2013. Design thinking: Past, present and possible futures. *Creativity and Innovation Management, 22*(2), 121–146.

Kastelle, T. 2014. *Making Ideas Real*. TEDxUQ 2014. [Online]. [Accessed 1 January 2021]. Available from: www.youtube.com/watch?list=PLsRNoUx8w3rOFE2Izzwuxiij5q1hh-D6qN&v=VcdX6Qz5-jw&feature=emb_logo

Kelley, T., Littman, J., & Peters, T. 2017. *The Art of Innovation: Lessons in Creativity from IDEO, America's Leading Design Firm*. London: Profile Books.

Kets de Vries, M. 2018. Dealing with disappointment: Research blog. [Online]. [22 June 2021]. Available from: www.kdvi.com/research_items/801

Kim, W.C., & Mauborgne, R. 2015. *Blue Ocean Strategy – How to Create Uncontested Market Space and Make the Competition Irrelevant*. Boston, MA: Harvard Business Review Press.

Knapp, J., Zeratsky, J., & Kowitz, B. 2016. *Sprint: How to Solve Big Problems and Test New Ideas in Just Five Days*. London: Bantam Press.

Knight, P., & Yorke, M. 2004. *Learning, Curriculum and Employability in Higher Education*. London: Routledge/Falmer.

Knight, R. 1994. Criteria used by venture capitalists: A cross cultural analysis. *International Small Business Journal, 13*(1), 26–37.

Ku, B., & Lupton, E. 2020. *Health Design Thinking: Creating Products and Services for Better Health*. Cambridge, MA: MIT Press.

Lakhani, K.R., & Panetta, J.A. 2007. *The Principles of Distributed Innovation – Innovations: Technology, Governance, Globalization*. The Berkman Center for Internet and Society Research Paper No. 2007-7. [Online]. [Accessed 22 November 2020]. Available from: https://ssrn.com/abstract=1021034

Leutert, W. 2021. Innovation through iteration: Policy feedback loops in China's economic reform. *World Development, 138*, 105–173.

Levin, P. 2005. *Successful Teamwork! For Undergraduates and Taught Postgraduates Working on Group Projects*. Maidenhead: Open University Press.

Lewrick, M., Link, P., & Leifer, L. 2018. *The Design Thinking Playbook*. Hoboken, NJ: Wiley.

Lewrick, M., Link, P., & Leifer, L. 2020. *The Design Thinking Toolbox*. Hoboken, NJ: Wiley.

Lewrick, M., Thommen, J.P., & Leifer, L. 2020. *The Design Thinking Life Playbook: Empower Yourself, Embrace Change, and Visualize a Joyful Life*. Hoboken: John Wiley & Sons.

Liedka, J., & Salzman, R. 2018. *Applying Design Thinking to Public Service Delivery*. [Online]. [Accessed 1 January 2021]. Available from: www.businessofgovernment.org/report/applying-design-thinking-public-service-delivery

Liedtka, J., King, A., & Bennett, K. 2013. *Solving Problems with Design Thinking: Ten Stories of What Works*. New York: Columbia University Press.

Liedtka, J., Hold, K. & Eldridge, J. 2021. *Experiencing Design: The Innovator's Journey*. New York: Columbia University Press.

Martin, R. 2009. *The Design of Business: Why Design Thinking is the Next Competitive Advantage*. Boston, MA: Harvard Business School Press.

Maxwell, A.L., Jeffrey, S.A., & Lévesque, M. 2011. Business angel early stage decision making. *Journal of Business Venturing, 26*(2), 212–225.

MIT. 2020. *Important Steps When Building a New Team.* [Online]. [Accessed 22 November 2020]. Available from: https://hr.mit.edu/learning-topics/teams/articles/new-team

Moran, J.W., & Brightman, B.K. 2001. Leading organizational change. *Career Development International, 6*(2), 111–118.

Morgan, T. 2017. *Collaborative Innovation: How Clients and Service Providers Can Work by Design to Achieve It.* New York: Business Expert Press.

Newman, K.M. 2016. Five science-backed strategies to build resilience. *Greater Good Magazine.* [Online]. [22 June 2021]. Available from: https://greatergood.berkeley.edu/article/item/five_science_backed_strategies_to_build_resilience

Norman, D. 2018. *Rethinking Design Thinking.* [Online]. [Accessed 22 November 2020]. https://jnd.org/rehtinking_design_thnking/

Office for Students (OfS). 2021. *Graduate Employment and Skills Guide.* [Online]. [Accessed 8 July 2021]. Available from: www.officeforstudents.org.uk/for-students/student-outcomes-and-employability/graduate-employment-and-skills-guide

Parhankangas, A., & Renko, M. 2017. Linguistic style and crowdfunding success among social and commercial entrepreneurs. *Journal of Business Venturing, 32*(2), 215–236.

Podolny, J.M., & Hansen, M.T. 2020. How Apple is organized for innovation. *Harvard Business Review, 98*(6), 86–95.

Pollack, J.M., Rutherford, M.W., & Nagy, B.G. 2012. Preparedness and cognitive legitimacy as antecedents of new venture funding in televised business pitches. *Entrepreneurship Theory and Practice, 36*(5), 915–939.

QS. 2019. *Global Skills Gap Report.* [Online]. [Accessed 16 May 2021]. Available from: www.qs.com/portfolio-items/the-global-skills-gap-report-2019/?utm_source=website&utm_medium=blog.

Rittel, H.W., & Webber, M.M. 1973. Dilemmas in a general theory of planning. *Policy Sciences, 4*(2), 155–169.

Sims, C., & Johnson, H.L. 2011. *Scrum: A Breathtakingly Brief and Agile Introduction.* Foster City, CA: Dymaxicon.

Standaert, L. 2015. *Prototypes, Not PowerPoints.* TEDxGhent. [Online]. [Accessed 2 January 2021]. Available from: www.youtube.com/watch?v=5jmYyOxX2RU

Stobierski, T. 2020. Five tips for managing change in the workplace. *Harvard Business School Online.* [Online]. [12 June 2021]. Available from: https://online.hbs.edu/blog/post/managing-change-in-the-workplace

Strunk, W., & White, E.B. 1999. *The Elements of Style.* 4th edn. London: Allyn and Bacon.

Sugerman, J. 2009. Using the DiSC® model to improve communication effectiveness. *Industrial and Commercial Training, 41*(3), 151–154.

Suleman, F. 2018. The employability skills of higher education graduates: Insights into conceptual frameworks and methodological options. *Higher Education, 76*(2), 263–278.

Sutton, R.I. 2001. The weird rules of creativity. *Harvard Business Review, 79*(8), 94–103.

Tidd, J., & Bessant, J. 2013. *Managing Innovation: Integrating Technological, Market and Organizational Change.* 5th edn. Hoboken, NJ: Wiley.

Tuff, G., & Nagji, G. 2012. Managing your innovation portfolio. *Harvard Business Review.* [Online]. [Accessed 22 November 2020]. Available from: https://hbr.org/2012/05/managing-your-innovation-portfolio

University of Birmingham. n.d. *A Short Guide to Reflective Writing*. [Online]. [Accessed 22 November 2020]. Available from: www.monash.edu/rlo/assignment-samples/education/ education-reflective-writing/reflective-writing-structure

Weber, E.P., & Khademian, A.M. 2008. Wicked problems, knowledge challenges, and collaborative capacity builders in network settings. *Public Administration Review, 68*(2), 334–349.

WEF. 2020. *The Future of Jobs Report*. World Economic Forum. [Online]. [Accessed 22 November 2020]. Available from: www.weforum.org/reports/the-future-of-jobs-report-2020

Whittington, R., Regnér, P., Angwin, D., Johnson, G., & Scholes, K. 2019. *Exploring Strategy*. 12th edn. Harlow: Pearson.

Zapfl, D. 2018. What types of innovation are there? *LEAD Innovation blog*. [Online]. [Accessed 22 November 2020]. Available from: www.lead-innovation.com/english-blog/types-of-innovation

INDEX

Page numbers in *italics* refer to figures.